T0323866

The New Beginning

The New Beginning
A Business Novel on How
to Successfully Implement
the Combination of the Theory
of Constraints, Lean, and Six Sigma
to Drive Profit Margins

Bob Sproull & Matt Hutcheson

Routledge
Taylor & Francis Group

A PRODUCTIVITY PRESS BOOK

First published 2021
by Routledge
600 Broken Sound Parkway #300, Boca Raton FL, 33487

and by Routledge
4 Park Square, Milton Park, Abingdon, Oxon OX14 4RN

Routledge is an imprint of the Taylor & Francis Group, an informa business

Library of Congress Cataloging-in-Publication Data
Names: Sproull, Robert, author. | Hutcheson, Matt, author.
Title: The new beginning : a business novel on how to successfully implement the combination of the theory of constraints, lean, and six sigma to drive profit margins / Bob Sproull & Matt Hutcheson.
Description: Boca Raton, FL : Routledge, 2021. | Summary: "This book is a sequel to the business novel, The Secret to Maximizing Profitability - A Business Novel on How to Successfully Combine the Theory of Constraints, Lean, and Six Sigma to Drive Profit Margins to New Levels. In The New Beginning, Tom Mahanan, Tires for All's former Director of Finance, who learned how to combine the Theory of Constraints with Lean and Six Sigma, and then applied it to Tires for All, to take his company to levels of profitability they had never experienced before. As a reward for his work, Tom was given a permanent seat on the Board of Directors, as long as he continued his improvement work at the remaining portfolio of companies owned by the Board of Directors. Tom performed extremely well, but one day he receives a life-changing phone call from his former mentor, Bob Nelson, the man who he had worked with at Tires for All to make amazing improvements. Bob asks him to play golf with him and two others, Jeff Johnson, from Toner International, and Pete Hallwell, the CFO at Maximo Health Center Complex. Pete and Tom share a golf cart during the round and begin chatting about the work Tom had done at Tires for All and the other portfolio of companies. Pete, who works for a healthcare complex of hospitals, is so impressed with the results Tom had achieved, that he invites him to lunch the following week. Tom accepts his offer of lunch and ultimately, Tom signs a consulting agreement with Pete. Tom had provided an example from a previous improvement effort where he worked with a hospital in Chicago to improve their Emergency Department time for STEMI-type heart attack patients. In his explanation, Tom presents a variety of improvement tools which includes the integration of the Theory of Constraints, Lean, and Six Sigma. Tom then meets with his current employer and specifically, the Chairman of the Board of Directors, Jonathan Briggs, to let him know that he will be resigning to form his own consulting firm. Jonathan then surprises Tom by offering him a consulting agreement to improve all of their portfolio companies. The remainder of the book is all about teaching companies how to combine the Theory of Constraints, Lean, and Six Sigma to obtain optimal results. In the final two chapters, a new problem surfaces, which is the Corona Virus. Essentially, this book teaches the reader how to successfully combine and implement the Theory of Constraints, Lean, and Six Sigma to produce results that many companies only dream of having. It covers a variety of different company types including manufacturing and healthcare"— Provided by publisher. Identifiers: LCCN 2020043209 |
ISBN 9780367688370 (paperback) | ISBN 9780367688387 (hardback) | ISBN 9781003139263 (ebook)
Subjects: LCSH: Theory of constraints (Management)—Case studies. |
Production management—Case studies. | Lean manufacturing—Case studies. |
Six sigma (Quality control standard)—Case studies.
Classification: LCC HD69.T46 S673 2021 | DDC 658.4/013—dc23
LC record available at https://lccn.loc.gov/2020043209

ISBN 13: 978-0-367-68838-7 (hbk)
ISBN 13: 978-0-367-68837-0 (pbk)
ISBN 13: 978-1-00-313926-3 (ebk)

Typeset in Minion Pro
by codeMantra

As we progress through our lives, we meet people who have an impact on our lives. Sometimes the impact is negative, but those people who made a really positive impact are the ones that truly matter. In my life, the most positive impact has been from my wonderful, loving and supportive wife, Beverly. Why has she been the person who had had the most positive influence on my life? The answer to that question could fill many pages but let me zero-in on just a few very apparent things. Beverly has been the most supportive person I have ever met. Her unconditional love is beyond what I ever expected before I met her. When we first got married, back in 1968, I truly didn't know what to expect from a wife. But what I did get was the most loving person I have ever met! Beverly gave me three wonderful children and as they were growing up, she taught them how to love others which has carried on in each of their marriages. She also taught each of them how to be great parents, by teaching them the value of listening, loving, and being devoted to their wonderful spouses. I dedicate this book to you Beverly and hope we have many more years together!

Bob Sproull

I would like to dedicate this book to Jesus Christ Our Savior, because without him nothing would be possible. To my loving wife Emily and daughters Ally and Madison without whom I would not be a father or husband. Thank you for always being supportive and encouraging in anything I strive to achieve. Also, to my father-in-law and author of many books (including this one). Thanks Bob for allowing me to be part of this book and most importantly part of your family. Your consistent love for not only our family, but for every human. You inspire me to be a better father, husband, and overall human being.

Matt Hutcheson

Contents

Foreword

The New Beginning as in Bob Sproull's previous books recommends using a procedure that combines the three main operational excellence approaches of Lean, Six Sigma, and the Theory of Constraints. The Theory of Constraints will tell you where to act—on the constraint—and then you use focused and prioritized Lean and Six Sigma. This manner of doing things is getting more and more pertinent year by year.

The world in which we operate is constantly becoming more volatile and less predictable, and this tendency will continue. Yet we are still using management practices that were designed for a much more stable environment. Companies still use annual budgets. When they sign off a budget, management claims that it has distributed the work equitably throughout the organization. Therefore, conveniently, they can ask everybody to work all the time. They will measure local efficiencies, and they will get upset when they see an idle resource, especially if it is expensive. They have yet to understand that their organization is now made up of just a few constraints surrounded by resources with excess capacity. They have yet to understand that one of the key challenges of modern operational management is learning to sensibly stop resources from over-producing.

"The sum of local optimums is not equal to the global optimum," Eliyahu Goldratt, the founder of the Theory of Constraints, said back in the 1970s, 50 years ago. Very few companies have taken this into account. Goldratt also said that the goal of an (for-profit) organization was to make more money now and in the future. In this book, the sequel to *The Secret to Maximizing Profitability*, Bob Sproull and Matt Hutcheson address those two interconnected goals.

To make more money now is ensuring sales and efficiency in the short and medium terms. Let's say that it is all about honoring the client orders that you have. To do this Lean and Theory of Constraints both seek to improve flow. So, the authors explain, among many other things, the Theory of Constraints' Drum Buffer Rope scheduling solution and the important notion of protective capacity. They also present the Distribution and Replenishment Solution that improves the management of the supply chain.

Beware if you think that you are already doing things this way. This approach is not daily or weekly bottleneck hunting. It is about finding the underlying structural constraint in the system. Too often people are hunting wandering bottlenecks. They are managing the waves of work. They are managing in the noise. The wandering bottlenecks will hide the underlying "true" bottleneck if you don't "learn how to see" the Theory of Constraints' way.

To make more money in the future, the second part of the goal is all about how your company should grow and become more profitable and more robust year after year. *The New Beginning* addresses this challenge, and (obviously?) it is important. Too many companies are floundering here. They have a high-level "vision" that is usually no more than a sentence or two about having good products, happy clients, a motivated work force, and so forth, but it doesn't define what you must do. So, and this is especially true of large corporations, most companies have some form of transformational roadmap and associated action plan. But these are usually built by top management in such a way that every department contributes. The "project" ends up having ten to twenty key top priority initiatives. This unfocused approach yields numerous steering committee meetings, very few departmental results because of managerial multitasking, and very few, if any, overall bottom-line results. Here the authors recommend using a "Goal Tree" and the Logical Thinking Process which it is part of. Having personally used this approach for many years I can vouch for its (extraordinary?) capacity to determine the few key actions an organization needs to do to quickly to move ahead and see the impact on the bottom line. So, let Bob and Matt explain to you, using the novel format story-telling of this book, all about: the Goal Tree, Critical Success Factors, Necessary Conditions, injecting solutions, span of control and sphere of influence, necessity-based logic and sufficiency-based logic. If your journey resembles mine, you will discover what I did—I thought I was logical because I was a successful engineer and I was wrong. This book does a great job of showing you how to apply some practical logical systems thinking to build for your company a beautiful, focused action plan that makes sense and enables you to improve much faster and go further than you thought possible.

The New Beginning also highlights the tendency companies have of spending too much time trying to save money and not enough time trying to make more money (increasing sales). It repeatedly emphasizes why you should move from a Cost World to a Throughput World. After you have read this book warning bells should resound whenever anyone talks to you about saving money.

The novel format of this book also facilitates the understanding of the problems inherent in the dry, but important subject of Cost Accounting. You will enjoy learning about Theory of Constraints' Throughput Accounting and the impact it can have on the bottom line through a new appraisal of your product mix.

For those who have read the last three books that Bob Sproull has authored or co-authored starting with the best-seller *Epiphanized: A Novel on Unifying Theory of Constraints, Lean, and Six Sigma*, you will be familiar with the business novel format he uses. Like the international blockbuster *The Goal* by Eliyahu Goldratt, you will be carried along by the storyline hardly noticing what you are learning. But in *The New Beginning* you will be skipping from one organization to another, thereby highlighting how this combined use of Theory of Constraints, Lean, and Six Sigma can be applied in any situation, whether a manufacturing company or a complex of hospitals.

I wish you all the best on your journey of open minded, focused, rapid, collectively motivating, logical, and systemic improvement and growth. Have fun.

Philip Marris
CEO Marris Consulting, Paris, France
Over 30 years of combining Theory of Constraints, Lean, and Six Sigma

Preface

This book is a sequel to Bob's book, *The Secret to Maximizing Profitability – A Business Novel on How to Successfully Combine the Theory of Constraints, Lean, and Six Sigma to Drive Profit Margins to New Levels*. Several of the readers of Bob's last book asked him to write a sequel as he had previously done by making *Focus and Leverage* the sequel to *Epiphanized: A Novel on Unifying Theory of Constraints, Lean, and Six Sigma*, two of his other books. This book will, once again, deliver a strong message on the impact the Theory of Constraints can have on all improvement initiatives, no matter what type of company you work in.

Chapter 1, entitled "Tom's New Beginning," is all about Tom Mahanan, the former Finance Director of Tires for All, who learned how to combine the Theory of Constraints with Lean and Six Sigma, and then applied it to Tires for All, to take his company to levels of profitability they had never experienced before. As a reward for his work, Tom was given a permanent seat on the Board of Directors, as long as he continued his improvement work at the remaining portfolio of companies owned by the Board of Directors. Tom performed extremely well, but one day he receives a life-changing phone call from his former mentor, Bob Nelson, the consultant who he had worked with at Tires for All to make amazing improvements.

In Chapter 2, entitled "The Phone Call," Tom receives a phone call from Bob Nelson, a former mentor and consultant with whom Tom had worked at Tires for All to achieve outstanding success. Bob invites Tom to play golf with him and two others, Jeff Johnson, from Toner International, and Pete Hallwell, the CFO at Maximo Health Center Complex. Pete and Tom share a golf cart during the round and begin chatting about the work Tom had done at Tires for All and the other portfolio of companies. Pete is so impressed with the results Tom had achieved that he invites him to lunch the following week. Tom accepts his offer of lunch and lets Pete know that he wants to teach him about the Theory of Constraints version of accounting known as Throughput Accounting.

In Chapter 3, entitled "The Meeting," Tom presents the details of Throughput Accounting to Pete and two of his employees who both work in accounting. The meeting goes well as they discuss other subjects related to the Theory of Constraints. In fact, the meeting went so well that Pete surprises Tom with an exclusive consulting offer with Maximo Health Center Complex of six different hospitals.

In Chapter 4, entitled "The New Direction," Tom returns home from his meeting with Pete Hallwell and discusses the consulting opportunity with his wife, who is fully supportive. Tom then contacts Bob Nelson to get his input into his decision on whether or not to accept Pete's consulting offer. Bob Nelson reassures him and lets Tom know that if he has consulting offers that he can't take on himself, he will refer them to him. Tom decides to accept the consulting offer, but when he "attempts" to resign from his Board seat, he gets a huge surprise.

In Chapter 5, entitled "Maximo Health Center Complex," Tom signs his consulting agreement and then discusses the need to develop a list of performance metrics that they would track as they proceed through their improvement journey. In this chapter, Tom provides an example from a previous improvement effort where he worked with a hospital in Chicago to improve their Emergency Department time for STEMI-type heart attack patients. In his explanation, Tom presents an improvement tool known as the Interference Diagram. Tom also meets with the Chairman of the Board of Directors, Jonathan Briggs, about a new list of portfolio companies for Tom to work with as part of his consulting agreement. One company, Simpson Water Heaters, stood out from the others because, in addition to their other poor performance metrics, their profit margins were negative.

In Chapter 6, entitled "Simpson's New Beginning," located in Detroit, Michigan, Tom meets with the new Plant Manager, Matt Maloney. Tom presents the basics of the Theory of Constraints and then a detailed presentation on Theory of Constraints' version of accounting known as Throughput Accounting. In this presentation, everyone in attendance gets to see how, by using this form of accounting, a different product mix can change the company's profitability. They also discussed the basics of Lean and Six Sigma, or at least how both had been used to improve Simpson's profitability, but not at the level they wanted or expected. Simpson's attempt to use Lean and Six Sigma was, of course, prior to having received assistance from Tom. The chapter ends with Matt asking Tom if there was a way to combine Lean and Six Sigma with the Theory of Constraints. Tom explained that they will see exactly how to combine the best of all three methods when he returns for another visit.

Chapter 7, entitled "Maximo Health Center Complex's New Beginning," begins with a review of potential performance metrics that they might use at this complex of hospitals to track their improvement results. Tom plans a visit to Maximo Health Center Complex to present the basics of Theory of Constraints, the importance of identifying the system constraint, plus a detailed look at Throughput Accounting to a group of leaders from each of the six hospitals within this complex. His presentation of Throughput Accounting includes a case study, of all things, a sock making company. At the conclusion of this training session, Tom invites Pete to a presentation on how to combine Lean, Six Sigma, and the Theory of Constraints, to be held at Simpson Water Heaters in Detroit, Michigan. Pete agrees to attend along with two LSS Black Belts from his complex of hospitals.

In Chapter 8, entitled "Simpson Water Heaters Next Meeting," Tom presents how best to combine Lean, Six Sigma, and the Theory of Constraints which will result in major improvements to profits. Tom explains that too many companies believe that the key to improving profits is through how much money can be saved, when in reality profit improvement should be based upon how much money can be made. Tom then presents a detailed look at how to combine these three improvement methodologies, the necessary tools, actions, and focus, and finally the expected deliverables. This chapter ends with Tom explaining that he would be back to Simpson Water Heaters to present several other key methodologies, namely Theory of Constraints' scheduling and replenishment methodologies, as well as something called the Goal Tree.

Chapter 9, entitled "The Next Step at Maximo Health Center Complex," begins with Tom going to Maximo Health Center Complex to present Theory of Constraints' Parts Replenishment Solution and the Goal Tree. He then explains the basics of how the Min/Max methodology works and why it typically results in excessive inventory with high levels of stock-outs. He then presents Theory of Constraints' Replenishment Solution and why it typically results in a 50% reduction in inventory while virtually eliminating stock-outs. Because of the length of time it takes to present this material, he reschedules his session on the Goal Tree for the following week.

In Chapter 10, entitled "Drum Buffer Rope at Simpson Water Heaters," Tom flies to Detroit to present the details of Drum Buffer Rope which Tom describes as a production planning and scheduling methodology. Tom explains that DBR is designed to regulate the flow of work-in-process inventory through a production line based upon the pace of the slowest resource. Tom explains that there are three schedules that must be maintained, namely shipping, the constraint, and material release. Tom finishes his presentation by describing the importance of something he refers to as protective capacity.

In Chapter 11, entitled "Maximo's Goal Tree," Tom presents a simple strategic tool used to create improvement plans. He explains that the Goal Tree is a logic diagram that helps companies understand why they are not achieving their goal. He then defines the span of control and sphere of influence that must both be defined before construction of a Goal Tree. Tom then presents the basic structure of the Goal Tree by defining the Goal, Critical Success Factors, and Necessary Conditions and then walks the team through the step-by-step process of how to create one. The team of high-level executives from Maximo then creates a high-level Goal Tree including lead and lag measures. Tom then explains the process of using the Goal Tree to assess their organization, which the leaders do. The chapter ends with Tom instructing the leaders to go back to their hospitals and create individual hospital Goal Trees.

In Chapter 12, entitled "Developing an Improvement Plan at Simpson," Tom explains that there is another part of the Theory of Constraints known as the Logical Thinking Tools. He explains that many people who have gone through training on these tools have come away not knowing how to use them. He then explains that the Goal Tree is a short-cut that can be used to assess a company's weak points. He then describes two types of logic, which are necessity-based logic and sufficiency-based logic. He then explains that the Goal Tree uses necessity-based logic. He goes on to explain the basic structure of a Goal Tree and then presents a case study of a manufacturing company creating a Goal Tree and then uses it to assess their company.

In Chapter 13, entitled "The Expanded Case Study at Simpson Water Heaters," Tom begins by discussing the value of performance metrics and defines them as feedback mechanisms that tell a company how well they're performing. Tom then completes the case study presented in the previous chapter, by inserting target levels for a company's Goal, Critical Success Factors, and many of the Necessary Conditions. The case study company then goes through an assessment of their company and then Tom describes how to insert various solutions at the base of the Goal Tree that should resolve most of the issues facing the company in question.

In Chapter 14, entitled "Maximo's Improvement Plan," Tom sets up a meeting at Maximo to review the individual Goal Trees from each hospital. The team from Maximo Oncology Hospital presents their Goal Tree, and Tom is impressed, especially with their use of lead and lag measures. The same team then presents their assessment results and completely surprises Tom by explaining that Maximo has decided to use the same Goal Tree at all of their hospitals. Tom then presents a healthcare case study involving a hospital that dealt with a STEMI-type heart attack that impresses everyone in attendance and then instructs the team on how to insert improvement initiatives onto the base of their Goal Tree. He finishes the discussion by explaining how to use several improvement tools, which includes a new tool, the Interference Diagram.

In Chapter 15, entitled, "More Training at Maximo," Tom introduces the team to Drum Buffer Rope, which includes the basic thinking behind how it works. He explains that organizations must focus on the system as a whole, rather than as isolated parts. He goes into detail on what a system is and why it's very important to think in terms of systems. Tom then briefly describes variation and how it can negatively impact any organization. He goes into detail summarizing Goldratt's Five Focusing Steps as well as the basics of Drum Buffer Rope. Tom then describes three different types of DBR which are traditional DBR, Simplified DBR, and Multiple Drum Buffer Rope. It is the concept of M-DBR that he believes Maximo should pursue and then schedules another meeting at Maximo.

In Chapter 16, entitled "Simpson Water Heaters' Goal Tree," before leaving their facility the last time, Tom had instructed Matt Maloney, the Plant Manager, to lead a team to create their own Goal Tree. When Tom arrived in the conference room to hear about Simpson's Goal Tree, he saw it on the screen in front of him. The team began presenting, but started with a review of their performance metrics, which were dreadful to say the least, especially with a negative profit margin. The team then presented their completed Goal Tree with each entity tying directly into their performance metrics. They then presented their assessment and listed two potential improvement initiatives. The team then presents another assessment of what they believed would happen if they successfully implemented both of the improvement initiatives. Based upon their implementation they then presented a future look at their performance metrics. Tom was impressed and decided to contact the other three portfolio companies for an update to their metrics.

In Chapter 17, entitled "The Board Meeting," Tom attends a meeting with the Board of Directors with his intention to provide an update on the four company's performance metrics. He presents the update and clearly there have been improvements to all of them. He then presents Simpson's Goal Tree, their assessment, future improvement efforts, and then a future assessment. The four improvement efforts included implementation of Drum Buffer Rope, Theory of Constraints' Replenishment Solution, Throughput Accounting, and, his very own, Ultimate Improvement Cycle methodology. The Board then surprises Tom by offering him a new consulting agreement whereby he would assist the Board on whether or not they should purchase new companies.

In Chapter 18, entitled "Maximo's Improvement Effort," Tom intends to follow up on two presentations he has already made, namely Drum Buffer Rope and possibly Theory of Constraints' Replenishment Solution. Although he had already presented both of these improvement initiatives, he wanted to do a follow-up session, especially on Drum Buffer Rope, just to make sure the teams understood everything necessary to do, in order to successfully implement both parts. In this session, Tom presented new details of Drum Buffer Rope and sent the team on a fact-finding mission to answer some unresolved questions.

In Chapter 19, entitled "Drum Buffer Rope at Maximo," Tom had scheduled another follow-up meeting to discuss more on Drum Buffer Rope. As he was ready to begin, Dr. Samuels entered the room and asked for permission to say a few words. To everyone's surprise, Dr. Samuels let everyone know that the hospital Board had decided to implement the team's recommendations on discharge policy changes and their housekeeping efforts, which pleased everyone. The team then presented three more recommendations on how to reduce hospital wait times. Tom finished the day with a new idea on Multiple Drum Buffer Rope for a hospital's Emergency Department and presented a drawing of his idea.

In Chapter 20, entitled "Simpson Water Heaters' New Initiative," Tom flies into Detroit to present the Theory of Constraints Replenishment Solution. Even though he had touched on this solution in another visit, in this trip he would present the details of how it works. He explains the pitfalls of using the Min/Max system which Simpson currently uses, with these pitfalls being excessive amounts of inventory while seeing regular examples of part's stock-outs. He then delivers the key messages associated with Theory of Constraints' Replenishment Solution with results being fifty plus percent reduction in inventory volume while stock-outs fall to nearly zero.

In Chapter 21, entitled "The End of the New Beginning," as Tom was driving home from Detroit, he began thinking about the offer the Chairman of the Board, Jonathan Briggs, had made to him about a new consulting agreement based upon helping them select future companies to purchase. Since Tom was a huge fan of the TV show, *Shark Tank*, you can only imagine what he would offer the Board as his payment structure. Prior to his trip to Chicago to present the latest performance metrics, Tom had an on-line meeting with each of the four portfolio companies to get an update on what they had implemented, and the results achieved. In this chapter Tom also requests and receives updates from all six hospital leaders and has a meeting to hear about them. The results presented were very good. He then flies to Chicago to meet with the Board of Directors and present the latest metrics. The results were astounding to the Board and needless to say, they were very happy. They were so happy that they offered to meet Tom's proposed payment structure for assisting the Board on new purchases, which surprised Tom. But what surprised Tom even more was an announcement his wife made to him on the phone.

In Chapter 22, entitled "The Virus," as Tom is excited about all of the great things happening around him, he learns about a new virus called the Corona Virus, or COVID-19, which is spreading rapidly across the globe. Tom researches the virus to find testing is a major issue in helping with the slow of the spread. His wife Beverly is also not feeling well and decides to see a doctor, since she is experiencing symptoms of this new virus. Tom decides to contact Chairman of the Board, Jonathan Briggs, to see if he had any contacts out in the field where the virus was starting to spread. Jonathan provides contact information for two doctors who are directly in the hot spots. Tom learns that along with testing for the virus, the shortages on ventilators to treat patients and masks to help protect against the spread had major issues with availability. He reaches out to two suppliers of these very important items to offer his free consulting services.

Chapter 23, entitled "The Webinar," begins with Tom presenting a webinar on the Theory of Constraints to Jefferson Ventilators and The Mask Makers. After presenting and implementing, both companies see an immediate increase (triple the rate) in production to the point of parts shortages effecting availability. Tom then presents how the Theory of Constraints' Parts Replenishment Solution can help resolve this issue.

Authors

Bob Sproull is an Independent Consultant and the co-owner of Focus and Leverage Consulting. Bob is a certified Lean Six Sigma Master Black Belt and a Theory of Constraints Jonah. He has served as a Vice President of Quality, Engineering, and Continuous Improvement for two different manufacturing companies, has an extensive consulting background in Healthcare, Manufacturing, and Maintenance and Repair Organizations (MRO), and focuses on teaching companies how to maximize their profitability through an integrated Lean, Six Sigma, and Constraints Management improvement methodology. Bob is an internationally known speaker and author of numerous white papers and articles on continuous improvement. Bob's background also includes nine years with the Presbyterian University Hospital complex in Pittsburgh, Pennsylvania, where he ran the Biochemistry Department at the Children's Hospital, performed extensive research in breakthrough testing methods, and assisted with the development of organ transplant procedures. Bob completed his undergraduate work at the University of Pittsburgh, PA, USA, and University of Rochester, NY, USA, with a dual Math/Physics major. A results-driven Performance Improvement Professional with a diverse healthcare, manufacturing, MRO, and technical background, he has significant experience appraising under-performing companies and developing and executing highly successful improvement strategies based upon the integration of Lean, Six Sigma, and Constraints Management methodology. Bob is the author of six books, *The Secret to Maximizing Profitability*; *The Problem-Solving, Problem Prevention, and Decision Making Guide*; *Theory of Constraints, Lean, and Six Sigma Improvement Methodology*; *The Focus and Leverage Improvement Book*; *The Ultimate Improvement Cycle: Maximizing Profits Through the Integration of Lean, Six Sigma, and the Theory of Constraints*; and *Process Problem-Solving: A Guide for Maintenance and Operation's Teams*. Bob is the co-author of *Epiphanized: A Novel on Unifying Theory of Constraints, Lean, and Six Sigma*, First and Second Edition, and *Focus and Leverage: The Critical Methodology for Theory of Constraints, Lean, and Six Sigma (TLS)*. Degrees, certifications, and memberships: Bachelor of Science Equivalent in Math and Physics, University of Rochester, Rochester, NY, USA; Certified Lean Six Sigma Master Black Belt; Kent State University Certified Six Sigma Black Belt; Sigma Breakthrough Technologies, Inc. TOCICO Strategic Thinking Process Program Certificate; TOC Thinking Processes (Jonah Course) L-3 Communications; Critical Chain Expert Certificate; Realization Technologies Lean MRO Operations Certificate, University of Tennessee, Knoxville, USA.

Matt Hutcheson is a Senior Logistics Administrator in the manufacturing field, with 17+ years' experience in warehousing, logistics, and supply chain. Degrees, certifications, and memberships: Associate's Degree CIS (Networking Emphasis), Trenholm Technical College, Montgomery, AL, USA; Masters Certificate in Supply Chain Management and Logistics, Michigan State University, East Lansing, MI, USA.

1

Tom's New Beginning

"Wow, I never dreamed I would get a check this big!" Tom Mahanan said, as he continued looking at his check and couldn't believe that he was holding his "royalty check" for $400,000! When Tom received his new role with the Board of Directors, he had done so without a major raise in his salary, but rather an agreement on a royalty check based upon profits. He was a big fan of the TV show *Shark Tank* and liked Kevin O'Leary's royalty offers. Tom Mahanan was the former Finance Director for Tires for All, and along with his royalty check, he had just been given a permanent seat on the Board of Directors from the Chairman of the Board, Jonathan Briggs. Over the past year, Tom had directed improvement efforts at six of the Board's portfolio companies and the improvement results were astonishing! Tom was on his way home to Western, PA, and as he sat in his first-class seat, he began thinking about all that he had accomplished over the past year.

Tom's leadership throughout the portfolio of companies had resulted in amazing results as evidenced in Table 1.1. On the six Portfolio Companies that Tom had fostered, the average % Profit Margins had increased from 8.3% to an astounding 27.6%! And the improvement had occurred in a relatively short period of time, which very much excited the Board of Directors. The other key metrics that had improved were the average % On-Time Delivery for the six portfolio companies listed in Table 1.1, which improved from 77.6% to 94.6%!

Other performance metrics that demonstrated improvement under Tom's leadership were average % Scrap for the six portfolio companies, which had improved from 5.9% down to 2.1%. In addition, the average % Rework improved from 9.4% down to 2.9%! Surprisingly, the average % Stock-Outs for the six portfolio companies had decreased

TABLE 1.1

Improvement Results

Company Name	% On-Time Delivery		% Scrap		% Rework		Stock-Out %		Efficiency %		%Profit Margins	
	Before	After	Before	After	Before	After	Before	After	Before	After	Before	After
Board of Directors Portfolio Companies												
Terox Automotive	79.6	91.6	4.1	2.1	8.8	3.2	10.7	1.1	91.9	62.1	4.9	27.9
Sweeney Automotive	69.5	94.3	3.8	1.5	7.6	2.1	11.7	0.9	93.4	71.2	6.1	22.2
Johnson Electronics	78.3	92.2	7.2	2.2	13.3	4.2	10.9	1.8	90.6	65.7	7.7	30.4
Westin Incorporated	80.4	96.5	9.5	1.3	11.4	2.7	8.8	0.7	85.6	69.3	8.8	25.6
Watson Steel Products	77.8	95.5	4.3	2.2	8.8	3.2	9.9	1.6	90.4	70.5	10.9	30.8
Semena Rubber Products	80.2	97.7	6.6	3.0	6.7	1.8	8.3	0.2	86.2	71.1	11.4	28.8

from 10.1% to 1.1%. And finally, the metric that surprised the Board Members the most was what happened to the average Efficiency % which dropped from an average of 89.7% to 68.3%! And these numbers did not reflect what had happened at Tires for All! Based upon these results and more, the Board gave Tom a permanent seat on the Board of Directors with one caveat. And that caveat was that Tom had to continue his continuous improvement work on all of their portfolio companies.

As he was flying home, Tom continued reviewing the results he had presented to the Board earlier that day. One metric that brought back happy memories for Tom was Tires for All's discovery relative to percent efficiency. Before he had begun his improvement learning journey, percent efficiency was considered a key metric that should be driven higher, especially by the Board of Directors. He thought to himself, "I'll never forget the look on the faces of the Board Members when I presented a run chart for this metric. This metric had been hovering around 95% before their improvement efforts had begun, but at the end of the day, it had dropped to nearly 60%!"

Tom reflected back to their Board meeting. Mark Roder, the General Manager at Tires for All, and Tom had walked inside the hotel restaurant and, to their surprise, were quickly greeted by several of the Board members. He remembered how they were led to a small conference room within the restaurant and were greeted by the Board Chairman, Jonathan Briggs. "Welcome to Chicago gentlemen," the Chairman said, and they all shook hands. "We're very happy you are here tonight, and we thought it might be a good idea if we discussed your performance metrics prior to our board meeting tomorrow." Jonathan had explained. "So, tell us Roger, why has your performance metric efficiency taken such a nose-dive?" Jonathan asked. Roger turned to Tom and whispered, "Tom, why don't you present this." Fortunately, Tom had decided to bring his laptop with him to dinner, just to practice his presentation, so Mark said, "I'd like to have Tom answer your question." And with that, Tom got out his laptop and began.

"I think the first thing I'd like to do is show you the history of our metric efficiency," Tom explained and brought up the plot of efficiency onto his screen (Figure 1.1). He remembered how surprised Mark was that he would start with this performance metric. Tom remembered that the Board members were shocked to see this graphic that demonstrated such a rapid decline in Tires for All's efficiency. Tom then explained, "At

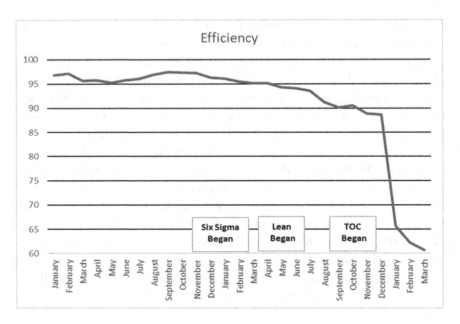

FIGURE 1.1
Performance Metric Efficiency %.

first glance, when you see this graphic image, you might be thinking that Tires for All is in serious trouble, but such is not the case."

Tom remembered how Jonathan had immediately responded and said, "That's exactly what I am thinking, but why are you saying you're not in trouble?" Tom had anticipated this response from the board and remembered putting his hand over his mouth to hide a smile. He then put up his next graph onto his screen (Figure 1.2) and said, "Contrary to what you might believe would be happening, here are our Profit Margins during the same time period," he explained. "How can that be?" Jonathan exclaimed! Tom remembered answering Jonathan's question very abruptly saying, "Because the belief that efficiency is a good performance metric is a false belief!"

His response stunned Jonathan who asked, "But, what about your metric for On-Time Delivery? How does it look?" And with that request, Tom flashed this graph (Figure 1.3) onto his laptop's screen.

Tom remembered exactly what Jonathan said after seeing this graphic. "I am totally confused by these graphs! You've got efficiencies nose-diving, while at the same time your profits and delivery metrics are

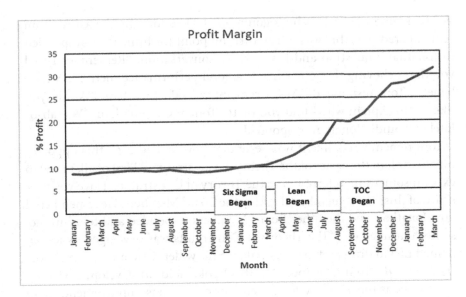

FIGURE 1.2
Tires for All's profits.

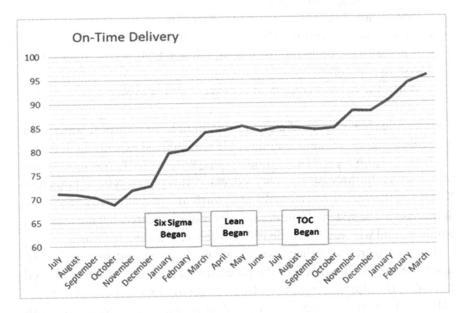

FIGURE 1.3
Tires for All's On-Time Delivery by month.

sky-rocketing upward? What's going on at Tires for All?" he asked. Tom remembered that this was a true turning point for him, as he responded to Jonathan's question and his ensuing conversation. "Remember I told you that believing that efficiency is a good performance metric is a false belief?" Tom responded. "Yes, I remember," said Jonathan. "Would you like me to explain why I told you that?" Tom asked Jonathan. "Yes, absolutely I would!" Jonathan responded.

Tom remembered, like it was yesterday, how he had used this opportunity to explain the basics of the Theory of Constraints. "First of all, I need to explain something referred to as the Theory of Constraints. Have you ever heard of this?" he remembered asking the Board Members. He remembered how Jonathan and the other Board Members responded and told him no, so he continued on. "The Theory of Constraints was developed by a man named Eli Goldratt and made popular in his widely read and quoted book, [1] *The Goal*," Tom explained. "In this book, Goldratt developed what he referred to as the 'Five Focusing Steps' for continuous improvement." Tom loaded a slide on his screen and said, "These five steps were:

1. Identify the system constraint.
2. Decide how to exploit the system constraint.
3. Subordinate everything else to the system constraint.
4. If necessary, elevate the constraint, but don't let inertia create a new system constraint.
5. When the current constraint is broken, return to Step 1."

Tom then loaded a figure of a piping system used to transport water onto his screen (Figure 1.4) and continued. He remembered explaining in detail, "What you see on my screen is a simple piping system used to transport water. Water, which in this case is gravity fed, enters this piping system, flows into Section A, then flows to Section B and so forth until it collects in a receptacle at the base of the system. If the demand for water increased, tell me what you would do and why you would do it?" he recollected asking Jonathan.

He remembered Jonathan looking at the diagram and saying, "Based upon the various diameters of the pipes, my guess is that you would need to modify the piping system by adding a larger diameter pipe in Section E." "Absolutely correct Jonathan!" he recalled responding to Jonathan. Tom then said, "So, you just completed the first two steps of Goldratt's Five

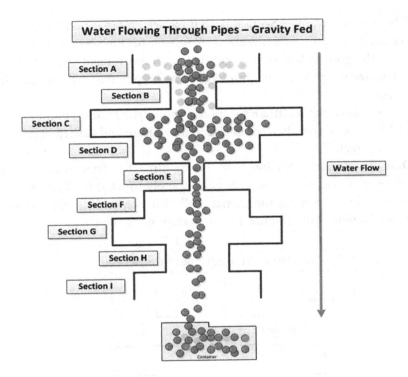

FIGURE 1.4
Piping diagram with constraint at Section E.

Focusing Steps. You identified the system constraint and then decided how to exploit it," Tom remembered saying. Tom then said, "The rest of the pipes were subordinated to the constraint, because they could only deliver water, based upon the output of the constraint."

Tom remembered continuing his explanation by asking, "Suppose there is another increase in demand for water from this system? What would you do and why would you do it?" he had asked Jonathan. Jonathan looked closely at the piping system and said, "In this case, once you opened up the diameter of Section E, the constraint moved to Section B of the piping system," he explained. "Basically, as you explained, you completed the first four steps of Goldratt's Five Focusing Steps, namely, identify the constraint, decide how to exploit it, and then everything else will be at the mercy of the constraint. Since we opened up Section E's diameter, we have completed Steps 4 and 5, because we have elevated the current constraint. We now have to move back to Step 1," he explained.

"The new constraint is Section B, so if we need more water, like Section E, we need to increase the diameter of Section B," Jonathan explained in detail. "The bottom line is, it's a continuous improvement process where new constraints pop-up and you have to be prepared to take action," he concluded.

Tom recalled that Jonathan's response was a true turning point for the Board Members. Tom then complimented Jonathan and flashed Figure 1.5 onto the screen.

Tom then remembered Jonathan asking him, "So, Tom, what was the purpose of this exercise and how does it apply to what has happened at Tires for All?" "Great question Jonathan!" Tom responded, and with that he posted a new figure (Figure 1.6) on his laptop's screen.

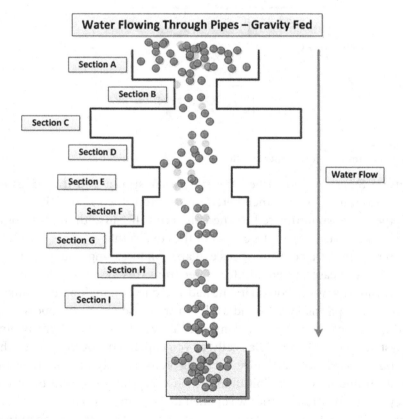

FIGURE 1.5
Piping system with a new constraint.

FIGURE 1.6
Simple 4-step process.

Tom then remembered how he had explained Figure 1.6, which was, "What you see here is a simple 4-step process with raw materials entering Step 1, are processed for 5 minutes and are then passed on to Step 2 and so on until the product exits Step 4 as finished product." "Thinking back to the piping diagram, what is the total processing time of the very first part through this process?" he had asked Jonathan. "The total time of the first part would just be the sum of the individual cycle times, for a total of 105 minutes," Jonathan responded. "Correct, now assuming this process has been up and running for a while, what is the output rate of this process?" Tom asked. Jonathan studied the drawing and said, "Since Step 3, at 60 minutes, is the longest cycle time, it seems to me that it would control the rate that products are made?" he asked in a question format. "You're right again Jonathan, Step 3 is this system's constraint," said Tom.

Tom chuckled to himself as he recalled what Jonathan said next, "I know what you're going to ask me next Tom, and the answer is, if we wanted to produce at a faster rate, we would need to reduce Step 3's cycle time because it is the system constraint." "Very good Jonathan, you're correct again," Tom had responded and then remembered asking, "So, here's a new question for you Jonathan. Assuming this company is measured by manpower efficiency, like Tires for All is, what happens to this process if every step is run to its full capacity?" Jonathan studied the drawing of this simple process and simply said, "Holy crap! Why didn't I learn this sooner?" he said openly. The rest of the board members were confused by what Jonathan had just said and one of them finally spoke up and said, "What did you mean Jonathan?"

Tom remembered smiling as Jonathan turned to the group and said, "Think about it everyone. If you run every step to its capacity, there's only one thing that will happen. The process simply becomes full of work-in-process inventory!" he exclaimed. "Does your next figure demonstrate this Tom?" he asked. "It most certainly does Jonathan," he replied and posted the figure (Figure 1.7) onto his laptop's screen.

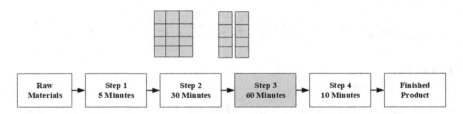

FIGURE 1.7
Process with excess work-in-process (WIP).

And then Tom remembered how this had become a true turning point moment for his career as Jonathan, without hesitation turned directly to Tom and began speaking, "What you have explained to us today, is mind boggling Tom! To think that all of the holdings in our portfolio are being run according to a metric like efficiency, is simply wrong!" he had stated emphatically. "Wow, to think that in less than thirty minutes, you have changed my thinking just blows me away Tom! And I want to thank you for sharing this very simple, but very valuable lesson with us!" he said. "Could you present this same material tomorrow to our Board of Directors Tom?" he asked. "Yes, of course, it's what I had planned to do anyway," Tom replied.

So, this was the start of Tom's new career as an "Improvement Consultant" that would change Tom's life forever. In effect, it was his new beginning. Over the course of the next year, Tom continued working to improve more of the Board's Portfolio Companies. The results he achieved were astounding to say the least! And then one day, Tom received a telephone call that would, once again, change the course of Tom's work life forever.

REFERENCE

1. Eliyahu M. Goldratt and Jeff Cox, *The Goal*, 1984, Great Barrington, MA: North River Press.

2

The Phone Call

"Hello, Tom Mahanan here," Tom said when he answered the phone. "Hi Tom, Bob Nelson here," Bob said. Bob Nelson, the owner of *Focus and Leverage Consulting*, was the man responsible for changing Tom's view of how companies can increase their profits to levels than most companies had never experienced! "Well hello Bob, it's so good to hear from you!" Tom responded. "How have you been Bob?" Tom asked. "I'm doing very well Tom and thanks for asking," Bob responded. "Well, what's up Bob?" Tom asked. Bob then said, "Tom, I was calling to ask you if you'd be interested in playing golf with me today? Two of my friends are going golfing today and we needed someone to complete our foursome," Bob added.

Tom responded by saying, "I'd be happy to play today...what time are you going?" "We have a tee time set up for 1:00 this afternoon," Bob said. "What course are you playing on Bob?" Tom asked. "I'm happy to say that we were able to get on Oakmont Country Club," Bob replied. "Oakmont, wow!" Tom exclaimed. "How were you able to get a round of golf on such a prestigious golf course?" Tom asked. Bob replied and said, "One of the guys we'll be playing with is a member there." "Jeff Johnson is the guy's name," Bob added. "Sounds great Bob, so you want me to meet you there?" Tom asked. "No Tom, I'll come pick you up about 12:15," Bob said. "Okay, see you then Bob," Tom replied.

Right on schedule, Bob pulled into Tom's driveway, and they loaded Tom's clubs into the car and off they went. Tom was very excited to be playing his first round ever on Oakmont Country Club. After all, Oakmont Country Club has hosted more major Championships than any other course in the United States, including eight U.S. Opens, five U.S. Amateurs, three PGA Championships, and two U.S. Women's Opens. Tom knew that Oakmont is perhaps the most difficult course in North America. It has 210 deep bunkers (personified by the Church Pews), hard and slick greens that slope away from the player, and tight fairways requiring the utmost driving precision. Tom has been an avid golfer for many years and remembered going to the 1973 U.S. Open. That year, Johnny Miller shot a final round 63 to win, and Golf Digest ranks Oakmont #4 in its most recent version of America's Top 100 courses. Tom was very excited so say the least!

"So, Bob, what have you been up to lately?" Tom asked. "I've been consulting as usual," Bob replied. "How about you Tom?" Bob asked. Tom then proceeded to tell Bob that he had been awarded a permanent seat on his company's Board of Directors, plus he told him about his huge royalty check. Bob just smiled and told him that he was very deserving of both the promotion and the large royalty check.

"You told me about Jeff Johnson, but who else are we playing golf with today Bob?" Tom asked. "The other guy's name is Pete Hallwell," Bob replied. "So who are these two guys Bob…how do you know them?" Tom asked. "Jeff Johnson is the CEO of a company I consulted for a few years ago," Bob replied. "I've never met Pete Hallwell," Bob added. "All I know is that he is the CFO of a Hospital complex located in Pittsburgh," said Bob. "What company does Jeff work for Bob?" Tom asked. "Jeff works for Toner International, a company that makes dry ink (toner) for copiers," Bob replied.

A short while later Tom and Bob arrived at Oakmont Country Club, ready for their round of golf. They walked into the club house, checked in, and attempted to pay for their round of golf. To their surprise, the round had already been paid for by Jeff Johnson. They both loaded their golf clubs onto a golf cart and then decided to go to the putting green to practice putting before their round began. As they were practicing, Jeff and Pete joined them on the putting green. "Good morning Bob," said Jeff as they shook hands. "Bob, I'd like you to meet Pete Hallwell," and the two of them shook hands. "Jeff and Pete, I'd like you to meet Tom Mahanan," and they both shook Tom's hand. After sharing a few pleasantries, it was time to go to the first tee.

They decided that Pete and Tom would ride together in one cart and Jeff and Bob would be in the other cart. They also decided to play team golf, with each team being the cart occupants. That is, Pete and Tom would be one team and Jeff and Bob would be the other team. Since apparently, they all averaged about the same scoring average when playing, the team with the lowest total score would be the winner. They all agreed that each player would put up $50 for the winning team to collect. The first hole was a 482-yard, par four hole, with numerous sand bunkers along the fairway. They flipped a coin to see which team would tee off first, and Pete and Tom won the toss.

Pete was the first to tee off and hit his drive down the center of the fairway, right around 285 yards. Tom was next to hit and hooked his drive into one of the fairway sand traps. Jeff was next to tee off and hit a beautiful drive down the center of the fairway about 20 yards ahead of Pete's drive. Bob's drive sliced and like Tom's drive went into one of the many bunkers. As they drove to their next shots, Tom asked Pete what kind of work he was involved in, and Pete responded by telling him that he was employed as the Chief Financial Officer at the Maximo Health Center Complex. He then explained that the Health Center Complex was a conglomeration of six different hospitals. He then asked Tom, "What do you do for a living?" Tom responded by saying that he was originally a Finance Director at a company named Tires for All, but that in recent years, he had become deeply involved in continuous improvement activities. He also explained that recently, he had been given a permanent board seat on his company's Board of Directors, provided he continued his continuous improvement work.

Tom and Pete arrived at Tom's ball which was buried in the sand trap. Tom estimated the yardage, took out his club, and struck the ball, which sailed to the front edge of the green. "Nice shot Tom!" Pete said. They then arrived at Pete's ball, and he managed to hit it within 3 feet of the pin. Meanwhile, Bob and Jeff had also played their second shots, and both had managed to hit the green. Bob was about 25 feet from the pin, and Jeff was within 15 feet for his birdie. Tom chipped up close to the pin and tapped in his par putt. Bob lined up his putt and rolled it to with 2 feet which he tapped in for his par. Jeff putted next and lipped out and then tapped his in for a par. Pete was last to putt, and although his putt was only 3 feet, he took his time reading his putt and then, like Jeff he lipped out his putt and had to settle for par. So, after one hole the match was tied.

As they continued playing, Tom and Pete kept chatting about their jobs as did Bob and Jeff. Pete was interested in learning why Tom had changed his career path from finance to consulting and asked him why he had made this change. "Good question Pete. For quite a few years I had been working in the finance arena for three different companies. In all of the companies I worked for, I had been using traditional Cost Accounting to make all of my company's financial decisions," Tom explained. "In my last job, we brought in an outside consultant, to help us improve our profitability, and it was this move that changed my entire approach to making financial decisions," Tom explained. "What do you mean that it changed your approach to making financial decisions?" Pete asked.

Before Tom could answer, they had arrived at the second hole which was a 340-yard par four, with, once again, numerous sand traps along the fairway. Tom was the first to tee off, and this time hit his drive down the middle of the fairway right around 290 yards. Pete was next and hit and he hit his drive right around 300 yards, again down the middle of the fairway. Jeff and Bob both hit their drives in the middle of the fairway right around 300 yards. Tom and Pete left the tee box, and Tom began answering Pete's last question about how he had changed his approach to making financial decisions. Tom began, "As I said, for years, probably just like you Pete, I had been using Cost Accounting to make my company's financial decisions. The fact is, I didn't know any other way to make financial decisions. But as I mentioned, at Tires for All we had decided to bring in an outside consultant to help us improve our profit levels," Tom explained.

Pete was listening attentively, and Tom continued. "We had tried both Six Sigma and Lean Manufacturing to improve our profits, but our profit levels still weren't high enough to satisfy our Board of Directors," Tom explained. "What were your profit levels Tom?" Pete asked. "When we started our improvement journey, our profits were right around ten percent," Tom stated. "And that wasn't good enough to satisfy your Board of Directors?" Pete asked. "Not even close!" Tom replied. Tom continued, "The Board of Directors actually was looking for Tires for All to double our profits to twenty percent!" He exclaimed. "Wow! That was a daunting task to say the least!" Pete responded. "Yes, it was, or at least I thought it was at the time," Tom said. "What do you mean, you thought it was?" Pete asked.

Just then, they arrived at Tom's ball. Tom pulled out a six iron and hit a beautiful shot to within 10 feet from the pin. "Nice shot," said Pete. Bob was next to hit, and he managed to hit it in one of the sand traps beside the green. Pete was next to hit, and like the first hole, he hit another great shot to within 4 feet from the pin. Jeff hit next and landed the ball about 20 feet from the pin. As they headed to the green, Pete repeated his question to Tom, "Tom, what did you mean when you said at the time, you thought improving your profit levels from ten percent to twenty percent was a daunting task?"

"What I meant was that, as you know, the overwhelming message from Cost Accounting is that if you want to improve your profit levels you need to look for new ways to save money," Tom stated. "What's wrong with that Tom?" Pete asked. "The bottom line is that there is only so much money that can be saved in any company," Tom explained. "The consultant we brought in explained that the key to improving profits is not through how much money you can save, but rather we should be looking for ways that will "make us money," and the two approaches are dramatically different," Tom said. "I'm confused," said Pete. "Please tell me more," he added. The foursome arrived at the second green with Bob checking his ball in the sand trap while the other three lining up their putts. Bob pulled out his sand wedge and hit it to within 10 feet from the pin. Jeff was next and hit a beautiful putt that dropped into the hole for a birdie. Tom was next, and like Jeff, he nailed his birdie putt. Pete then took his time and lined up his four-footer, but like the first hole, he missed his birdie opportunity. So, after two holes, the match remained all square.

The third hole was another par four at 428 yards with numerous sand traps on either side of the fairway. Tom was the first to tee off and managed to hook his drive into a massive sand trap along the left side of the fairway. Jeff was next to hit and once again hit a beautiful drive up the middle of the fairway estimated to be 305 yards. Pete then hit his drive around 290 yards, again in the center of the fairway. Bob was last to hit and pushed his drive into a trap along the right side of the fairway.

Tom and Pete climbed into their cart, and Pete repeated his question, "Tom, why did you say that saving money is different than making money?" Tom responded and said, "Pete, in order to explain this difference, I need to explain something referred to as the Theory of Constraints." "The theory of what?" Pete asked. "It's called the Theory of Constraints and it was developed by Dr. Eliyahu Goldratt back in the 1980s," Tom explained. "Let me try to explain the basics of this theory," Tom said. "The Theory of Constraints is basically a management paradigm that states that in any manageable system, you are limited on how much of your goal you can achieve, by a very small number of constraints, or as they're also known, bottlenecks. Goldratt explained that there is always at least one constraint, and the Theory of Constraints uses what he sometimes called, a *focusing process*. The first thing you must do is identify your constraint and then exploit it to maximize its throughput potential. You must then subordinate the rest of the organization to it. When Goldratt introduced the world to the Theory of

Constraints, he used a chain analogy to explain this concept and explained that a chain is no stronger than its weakest link," Tom explained. "Are you with me so far Pete?" Tom asked. "I'm not sure Tom," Pete responded.

They arrived at Tom's ball, and by the look on Tom's face, you could tell that he wasn't happy with where his ball was. It seems that his ball was buried in the sand as he could only see the top of it. He pulled out his three iron, took a huge swing, but only managed to move the ball about 50 yards. Bob was next to hit, and like Tom, he was in a sand trap. He managed to move the ball just off the edge of the third green. Pete was next to hit, and once again, he hit a beautiful shot to within 7 feet from the pin. Jeff was last to hit and landed on the green about 15 feet from the pin. Tom and Pete began driving toward the third green until they came to Tom's ball. Tom was about 75 yards from the pin, so he used his pitching wedge and nearly holed the shot, but because the greens were so fast, his ball rolled 20 feet past the pin.

Everyone putted well except for Pete, as like the first two holes, he missed another opportunity for a birdie. In fact, he ended up three-putting from 7 feet for a bogey. Pete and Tom were now two shots behind as they moved to the fourth hole's tee box. Hole number four was playing at over 600 yards with a severely undulating green. So, when you take into account the speed of these greens and then add undulations, this was seen as the hardest hole on the golf course. Jeff was the first to tee off, and like the first three holes, he hit a beautiful drive up the center of the fairway. Bob hit next and hit a nice drive up the right-hand side of the fairway. Tom also hit a good drive up the left-hand side of the fairway. Pete was the last to hit and nailed his longest drive of the day, well over 300 yards in the center of the fairway.

As Tom and Pete drove their cart, Tom tried once again to explain the Theory of Constraints. "Pete, I want to try a different approach to explain the Theory of Constraints," he said. "Pete, if I were to ask you what your goal is when you play golf, what would you say it is?" Tom asked. Pete, with a quizzical look on his face, said, "I think it would be to shoot even par? So after the first three holes today, what would you say is preventing you from reaching your goal?" Tom asked. "That's easy, if I could make a putt or two, or at least make my short putts, I could have been at even par," Pete said. "So, the factor that is preventing you from making pars is your putting?" Tom asked. "Yes, that's pretty obvious," Pete replied. "Pete, then putting is your constraint," Tom said. "If you want to move closer to your goal of shooting even par, you have to come up with a way to make more putts, right?" Tom asked. "I see your point Tom, my putting is my constraint," Pete replied. "If I want to make more pars, I need to correct or improve my putting," he added. "That's correct Pete," Tom replied. "Your focus doesn't need to be on driving or iron shots. It needs to be on your putting," Tom added. "I truly do understand your point Tom," Pete replied. "So, can you tell me more about this Theory of Constraints Tom?" Pete asked. "I mean, I understand about the constraint as it applies to my golf game, but how does it apply to our jobs?" Pete added.

And with that request, Tom began his explanation again. Tom pulled out his cell phone from his pocket and loaded a diagram onto his screen (Figure 2.1). "What you see here is a simple cross section of a piping system used to deliver water through a series of pipes using only gravity for the water to flow. Water enters into Section A, then flows into Section B and continues flowing until the water reaches and collects in the receptacle at the base of the piping system. So Pete, if you wanted more water

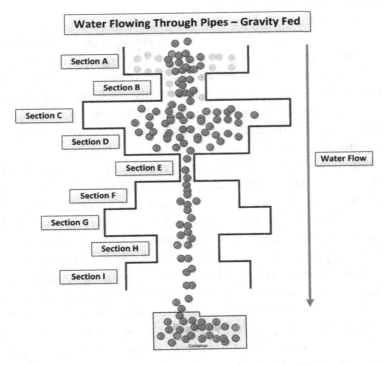

FIGURE 2.1
Piping system with Section E as the constraint.

to flow through this system, what would you do and why would you do it?" Tom asked.

Pete looked at Tom's drawing and then said, "Well based on what you explained about my golf game, it seems to me that the only way to get more water to flow would be to insert a wider diameter pipe in Section E." "And why do you think this would be the way to get more water flowing through this piping system?" Tom asked. "Because Section E's diameter is the smallest diameter pipe, so water tends to back up in front of Section E," Pete responded. "That's correct Pete," replied Tom.

They were now ready to hit their second shots on this very long par five hole. Both Jeff and Bob hit their shots and managed to stay out of any sand traps, but unfortunately, Bob hit his drive into the rough with the grass being about 4 inches long. Tom hit next and hit a very good three wood up the center of the fairway. Pete was last to hit and hit an excellent three wood up near the green. Pete and Tom got back into their cart and without hesitation, Pete said, "Can you please tell me more about what you call the Theory of Constraints?"

With that, Tom loaded another figure on his cell phone's screen (Figure 2.2). "What you see here is the same piping system, only this time we have taken your suggestion and inserted a larger diameter pipe in Section E and as you can see, more water is now flowing. So Pete, tell me what you see now," Tom said. Pete reviewed this new image and then said, "Well for me, it appears as though the constraint has moved to Section B?" he said in a question-like statement. "That's absolutely correct Pete!" Tom said emphatically.

"So, Tom, how does this piping system example relate to our everyday jobs?" Pete asked. And with that question, Tom again loaded a new image onto his phone (Figure 2.3). "So, Pete, here is a very simple process with four steps and the time required to complete each of the four steps. In this example we are looking at a simple manufacturing process. Raw materials enter into the process at Step 1 which takes 5 minutes to complete. The work at Step 1 is completed and then the semi-finished material is passed on to Step 2, which takes 30 minutes to complete. When completed, Step 2 passes its semi-finished product on to Step 3. Step 3 requires 60 minutes to process the in-coming material and then passes it on to Step 4, which takes 10 minutes to transform the material into a finished product," Tom explained. "With the piping system example in mind, where is the constraint in this process?" he asked. Pete then studied the new image on

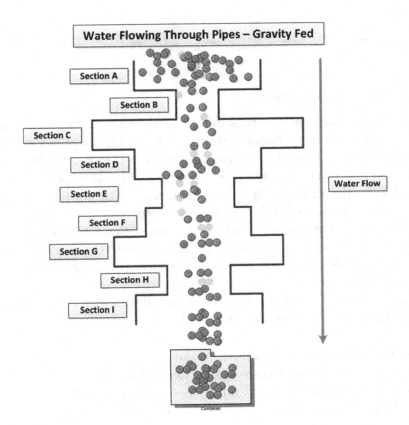

FIGURE 2.2
Piping system with Section B as the constraint.

Tom's phone and said, "I think because Step 3 takes 60 minutes to complete, it would have to be the constraint." "Good job Pete!" said Tom.

They now arrived at Tom's ball, and after studying the yardage to the pin, he pulled out a seven iron and hit it onto the green about 30 feet from the pin. Jeff and Bob both hit their shots, and both had birdie putts. Not close putts, but birdie putts none the less. Pete, who was just off the green, studied his next shot as though he was lining up a putt. He decided to use his putter for this shot and stroked the ball, and to his surprise, he made the putt for an eagle! Everyone else two-putted for pars, but because of Pete's eagle, the match was all square again. Needless to say, Pete was very excited about his eagle, especially since it was considered the hardest hole on the golf course!

FIGURE 2.3
Simple 4-step manufacturing process.

When Tom and Pete were back in their cart, Tom pulled up the image on his phone again and began speaking. "Pete, in this image of a manufacturing process (Figure 2.3), if you were now forced to produce product at a faster rate, what would you have to do and why would you do it?" Tom asked. Pete studied Tom's sketch again and said, "Well just like the piping diagram, if we needed more product to satisfy more orders, we would have to reduce Step 3's time." "And why did you say that Pete?" Tom asked. "Because it is the constraint, and the constraint controls the output of any process?" he said in a question-like manner. "Exactly correct Pete!!" said Tom enthusiastically.

Tom continued, "Goldratt presented the world with what he referred to as the Five Focusing Steps which are:

- Step 1: Identify the system constraint.
- Step 2: Decide how to exploit the system constraint.
- Step 3: Subordinate everything to the system constraint.
- Step 4: If necessary, elevate the system constraint.
- Step 5: When the constraint is broken, return to Step 1, but don't let inertia create a new constraint."

"What do you mean by subordinate, Tom?" Pete asked. "Let me ask you another question Pete," Tom replied. "Thinking back to our simple four step process presented earlier, what would happen to this process if every step ran at its full capacity?" Tom asked. "I'm not sure what you mean?" Pete replied. Tom loaded a new image onto his cell phone of the same four-step process and added work-in-process inventory to it (Figure 2.4).

"What you see here is what happens to the same 4-step process if the steps in front of the constraint are permitted to run at their full capacity. The system becomes clogged with WIP inventory which encumbers the process and needlessly ties up excessive cash," Tom explained. "So, the concept of subordination simply means, in real terms, that non-constraints should never outpace the system constraint. You can imagine what this

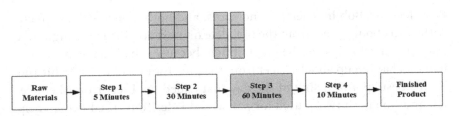

FIGURE 2.4
Simple 4-step process with excessive WIP inventory.

process might look like if it ran for three shifts at maximum capacity at each step," Tom explained. "That is the essence of the basics of the Theory of Constraints Pete," Tom added. "But having said that, some time I'd like to show you a different form of accounting known as Throughput Accounting," Tom said. "Why don't we get together for lunch one day next week Tom?" Pete asked. "Just let me know what day and time works for you Pete," Tom replied.

"Before we finish today, I see how this works for a manufacturing process, but what about a service industry like my hospitals?" Pete asked. "The bottom line is that exactly the same principles apply to service industries that apply to manufacturing," Tom explained. "How could that be Tom?" Pete asked. "Pete, your hospitals have processes just like a manufacturing company does," Tom explained. "And each step in your processes have a cycle time to complete each of the steps," Tom continued. "When we get together next week, I'll get into this in more detail," Tom added.

The rest of the day was spent playing the remaining holes, and in fact, as they approached the 18th hole, they were all tied. This is by far the most picturesque hole at Oakmont and perhaps the greatest finishing par 4 in golf. If you want to score well, you have to drive the ball in the fairway to avoid what they call the "chip out" bunkers on the left and right. The yardage on this hole was 484 yards and Pete was the first to hit his driver. He hit it really well and kept it out of the bunkers. Jeff hit next, and he too hit an excellent drive right down the middle of the fairway. Bob hit next, and he too kept it out of the bunkers and in the fairway. Tom stepped up next and hit his best drive of the day, nearly 320 yards down the center of the fairway.

As they drove up the fairway toward their balls, Tom and Pete reflected on their day. Pete was very appreciative of all that Tom had taught him and told him he was very anxious to hear about Throughput Accounting.

Both Jeff and Bob hit their second shots, and both landed on the green, with both about 20 feet from the pin. Pete hit next and hit a very high shot that landed very close to the pin, but then because it had so much spin on it, it had backed up about 15 feet from the pin. Tom was the last to hit and hit his best approach shot of the day that ended up 4 feet from the hole. Jeff and Bob both two-putted for par, as did Pete. Tom asked Pete to help him read his putt, which he did. Tom knew that if he made this putt, he and Pete would be one hundred dollars richer. He stood over his putt and stroked it, and it went around the cup before it fell into the hole for the match winner. Pete and Tom hugged each other in celebration and then collected their winnings.

It was a good day for Pete and Tom, but especially for Pete. He felt a new-found desire to learn more about the Theory of Constraints, but more importantly, Throughput Accounting. Like Tom, Pete had always spent his days working in the financial field, and he was anxious to learn more from Tom. And that day would come one day next week.

3

The Meeting

Pete contacted Tom early Monday morning and told him that if he could meet on Wednesday at 9:00 am, he would free up that day and time to meet with him. He also reiterated how excited he was to learn about Throughput Accounting. Tom agreed on the date and time, and decided to create a slide deck on Throughput Accounting. He decided to use the same slide deck that he used at Tires for All since it seemed to resonate with everyone and they were able to take it and use it in their financial decision-making.

It was now Wednesday morning, and Tom left for his appointment with Pete. He arrived right on schedule, and the security guard called Pete to let him know that Tom was in the lobby. Shortly thereafter Pete arrived in the lobby and signed in Tom. They took the elevator to the seventh floor and shared pleasantries with each other. "Tom, I want you to know how much I enjoyed playing golf with you," said Pete. "In addition to winning, I just learned so much during our round," he added. "I enjoyed it too Pete," Tom replied. The two of them went to a conference room, and Pete let Tom know that he had invited a couple of his employees to join them, so they could learn about Throughput Accounting as well. The two employees arrived and introduced themselves to Tom. "I am Cindy McPherson and I am a Cost Accountant," she said. "And I am Bruce Johnson and I am the Accounting Manager here at Maximo Health Center Complex."

Tom began, "Before I begin, I want you all to know that I had been a Director of Finance for quite a few years and I was a strong advocate for the principles of Cost Accounting. I had never been exposed to the Theory of Constraints or Throughput Accounting, but after I heard about both, it absolutely changed my approach to financial decisions as soon as I learned what it had to offer. So, since all of you are involved in financial decisions, I want you to pay close attention to what I have to say today. I truly believe that if you listen to what I have to say, with an open mind, it will absolutely change your approach to making money for your hospital complex. But before I begin, I think it's important for both Cindy and Bruce to hear a bit about the Theory of Constraints," Tom explained.

Tom took his time and presented the same graphics that he had shown Pete on the golf course. He began with his piping system and asked the same kind of questions he had asked Pete. He then presented the simple 4-step process and, again, asked questions similar to what he had asked Pete. He then presented Goldratt's Five Focusing Steps, and both Cindy and Bruce seemed to "get it" like Pete had. They both asked good questions along the way, and when Tom was satisfied that they both understood the basics of the Theory of Constraints, he began his discussion on Throughput Accounting.

Tom began again, "The primary focus of Cost Accounting, as you all know, is per part or per unit cost reductions. Because perceived cost reductions are viewed so favorably, is it any wonder why there is so much emphasis on measuring the performance metric efficiency? I assume you use that metric here, correct?" They all indicated that it was one of their key metrics. Tom began again, "And yet cost reductions don't seem to be the answer for most companies. There have been very many highly efficient companies that have come close to going out of business or have actually gone out of business. Have you ever heard of a company that has saved themselves into prosperity?" he asked rhetorically, and he noticed heads bobbing up and down in agreement.

"Many companies will categorically state that the primary goal of their company is to make money, and yet they spend the largest portion of their time trying to save money. It would almost appear as if they've forgotten what their goal really is. I'm here to tell you that the strategy you use to make money, is infinitely different than the strategy you would use to save money," he explained. He continued, "For most companies, the assumption is that the actions required to save money are the same actions required to make money. That is, if you somehow save enough money, it's believed in many cases to be the same as making money, but believe me this is absolutely not true," he explained. "Any questions so far?" he asked, but there weren't any, so he continued.

"These two approaches to making a profit are opposite in their thinking, and each one takes you in a very different direction with absolutely different results. If the goal of your company is to save money, then probably the best way to accomplish your goal might be to just go out of business. Think about it, wouldn't this action save you the maximum amount of money!" Everyone chuckled at what Tom had just said. "However, if the goal of your company is to make money, then a much different strategy must be used and that is by maximizing throughput through the system, or in your case maximizing the number of patients you see and treat," Tom explained. Cindy raised her hand and said, "I'm confused Tom. If you save enough money, won't you end up making money?" Tom responded and said, "I used to think along those same lines Cindy when I worked in Finance, but what I learned changed my approach completely. Stay with me and I'll show you why," he said.

"Maybe it's possible that some of the Cost Accounting rules and methods might be wrong and might mislead you into thinking some results are better than they really are. Is it possible that there might be another way to look logically at the practice of Accounting, that will truly get us closer to our goal of making money? What if there was another way? A way that provides an alternative accounting method that allows us to consider abandoning or even ignoring the Cost Accounting rules that are causing so much trouble? I want to now present a look at Throughput Accounting, but before I do, I want everyone to understand that we can't totally abandon Cost Accounting, simply because it's required by law when we report our results. What I'm about to explain though is a better way to make *real time* financial decisions," he explained to a very captive audience, especially Pete. "Any questions before I explain Throughput Accounting?" Tom asked. There weren't any, so Tom began again.

"As I mentioned, Throughput Accounting is not an attack on Cost Accounting, but rather a different way to look at the accounting measures and manage the company at a much higher success and profitability level. In its basic form, Throughput Accounting uses primarily three basic performance metrics which are Throughput (T), Investment/Inventory (I), and Operating Expense (OE). These three metrics are a simplified methodology that removes all of the mystery of Accounting and rolls it into three simple measures. So, let's look at the definition of these three, primary metrics," he said and posted a new overhead on the screen (Figure 3.1).

- *Throughput* is the rate at which inventory, or in your case patients, is converted into sales or revenue. If you make lots of products and put them in a warehouse, or in your case, see lots of patients and have them wait in waiting rooms, that is not throughput, it's just inventory. The products or services only count as Throughput if they are sold to the customer and you receive fresh money back into the business system.

- *Investment/Inventory* is the money an organization invests in items that it intends to sell or treat. This category would primarily include inventory, both raw materials and finished goods. It also includes things like buildings, machines and other equipment used to make products for sale, knowing that any, or all of these investments, could at some point in time, be sold for cash.

- *Operating Expense* is all of the money spent generating Throughput. This includes things like, rent, utilities, phone, benefits, wages, etc. It is any money spent that does not fit within one of the first two Throughput Accounting categories.

FIGURE 3.1
Definitions of T, I, and OE.

Tom then said, "When you read and understand these definitions, it seems likely that all the money within your company can be categorized to fit within one of these three measures." He then asked if there were any questions or comments, but again, there were none. This audience was captivated by what Tom was saying.

Tom then explained, "In thinking about Throughput Accounting, it's important to consider the following thoughts. Throughput Accounting is neither costing nor Cost Accounting. Instead, Throughput Accounting is focused on cash without the need for allocation to a specific product, which is very different than Cost Accounting." He continued, "This concept includes the variable and fixed expenses for a product or service. The only slight variation would be the calculation for Total Variable Cost (TVC). In this case the TVC is a cost that is truly variable to a product or service, such as raw materials, paying a sales commission or shipping charges."

Tom continued, "The sum total of these costs becomes the Totally Variable Costs or TVC. TVC is only the cost associated with each product or service. Some would argue that labor should also be added as a variable cost per product, but this is simply not true! Labor is no longer a variable cost, it's a fixed cost. Think about that! In terms of hourly labor measures, you pay employees for vacation, holidays and sick leave. You even pay them while they are making nothing or servicing no one! The employees cost you exactly the same amount of money, whether they are at work or not. Using this example, labor is an Operating Expense and not a variable cost associated with products or services, which is a vastly different concept than how Cost Accounting treats labor," Tom explained and then inserted a new slide onto the screen (Figure 3.2).

- Throughput (T) = Product Selling Price (SP) – the Total Variable Cost (TVC). Or simply

  $T = SP - TVC$.

- Net Profit (NP) = Throughput (T) minus Operational Expense (OE). Or $NP = T - OE$

- Return on Investment (ROI) = Net Profit (NP) divided by Inventory (I).

  Or $ROI = NP/I$

- Productivity (P) = Throughput (T) divided by Operating Expense (OE).

  Or $P = T/OE$

- Inventory Turns (IT) = Throughput (T) divided by Inventory Value (IV).

  Or $IT = T/IV$

FIGURE 3.2
Throughput Accounting definitions.

"Are there any questions about what I've presented so far?" he asked. Cindy raised her hand and asked, "Where did all of this come from Tom?" Tom responded, "Throughput Accounting was proposed by Dr. Eliyahu M. Goldratt as an alternative to traditional Cost Accounting in his and Jeff Cox's classic novel, [1] *The Goal*." "Okay, thank you." Cindy responded. Tom added, "I would encourage you to get a copy of their book or a book entitled, *Epiphanized* by Nelson and Sproull."

He continued his explanation, "Some would argue that Throughput Accounting falls short because it is not able to pigeon-hole all of the categories of Cost Accounting into Throughput Accounting categories. Things like interest payments on loans, or payment of stock-holder dividends, or even depreciation of machines or facilities. However, this argument is invalid. Ask yourself, which one of those specific categories can't be placed into one of the Throughput Accounting categories?" Tom said.

"The baseline Throughput Accounting concept is really very simple. Think of it this way. If you have to write a check to somebody else, it's either an Investment (I) or it's an Operating Expense (OE). It's an Investment, if it is something you can sell for money at some point in time. It's an Operating Expense if you can't. Just put this debt in the category that makes the most sense. On the other hand, if somebody is writing a check to you, then it's probably Throughput (T). Cost Accounting rules have made it much more complicated than it needs to be. And when you make it that complex and difficult, the stranglehold that Cost Accounting has on your thinking becomes even more obvious," Tom explained.

"Throughput Accounting is really focused on providing the necessary information that allows your decision-makers, like all of you, to make better decisions in real time. If the goal of your company is truly to make more money now, or make more money in the future, then any decisions being considered should get your company closer to the goal and not further away. Effective decision-making is well suited for an effective Throughput, Inventory, and Operating Expense analysis. This analysis can show the impact of any local decisions on the bottom line of the company," Tom explained. Bruce Johnson then asked, "Why has this form of Accounting not been made more well-known? I mean, based on what you've explained so far, why isn't it taught more in graduate schools?" he asked. "I wish I had a good answer for you Bruce, but I don't. All I know is that when I learned about it, it changed my whole approach to how companies should go about making better profits," he responded.

He then said, "Ideally good business decisions should cause these three things to happen. First, Throughput (T) should increase while, at the same time, Investment/Inventory will either decrease or stay the same. It is possible that Investment/Inventory can go up as long as the effect on Throughput is exponential. In other words, sometimes a very well-placed investment can cause the Throughput to skyrocket. The third thing that will happen when a good decision is made is that Operating Expenses will either decrease or stay the same. It is not always necessary to decrease Operating Expenses in order to have a dramatic effect on Throughput and ultimately profits. Consider the situation where the Throughput actually doubles and you didn't have to hire anyone new to do it, nor did you have to lay anyone off."

"The decision-making process becomes much easier when these factors are considered. The movement either up or down, of these three measures should provide sufficient information for good strategy and much better decisions. Any good decision should be based on global impacts to the company, and not just a single unit or process in isolation. If your thinking is limited to the lowest level of the organization, and you are focused on the wrong area, then the positive impact will never be seen or felt by the entire organization," Tom explained.

And again, Tom continued, "If we compare these two concepts at the highest level, then Cost Accounting is all about the actions you take to try and save money, while Throughput Accounting is all about the actions you take to make money. Once you've made the cost reductions and you still need more, what do you do next? Where else can you reduce costs? On the other hand, making money, at least in theory, is infinite. What is the limit on how much money your company can make now?" Tom asked rhetorically.

"In conclusion, the Throughput Accounting cost model contains only Total Variable Cost (TVC) and Throughput (T). The calculation is simple: Throughput = Selling Price − Totally Variable Costs. Throughput, in essence, equals the dollars remaining from selling the product, or delivering the service, after you have subtracted the Totally Variable Cost. Nothing is allocated, nothing is assumed, it's just a simple cash calculation from the sale," he explained. "The bottom line is this, if you have sales that you can't meet, or services you can't deliver, it's time to focus on your constraint and drive Throughput higher and higher. When Throughput increases and Operating Expenses decrease or remain the same, your profit margins will increase proportionally," Tom stated.

Tom continued and explained, "this is what we did at Tires for All and our margins increased dramatically. Before I conclude, I want to show you several run charts of our key performance metrics, and with that said, he posted these run charts (Figures 3.3–3.6). Here are our run charts for Profit Margins, Efficiency, On-Time Delivery, and Stock-Out Percentage and as you can see everything improved over time except for our Efficiency. In fact, if you compare our profit margins to our efficiency numbers, they are polar opposites. That is, as our efficiency decreased, our profit margins increased at the same time. What conclusions can you draw?"

With all this being said about the accounting method comparison, Tom recommended that everyone take a break, but to be back in fifteen minutes. Before they left, he asked if there were any questions, and Pete raised his hand. "In your last graph, you show stock-outs decreasing dramatically. Why did this happen?" "Hold that question until we come back," Tom said.

Pete stayed behind to speak with Tom. "Tom, I have to tell you, that was one of the finest presentations I have ever heard!" "Well thank you Pete, can I ask what you liked about it?" Tom asked. "So many things Tom. You took a very difficult subject and made it seem so easy, but what I really liked is that you have convinced me that our company needs to

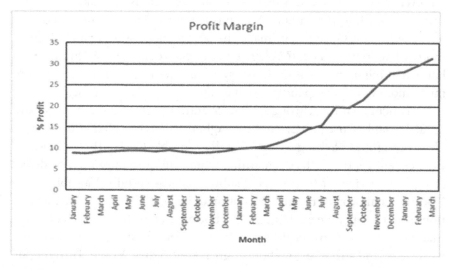

FIGURE 3.3
Profit Margins.

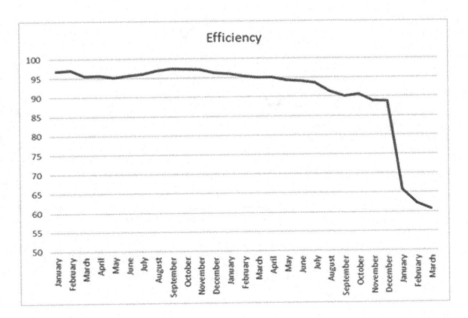

FIGURE 3.4
Efficiency.

FIGURE 3.5
On-time Delivery.

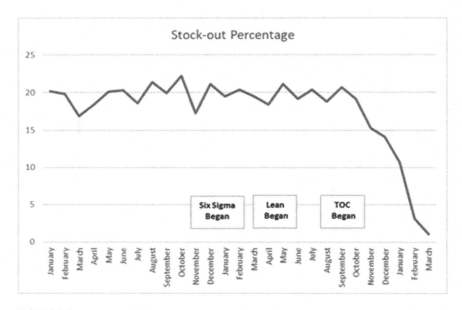

FIGURE 3.6
Stock-out Percentage.

implement Throughput Accounting!" Pete replied. "It's as though we have been tripping over dollars to pick-up pennies!" he added.

"Like I told this group, throughout my career, I have been working in the financial world in some capacity, but once I heard about Throughput Accounting, and what it can do for a company, I was convinced immediately that Tires for All needed to apply this method to our financial decision-making process!" Tom explained. "And the good news is, once we focused on increasing Throughput, our profitability dramatically improved to the level we now have," he added. "When everyone comes back from break, I want to say a few words to Cindy and Bruce, before you begin speaking again," Pete said.

When Cindy and Bruce were back in the conference room and seated, Pete began speaking. "I don't know about everyone else, but once I heard what Tom had to say about Throughput Accounting, I was convinced that this has to be embraced by our company. I say this, not because I want everyone to abandon Cost Accounting, but rather because I am convinced that in terms of real-time financial decisions, Throughput Accounting is much superior to it. So, with this in mind, I want our company to begin using Throughput Accounting to this end. I truly believe that by coupling our decision to eliminate driving efficiencies higher in non-constraints, with driving Throughput higher, the profitability of our companies will skyrocket!" And with that, he turned the podium back over to Tom.

"Thank you, Pete for your kind words about my presentation on Throughput Accounting," Tom said. "Do any of you have any questions for me about anything I presented to you today?" Tom asked. Pete raised his hand and said, "Before I met you, I had never heard about the Theory of Constraints, and I must say, it has changed my thinking going forward. My question is a general one in nature. What else can the Theory of Constraints do for our company?" he asked.

Tom looked at the audience and said, "The Theory of Constraints has so many facets to it. For example, earlier I presented run charts for on-time delivery and stock-out percentage. The Theory of Constraints version of its parts replenishment solution is completely different than what you are probably using. Imagine, for example, that you could very easily implement a procedure that could reduce your medical products inventory by fifty percent, while virtually eliminating stock-outs," he explained. "The Theory of Constraints also has its own version of a scheduling system that is far superior to what you're probably using now. This system is known as Drum Buffer Rope," Tom said. "In addition, the Theory of Constraints has a logic-based method that will help you plan your future improvement initiatives," Tom added. "The list goes on and on as to what the Theory of Constraints can do for you," Tom said.

"So, Tom, would you be interested in helping us learn more about the Theory of Constraints and all that it has to offer?" Pete asked. "What are you suggesting Pete?" Tom asked. "I was thinking that our company, Maximo Health Center Complex, could offer you an exclusive consulting agreement to come in and change our approach to running our business," Pete replied. "To be honest Pete, I had never considered working as a freelance consultant before," Tom said. "We think you'd be a fantastic consultant Tom, so please consider my offer," Pete said. "Would you at least consider my offer?" Pete asked. "I'll have to give this some thought Pete," Tom replied, and with that, Tom said that he had to leave to go to a meeting with my Board of Directors.

4

A New Direction

On his way back home from Maximo Health, Tom kept thinking about the offer he had just received from Pete Hallwell. Tom was very happy with his current role and had never considered becoming a consultant before. As he drove home, he thought that maybe he should call Bob Nelson, the owner of *Focus and Leverage Consulting* just to discuss this opportunity with him. Tom had so many unanswered questions in his mind about this potential opportunity, so he thought maybe Bob Nelson could help him answer some of his questions.

Tom pulled into his driveway, and his three children came running out of his house to greet him. Tom's three kids were named Tom Junior, Robert, and Susie, and he loved them dearly. His lovely wife Beverly was inside cooking dinner. Tom and his three children went into his home, and Susie shouted, "Mommy, Daddy's home!" Tom went over and kissed her on the cheek and whispered in her ear, "Honey, after dinner, I have something we need to talk about, and I need your advice." "Is it something serious honey?" she asked. "No, nothing serious, just an opportunity I want to talk to you about," Tom replied. They all sat down to dinner, and when dinner was over, the kids went into the family room to watch TV.

Tom and Beverly went into Tom's home office, and Tom began. "Honey, today I met with one of the men I played golf with on Saturday," Tom said. "I went there because, during our round of golf, we had talked about the Theory of Constraints and more specifically, Throughput Accounting," Tom explained. Beverly was well aware of both the Theory of Constraints and Throughput Accounting because she and Tom had talked about both subjects many times. "Anyway, this man works as the CFO of Maximo Health Center Complex, and he wanted me to come there and explain

Throughput Accounting in more detail," Tom said. "So, what's the problem Tom?" Beverly asked.

"There's no problem, but there may be an opportunity that I had never considered before," Tom replied. "An opportunity?" Beverly asked. "Yes, after I made my presentation, the CFO, Pete Hallwell, asked me if I would be interested in coming to Maximo Health Center Complex and become their exclusive consultant," Tom explained. "So, what's your issue Tom?" she asked. "Honey, the job I have is a great job and it pays so well," he explained. "And?" she asked. "The fact of the matter is that I love consulting and I see this as an opportunity to go off on my own and try something new, just like Bob Nelson," Tom said. "Honey, no matter what you decide to do, I will support your decision," Beverly added. "Here's what I was thinking honey," Tom said. "I thought it might be a good idea if I had a conversation with Bob Nelson about the pros and cons of becoming an independent consultant," Tom added. "I think that's a great approach Tom, so I would do it if I were you. As I said, no matter what you decide to do, I will support your decision," Beverly said.

After talking with his wife, he decided to call Bob Nelson and set up a meeting with him. "Hi Bob, it's Tom, how are you?" Tom asked. "I'm fine Tom, what's up?" he asked. "Do you have time to meet with me to chat about an opportunity I've been given that could change my whole direction in my work life?" Tom asked. "Well sure I do. When would you like to meet?" Bob asked. "Are you free tomorrow maybe for lunch?" Tom asked. "Where would you like to meet Tom?" Bob asked. "I was thinking that we could meet at Feroni's Restaurant around 12:00? Does that work for you Bob?" Tom asked. "It sure does Tom, I'll meet you there," Bob replied.

Right on schedule Bob and Tom arrived at the same time, got a table, and ordered lunch. "So, Tom, what is it you wanted to talk about?" Bob asked. "Well, remember when we played golf on Saturday?" Tom asked. "Yes, I do Tom, you shared a cart with Pete Hallwell and collected fifty dollars from each of us," Bob replied. "During our round of golf, we got on the subject of the Theory of Constraints and more specifically, the basics of Throughput Accounting," Tom explained. "After the round, Pete asked me to come to his company to share my knowledge of Throughput Accounting. When we were all finished, Pete offered me an opportunity to come consult for his company," Tom said. "That's great Tom, you must have really impressed Pete for him to make an offer like that!" Bob said. "Apparently I did Bob, but here's my question for you," Tom replied. "Should I take advantage of this opportunity?" he asked. "Tom, is it something you want to do?" Bob asked. "I'm not sure Bob, that's why I wanted to meet with you today," Tom said.

"Tom, this has to be your decision," Bob said. "I know that Bob, but I have many unanswered questions floating through my mind," Tom replied. "Such as?" Bob asked. "Well, I'm a pretty practical person," said Tom. "Having a regular paycheck and knowing where I'm going everyday gives me a sense of security," Tom said. "I'm not sure it's something that I want to give up," Tom explained. "If it makes you feel any better, I had the same concern before I started consulting," Bob replied. "What else are you concerned about Tom?" Bob asked.

"I'm thinking that giving up a steady paycheck might be intimidating. But regardless of how strong my consulting skills might be, I would think that every business owner has to embrace some level of uncertainty. I would also think that it can be very difficult to predict how many new clients I can bring on board, and exactly how much and when they'll pay you," Tom explained. Bob interjected, "You also have to factor in expenses like home office equipment, software and even things like insurance. As an independent consultant, you also need to get comfortable with the difference between gross revenue and net pay." "It seems like there are so many uncertainties by going independent," Tom replied.

Bob then said, "To account for the increased expenses, when I first started my business, I created a business checking account, and every two weeks, I paid myself a relatively conservative salary from that account. At the end of my first year, I even gave myself a 'bonus' with the money I had accumulated in my business account. I did all this just to make my transition from employee to independent consultant less stressful." "I really like that idea Bob!" Tom exclaimed. "What else?" Tom asked.

"When you're working on your own, your throughput is directly responsible for your paycheck. One thing I did was to use a VIP email address for my clients so that I could respond as quickly as possible. The other reason for doing this is because I wanted to set the expectation that I would always be available. You would also have to keep track of the necessary accounting tools, in order to make sure you always account for billable time. When I started, I set up a simple Excel file to make this easier. I then made the jump to QuickBooks in order to cut down on my time to update my Excel spreadsheets," Bob explained. "I like that idea too Bob!" Tom replied. "The flip side of the increased overhead is that you will then have control over your own schedule. I remember when my daughter was born, I gave myself a very generous paternity leave. What you end up with is a very flexible schedule and trust me, this flexibility is absolutely worth the extra effort required to keep your business running smoothly," Bob explained.

"If I take this opportunity, do you think I should work from home or should I rent an office space?" Tom asked. "When I first started, I absolutely worked from my home, and the good news is, your office space is tax deductible," Bob explained. "How about hiring someone to do things like take care of your books or scheduling your work?" Tom asked. "In time, I did hire help and that help was my wonderful wife," Bob said with a smile. "Nice idea Bob and I think my wife would enjoy working with me," Tom replied.

"One of the great benefits of working for yourself is the ability to take on more or less work, hire or not hire, keep a home office or rent an office—it's all up to you. My recommendation is that you take it one step at a time, just to make sure that you maintain your sanity. You may be wondering how you go about getting more clients, after your first assignment runs out?" Bob asked rhetorically. "Yes, how do you go about getting more clients Bob?" Tom asked.

"One of the first things you need to do is create a website. Your website should include things like your list of accomplishments, past and present clients, testimonials from past clients, you're approach to continuous improvement, any training you can provide, and anything else you can use to market yourself," Bob explained. "When I first started, I created a flyer that summarized all of the things I just mentioned and then mailed it out to numerous potential clients. And here's something else as you're making your decision, because I know you and what you're capable of. If I get requests that I can't honor, because of time constraints, I will send them your way," Bob said. "You will send me potential clients?" Tom asked. "Yes, I would be happy to do that!" Bob said with a touch of emotion.

"So, based on everything we've talked about today, what do you think your final decision will be Tom?" Bob asked. "Well, I feel much more confident that I can make this work, so right now I'm leaning toward accepting his offer," Tom responded. "I think that is a wise decision for you Tom, simply because I think you will absolutely succeed," Bob replied. And so, with their lunch meeting completed, they said their goodbyes. As they were walking out, Bob turned to Tom and said, "And Tom, if you need any help creating your website, I'm always available to assist you in any way that

I can." "Thank you so very much for everything today Bob, and I will probably take you up on your offer to help me with my website," Tom replied.

Tom went home and let his wife Beverly know that he had made his final decision to accept Pete's offer to consult for his company. He also told Beverly that he would not be immediately quitting his current position on the Board of Directors, as he had things to do before that happens. Beverly was fully supportive of his decision and even told him that if he needed help getting ready for his transition that she would be ready and willing to help in any way she can.

The next morning, Tom put in a call to Pete, just to let him know that he would accept Pete's offer. Pete didn't answer the phone, so he left a voice mail for Pete to return his call. Later that day, Pete returned his call and they worked out the details of his contract. His contract was to be paid on an hourly rate of $300/hour, with an average of forty hours per month that he must work. Pete agreed to it, so what they set up was a monthly payment of $12,000. The contract was guaranteed for one year, so, in effect, Tom's annual "salary" would be $144,000. In addition to the hourly rate, Tom also negotiated that he would receive "five percent" of the improvement in profit margins and that the margins would be calculated based upon Throughput Accounting and not Cost Accounting. The good news for Tom was that there was no exclusivity on his part, so he was free to take on other clients throughout the year. All he had to make sure of was that he gave Pete's company a total of 480 hours of work for the entire year. Both Pete and Tom were very happy with this contract.

After the phone call, he let his wife know what he had negotiated, and she was very happy with the contract he had agreed to honor. He then called Bob Nelson to get his opinion on his contract, and Bob told him that he thought it was a very reasonable contract. So, the stage was now set for Tom to let Jonathan Briggs, the Chairman of the Board, know what his plans were going forward. To that end, he scheduled a meeting with Jonathan for the next day. Tom was very curious as to what the reaction might be when he told the Board of Directors that he would be leaving. Jonathan asked him what the meeting would be about, so he told him that he had been offered a new position as an independent consultant. Needless to say, Jonathan was flabbergasted when he heard this news.

The next day Tom arrived for his meeting with Jonathan and perhaps some of the other Board Members. He went directly to Jonathan's office and after exchanging a few words, Jonathan told Tom that they needed to go to the Board Room to have this meeting. Surprisingly, when they walked into the Board Room, the entire Board of Directors were seated and ready to hear what Tom had to say. After reintroducing Tom to the Board, Jonathan handed the floor over to Tom and Tom began.

"It is with great reluctance that I am announcing my resignation and will be starting my own consulting firm effective in two weeks," Tom said. To Tom's surprise, what he heard next was applause from the Board Members. He thought to himself, "Were they happy to see me leaving?" Jonathan then stood up and said, "We, the members of the Board of Directors, want to thank you for the amazing work you have done for our portfolio of companies!" And then the applause started again. "And in appreciation for the work you have done for us, we would like to offer you a contract to continue consulting for us, not as an employee, but as an independent contractor," Jonathan said. "And with that, this meeting is adjourned," Jonathan said. "Tom, let's you and I go to my office to work out the details of your new contract," Jonathan said.

"So, Tom, let's hear about the contract conditions you just signed?" Jonathan said. Tom laid out the conditions of the contract he was to sign with Maximo Health Center Complex. Jonathan then said, "Rather than having lots of negotiations, let's say we use the same contract details for you with our Board of Directors?" "You mean the same number of hours, for the same pay, with the same bonus?" Tom asked. "Yes, that's exactly what I mean," Jonathan replied. "But if you work more hours than the agreed upon forty hours, we'll just add that onto your bonus check," Jonathan added. "I'll take that offer Jonathan," Tom replied. "I'll have our legal department write up your contract so we can sign it tomorrow," Jonathan said. "Sounds like a plan Jonathan," Tom replied. "Oh, and one other thing," said Jonathan. "As a token of our appreciation for the work you have done for us over the years, as part of our consulting agreement, you get to keep your health insurance!" Jonathan said.

Tom returned home, full of excitement about his new venture. While he had originally been worried about the financial end of his consulting venture, at the end of the day, he would actually be making close to what he had been making for the past year. Actually, if he did his math correctly, he had the potential to make more money consulting. Plus, he still has health insurance! He couldn't wait to get home to his wife and share the good news. "Honey, you're not going to believe the two consulting agreements I made today! I told you about the one with Maximo Health Center

Complex, but today I went in to resign my current role with the Board of Directors. They shocked me by first giving me a round of applause, which at first, I thought they were happy to see me resign. But I was so very wrong!" He explained the details of his new deal, and she put her arms around him and kissed him on the cheek. "Tom, I am so very proud of you!" she said. "So, when do you start honey?" she asked. "With the Board of Directors, I start tomorrow and with Maximo Health Center Complex, I start in two weeks!" he said with excitement.

Tom reported to work with the Board of Directors the next day and it seemed as though nothing had changed since he had the same office that he always had. He had a list of projects that he had been working on and all were doing very well. As he was sitting at his desk, there was a knock on his door and in came Jonathan. "Welcome back Tom," Jonathan said. "What are you working on today?" he asked. "I'm looking at the list of improvement projects I have going on at Semena Rubber Products," Tom replied. "I see that their profit margins are now up over 30% as of last week," he added. "Tom, I have a list of other companies that you haven't worked with yet, so I'd like to go over some of these with you," said Jonathan. "Sounds good Jonathan," Tom replied.

Jonathan showed Tom a list of four companies, owned by the Board of Directors, along with six key metrics these companies have been tracking and the person in charge (Table 4.1). Tom looked at the list and said, "Not surprisingly, these metrics are very close to the six companies I have worked with in the past year, except for Simpson Water Heaters." "Yes, you're absolutely right Tom," Jonathan replied. "Simpson Water Heaters is so bad, it's on the verge of shutting down!" he added. "The Board of Directors met yesterday afternoon and we all decided that these companies are where you should focus your improvement efforts," Jonathan explained. "And we'd like you to start with our water heater company," he added. He continued, "We're very confident that the other companies you've already 'fixed' will not need your input any longer, simply because you have given them the right kind of training, mindset, and controls to be able to continue performing." "I do understand Jonathan, and I will get to work on them right away," Tom replied. "Alright Tom, and good luck with your new consulting business," Jonathan said.

So, the stage was set for Tom's new venture with four new companies added to his list. Tom spent the rest of the day reading about these four companies and imagining what he would need to do to turn them into

TABLE 4.1

Four New Portfolio Companies

Company Name	% On-Time Delivery	% Scrap	% Rework	Stock-Out %	Efficiency %	% Profit Margins	Person in Charge
Tamsen Auto Parts	68.9	4.8	10.1	11.2	95.4	5.7	Bill Dawson
Simpson Water Heaters	68.1	8.8	15.6	19.1	94.7	−1.2	Matt Maloney
Watson Rubber Articles	70.9	6.8	8.8	9.9	88.7	7.8	Sarah Johnson
Jackson Electronics	75.4	4.9	14.2	13.4	89.9	9.1	Tim Selsa

much more profitable companies. He thought to himself, "The good news is, these new companies probably will be performing the way his other six companies were when he began his improvement efforts." So, with this in mind, he made a series of phone calls to each of these new companies to introduce himself and to set the stage for a visit to each one.

Tom also searched the internet for information on Maximo Health Center Complex, looking for what type each of the six hospitals were. He found that one of the hospitals specialized in children, one focused on pregnant women, one specialized in elderly people, and the remaining three hospitals were general hospitals, with one of them being affiliated with a local university, which meant there were probably many interns there. One thing Tom was sure of, and that was that he would be very busy over the next year, especially with the portfolio company that's losing money!

5

Maximo Health Center Complex

Bright and early, Monday morning, Tom called Pete Hallwell, the CFO at Maximo Health Center Complex. "Hello, this is Pete Hallwell, how can I help you?" Pete said when he answered the telephone. "Good morning Pete, this is Tom Mahanan," Tom said. "Well hi Tom, what can I do for you?" Pete asked. "One thing I was calling about was to find out if you have my consulting contract ready for me to sign?" Tom said. "Yes, I have it right here on my desk, whenever you're ready to come and sign it," Pete replied. "Great, I'll come in later today," Tom said.

"The other thing I was calling about was to ask you if you could have someone put together a list of performance metrics that your hospitals track on a regular basis?" he asked. "Are you talking about things like efficiencies, profit margins, etc.?" Pete replied. "Yes, that's exactly what I'm referring to Pete," Tom said. "Do you want to see all of our metrics, or are you more interested in those that relate to patient flow through our various hospital segments?" Pete asked. "I think as a starting point, just those metrics that tie into patient flow, but of course, I'm interested in profit margins as well," Tom replied. "I'll have someone put together the list of metrics and when you come in to sign your consulting agreement, we can look at the list and see if we've covered everything," Pete said. "Sounds good Pete, what time would you like me to come in?" Tom asked. "How about 1:00 pm?" Pete replied. "Sounds like a plan Pete, I'll see you then," Tom replied.

Later that day, Tom arrived at Maximo Health Center Complex, signed in and the security guard called Pete to let him know that Tom was in the lobby. Moments later, Pete arrived, and the two of them went to Pete's office. "Here is your contract Tom, so take a minute to look it over and if it looks good to you, go ahead and sign it," Pete said. Tom took several minutes to look it over and said it looked good to him, so he signed it.

Pete then reached in his desk drawer and pulled out a document that summarized some of the performance metrics tracked by the Maximo Health Center Complex. Tom looked it over and said, "Tom, while these are no doubt important metrics for you company, what I'd like to do is simplify this list and boil it down to just a few key metrics that focus on the flow of patients through your hospitals," Tom explained. The list presented by Pete included five different categories as follows:

- Volume Metrics
- Revenue Leakage Metrics
- Utilization Metrics
- Quality Metrics
- Financial Metrics

Pete then pulled out a different sheet of eight key metrics that Maximo Health Center Complex tracked on a regular basis. Tom reviewed this list, and once again, he indicated that he wanted to simplify the list of key metrics that he believed would be better to track (Table 5.1).

"Let me review this list of metrics and I'll give you my thoughts on what simple metrics we can track to measure the impact of our improvement efforts," Tom said. "Just off the top, I'm thinking that one of the metrics

TABLE 5.1

Key Hospital Performance Metrics

Metric	Metric Description
Average Hospital Stay	Appraise the amount of time your patients are staying in your hospital after admission?
Treatment Costs	Calculate what a patient costs your facility?
Hospital Readmission Rate	Calculate how many patients are coming back after they are discharged?
Patient Wait Time	Calculate your patient satisfaction score by assessing their average wait time.
Patient Satisfaction	How patients felt while being taken care of in your hospital?
Patient Safety	Identify any incidents happening in your hospital and reduce the patients' exposure to further risk?
ER Wait Time to See a Doctor	Evaluate the time patients spend from checking in to the ER until they see a doctor.
Costs by Payer	Evaluate which type of health insurance they have and what it costs.

we will use is % Profit, but we'll use Throughput Accounting's calculation to get your margins," Tom added. "I think another metric we could track would be your average hospital stay, since if we could reduce that number, it would be the equivalent of an increase in Throughput. Maybe another metric we could track would be patient wait times, simply because if we could reduce that, it would translate into your hospitals ability to see more patients in a given period of time," he added.

"Another metric that I'm certain you track is efficiency or some derivative of it. We want to be able to drive this metric lower, simply because the only place it matters is in the system constraint," Tom explained. "As a matter of fact, I think one of the things you should do in advance of our improvement efforts, would be to put together a process map on several of your key processes. Maybe something like your surgical process, or maybe even you Emergency Department process. If we can shorten these, the net result is being able to see more patients, which translates into increased revenue, and therefore, improved profit margins. Let me get back to you on a final list, but until I do, have someone create some process maps on some of your key processes," Tom explained. "For example, I once consulted for a hospital Emergency Department, where we were looking at Door to Balloon (D2B) Time for patients with STEMI type heart attacks. So, if you could get someone to map out this process and include cycle times for each of the major steps in this procedure, we could set up a team on this one," Tom explained. "I remember we were able to reduce the D2B Time from a median of 66, down to a median of around 53 minutes, which in this type of heart attack was a very significant improvement, simply because the longer the duration of this type of heart attack, the more damage is done to the heart," Tom added. Tom continued, "One day I will give you the details of this case study and discuss several of the tools that this team used."

As Tom was driving home, he began thinking about what should be included in Maximo Health Center Complex's list of performance metrics. He thought to himself, "Maximo Health Center Complex's profits are all tied to the number of patients they can see and treat, so there has to be a metric centered around this." He continued thinking, "One of the keys to increasing the number of patients seen and treated revolves around patient wait times, and I know they already measure patient wait time, so this should be one of the key metrics to track. I think another metric that ties into both of these metrics is another metric they already measure and that is, average hospital stay, so that should be another one.

Just like Saint Mary's hospital that he had worked with to reduce, STEMI heart attack treatment time, and maybe even other Emergency Department repetitive conditions, he believed that one of the key metrics should be focused there. One thing Tom knew for sure was that hospitals have many different opportunities that could be addressed to drive profitability upward. "There are numerous treatment clinics that would benefit from my integrated Theory of Constraints, Lean, and Six Sigma," Tom thought to himself. Tom made mental notes of all he had considered during his drive home until he pulled into his driveway.

Tom grabbed his briefcase and walked in his front door. His wife Beverly was in the kitchen making dinner and said, "Hi honey, how did your meeting go with Maximo Health Center Complex?" "It actually went very well, and I was able to sign my contract with them," Tom replied. "What are you making for dinner honey?" Tom asked. "Your favorite meal, Chicken Divan," she replied. "Oh, thanks honey, I'm in the mood for that," Tom said. "Need help with anything honey?" he asked. "Nope, I have everything under control," she said. "OK, I'll be in my office, so let me know if you need anything," Tom said.

Tom recollected his thoughts on Maximo Health Center Complex's performance metrics and decided to make a list that he could review with Pete Hallwell. After thinking through his list, Tom's final list was condensed to the following five metrics:

1. % Profit Margins
2. Average Hospital Stay
3. Patient Wait Times
4. Patient Satisfaction
5. Efficiency % or Utilization

He thought to himself, "These metrics are the global metrics that we can track for the entire company, but I'm certain that there will be many more specific metrics which will be tied to each of the improvement projects as the teams attack different problems within each of the hospitals."

Tom now turned his attention to one of the portfolio companies he had discussed with Jonathan Briggs, Simpson Water Heaters. Tom thought to himself, "I really don't know anything about water heaters and how they are produced, so I'm going to need some help with this one." Tom decided to call Jonathan and ask him some questions about this company. Tom dialed Jonathan's number, and within two rings, his call was answered, "Hello, Jonathan Briggs here, how can I help you?" "Hi Jonathan, it's Tom Mahanan," Tom replied. "Hi Tom, what's up?" Jonathan asked. "I want to get started on Simpson Water Heaters right away, so I need a contact at their location, and by the way, where are they located?" "They're located in Detroit, Michigan, and I think the best contact would be their Plant Manager, Matt Maloney," Jonathan said.

"Can you tell me something about his background Jonathan?" Tom asked. "Matt is a relatively new hire for Simpson Water Heaters and prior to coming on board, his background was in Logistics," Jonathan replied. "I've met Matt and, as you will see, he is very impressive!" Jonathan added. "Why do you say he's very impressive Jonathan?" Tom asked. "For one thing, he is always looking for better ways to do things," Jonathan said. "One of the reasons he was hired was that he has some experience with the Theory of Constraints, so that alone qualified him for this position," Jonathan added. "That's great Jonathan, we both know that this will be a quality that will 'speed-up' their improvement," Tom said. "How long has he been there at Simpson Water Heaters and do you have his phone number?" Tom asked. "Just three weeks, and his phone number is on our website," Jonathan replied. "OK, thanks Jonathan," Tom said and with that he ended the phone call.

Tom decided that he might as well contact Plant Manager, Matt Maloney, now, so he got on the Board's website and got his phone number. He dialed the number and within three rings, someone answered the phone. "Hello, Simpson Water Heaters, this is Emily Johnson, how can I help you?" she asked. "Hi Emily, this is Tom Mahanan, and I'm trying to reach Matt, is he available?" Tom asked. "He's out on the production floor somewhere, do you want me to go find him?" asked Emily. "No, just tell him to call me today when he gets a chance," Tom replied and gave Emily his phone number. "I will do that Tom," she said, and the call ended.

An hour later, Tom received a call from Matt Maloney that Tom answered and said, "Hello, this is Tom Mahanan." "Hi Tom, this is Matt Maloney returning your call," Matt said. "Hi Matt, thanks for returning my call," Tom replied. "Matt, not sure if you know me or not, but I am working with the Board of Directors for Simpson Water Heaters. I called Jonathan Briggs and asked him for a contact at your company and he gave me your name," Tom explained. "Just so you know, I worked directly with the Board of Directors and had been in charge of the portfolio's continuous improvement efforts. Within the last week, I resigned that position and became an independent consultant, but to my surprise, the Board hired me right back for consulting purposes," Tom explained. "Because of your company's dreadful numbers, especially the % Profit Margins, I will be coming to Detroit to start a continuous improvement effort," Tom added.

"I know you've only been there a short period of time, but I also know you have some experience with the Theory of Constraints and Theory of Constraints plays a big part in my improvement methodology," Tom explained. "So Matt, tell me about your experience with the Theory of Constraints?" Tom asked. "Well, my experience is somewhat limited, in that I tried to implement it at the company I worked for and it was flat-out rejected by the leadership," Matt explained. "Do you know why they rejected it Matt?" Tom asked. "The CEO of that company told me that, based upon what he had heard about the Theory of Constraints, their company's Efficiency % would take a nosedive and he wanted nothing to do with it!" Matt exclaimed. Tom just chuckled and said, "Does not surprise me one single bit Matt." "What I'd like to do is come visit your company and explain my method to you," Tom said. "And for the record, Jonathan Briggs, the CEO of the Board of Directors is solidly behind my method," Tom added. "Great news Tom, so when would you like to come here?" Matt asked. "Next week some time, so look at your schedule and get back to me on the best day to come," Tom said. "Will do Tom," Matt said.

Later on, in the day, Tom received an email from Matt Maloney, and in it, he had suggested that Tuesday would be the best day for him to meet with Tom. Tom looked at his schedule and returned Matt's email indicating that Tuesday works for him and that he would be there Tuesday morning around 8:00 am. Tom also suggested that they should meet in their conference room and that he should invite anyone he feels should be there. Tom also let Matt know that one of the things he wanted to do was present his methodology which he referred to as the *Ultimate Improvement Cycle* which should take a couple of hours to present. Later in the day, Tom received a reply from Matt, indicating that he would set everything up for their meeting.

So, the stage was set to hopefully turn Simpson Water Heater's negative profits into positive ones. Tom then thought about all he wanted to do with Matt while he was there, but at least he knew he didn't have to convince Matt of the power of the Theory of Constraints, and that was a good thing. Tom thought about what else he should present, so he reviewed their key metrics in Table 5.2.

TABLE 5.2

Performance Metrics for New Companies

Company Name	% On-Time Delivery	% Scrap	% Rework	Stock-Out %	Efficiency %	% Profit Margins
Tamsen Auto Parts	68.9	4.8	10.1	11.2	95.4	5.7
Simpson Water Heaters	68.1	8.8	15.6	19.1	94.7	−1.2
Watson Rubber Articles	70.9	6.8	8.8	9.9	88.7	7.8
Jackson Electronics	75.4	4.9	14.2	13.4	89.9	9.1

It was clear to Tom, after reviewing these metrics, that there was much work to do. For each of the six key metrics, Simpson Water Heaters was performing the worst of the four companies. Their % On-Time Delivery was right around 71%, their scrap stood at almost 9%, and their rework was approaching 16%! In addition, their Stock-Out % was 19% which probably tied directly into their abysmal % On-Time Delivery. Their Efficiency % was almost 95% which clearly was tied to their −1.2% Profit Margins! After reviewing these metrics, Tom knew that these were clearly a part of a broken system!

Tom thought about how he might present this opportunity to the employees in the conference room and he decided that he would present the before and after results for the original portfolio of companies as depicted in Table 5.3. He believed that once they saw these results, they would most likely buy-in to his improvement methodology. At least he hoped that it would have this affect.

Tom knew that in order for Simpson Water Heaters to reach the improvement levels seen in Table 5.3, they had to learn about things like Theory of Constraints' version of accounting known as Throughput Accounting, plus the Theory of Constraints Replenishment Solution, and Theory of Constraints' scheduling system referred to as Drum Buffer Rope. He decided that during his visit, he would at least touch on these three methods. But to him, the most important point he must deliver was the basic concept of a system constraint. In fact, Tom decided that he would begin his presentation with this subject. So, with these thoughts in mind, Tom was ready for his trip to Detroit the following week.

TABLE 5.3

Before and After Results

Company Name	%On-Time Delivery		% Scrap		% Rework		Stock-Out %		Efficiency %		%Profit Margins	
	Before	After	Before	After	Before	After	Before	After	Before	After	Before	After
Board of Directors Portfolio Companies												
Terox Automotive	79.6	91.6	4.1	2.1	8.8	3.2	10.7	1.1	91.9	62.1	4.9	27.9
Sweeney Automotive	69.5	94.3	3.8	1.5	7.6	2.1	11.7	0.9	93.4	71.2	6.1	22.2
Johnson Electronics	78.3	92.2	7.2	2.2	13.3	4.2	10.9	1.8	90.6	65.7	7.7	30.4
Westin Incorporated	80.4	96.5	9.5	1.3	11.4	2.7	8.8	0.7	85.6	69.3	8.8	25.6
Watson Steel Products	77.8	95.5	4.3	2.2	8.8	3.2	9.9	1.6	90.4	70.5	10.9	30.8
Semena Rubber Products	80.2	97.7	6.6	3.0	6.7	1.8	8.3	0.2	86.2	71.1	11.4	28.8

6

Simpson's New Beginning

Right on schedule, Tom arrived at Simpson Water Heaters and was met in the lobby by Matt Maloney. "What time have you scheduled our session for Matt?" Tom asked. "We're scheduled to start at 9:00," Matt replied. "It's only 8:00 now, so could you show me your manufacturing process?" Tom asked. "Be happy to, where would you like to start, Tom?" Matt asked. "Let's start at your raw material receiving department and work our way through your process all the way to shipping," Tom replied. The two of them walked to the back of the plant to receiving. "I'm not interested in the details Matt, just the flow from raw materials to shipping," Tom said.

The two of them walked the process with Tom making notes as he progressed through the entire process. When they arrived at the warehouse and shipping, Tom was amazed at the level of inventory of finished and semi-finished water heaters existed in the storage racks. Tom asked Matt, "Do you have orders for all of these tanks?" "No, we do not Tom and as you can see, many of them are not even complete," Matt responded. "Why do you have such a mountain of inventory if you don't have sales?" Tom asked. "That was one of the first questions I asked when I started this job and the response floored me," Matt said. "It seems that everyone is so focused on keeping their efficiencies high, that they just continue making water heaters," Matt added. Tom made a note on his iPad, and it was now time to move to the conference room for his presentation.

When everyone was seated, Matt introduced Tom and Tom began. There were seven people seated, so Tom's first question was for everyone to introduce themselves and state their role at Simpson Water Heaters. "I am Nancy Watson and I am the Accounting Manager." The introductions continued, "I am Greg Thompson and I am the Production Manager." "I am Cynthia Eberstein and I am the Quality Manager."

"I am Bill Gregory and I am the Shipping Manager." "I am Ted Russell and I am the Purchasing Manager." "I am Terry Jones and I am the Engineering Manager." "I'm very happy to meet everyone, so let's get started. I want everyone to listen with an open mind on what I have to say today," Tom said. With the introductions complete, Tom opened his laptop, pulled up a file, and began.

"The figure you see on my screen (Figure 6.1) is the cross section of a simple, gravity fed, piping system used to transport water. As you can see, water enters into this system through Section A, then flows into Section B, then Section C and so forth until it exits Section I and is collected in a receptacle at the bottom of this system." "So, here's my first question for you," said Tom. "If you were asked to increase the flow of water through this system, what would you need to do to make this happen?" Tom asked. The group studied the drawing until Terry Jones raised his hand and said, "Couldn't you just turn the pressure up higher?" "No Terry, as

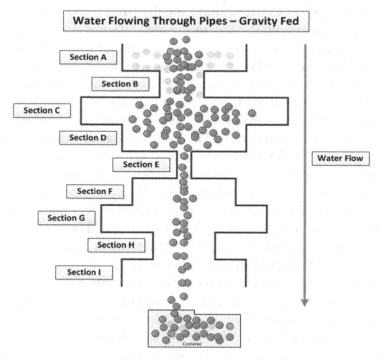

FIGURE 6.1
Piping system used to transport water.

I explained, this system is a gravity fed system," Tom replied. "Look closer, he said to the group," he added.

Greg Thompson, the Production Manager, raised his hand and said, "It seems to me that if you wanted more water to pass through this piping system, you would need to open-up the diameter of the pipe in Section E." "And why is it that you think this, Greg?" Tom asked. "Well, for me the reason is that Section E is what is limiting the flow of water because it's the smallest diameter pipe in the system?" he said in a question. "Greg, you're absolutely correct in your assessment of this system!" Tom exclaimed. "Does everyone see what Greg explained?" he asked, and it appeared as though everyone did.

"So, Greg, one more question for you. What would determine how large the new diameter of Section E should be?" Tom asked. Greg looked at the drawing again and said, "I think it would depend on how much more water is required?" again responding in a question-type format. "Once again you are correct Greg, it would depend upon the new demand requirement," Tom replied. "So, based upon what Greg has instructed us to do, the new system might look like this," and Tom flashed a new figure (Figure 6.2) on his laptop screen.

"Here you see the same piping system, but it now has Section E's new diameter," Tom explained. "So, my next question for the group is, if there was another increase in demand for water, what would you have to do and why would you do it?" Tom asked. Nancy Watson raised her hand and said, "Clearly, based upon what we learned on Section E, you would now have to enlarge Section B's diameter." And then she added, "And the new diameter would be based upon the new demand requirement." "Very well said Nancy!" Tom exclaimed. "Any questions so far?" Tom asked the group.

Ted Russell, the Purchasing Manager, raised his hand and asked, "With all due respect, what has this piping system got to do with how we make water heaters?" "Great question," Tom said as he flashed a new figure on his laptop screen (Figure 6.3). What you see here is a very simple, 4-step manufacturing process used to make something. Raw materials enter Step 1 are processed for 5 minutes and then passed on to Step 2, which takes 30 minutes to process, before passing it on to Step 3, which requires 60 minutes to complete before passing the semi-finished product on to Step 4, where it's completed as a finished product in 10 minutes.

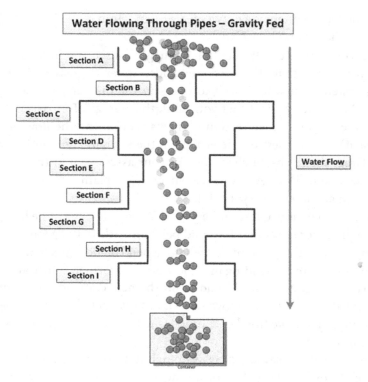

FIGURE 6.2
Piping system with Section E's diameter enlarged.

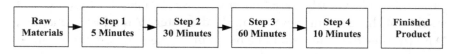

FIGURE 6.3
Simple manufacturing process.

"Using the piping system as a reference guide, what if there was a surge in demand?" he asked. "What would you do and why would you do it?" he added. Matt Maloney, the Plant Manager spoke up and said, "Well, based upon what we just heard about the piping system, it seems obvious to me that we would have to reduce the cycle time on Step 3, because it is the equivalent to Section E of the piping diagram. And how much time we would have to reduce the cycle time would be completely dependent upon how much more finished product would be required. "Absolutely correct Matt!" Tom responded.

"So, one more question for you Matt," Tom said. "How fast should Steps 1 and 2 be running and why?" Tom asked. "Well, in order to avoid a build-up of work-in-process inventory, Steps 1 and 2 should be producing at the same rate as Step 3," Matt explained. "But Matt, what would happen to the efficiencies of Steps 1 and 2 if they stopped producing at their capacity?" asked Nancy Watson, the Accounting Manager. Tom put his hand over his mouth to avoid anyone seeing his smile. Matt then said, "Nancy, it would seem to me that efficiency is not a good metric for us!" "Why Matt, we've been tracking efficiencies for as long as I've worked here and based upon what I've seen from the Board's reports, our efficiencies are one of the best in their portfolio of companies?" Nancy responded. "Yes, that's true, but our profit margins are the absolute worst of all the portfolio companies," Matt responded with emotion.

Tom suggested that everyone take a brief break, while he loads the next part of his presentation. Matt stayed behind and said, "Tom, I have never seen this material presented in this way before, and I have to tell you, it was impressive and so easy to understand!" "I'm happy you are enjoying it so far Matt, but I think the next part will also be enjoyable as well," Tom responded. "What is it the you're going to be presenting next Tom?" Matt asked. "The next section will be Goldratt's Five Focusing Steps and then on to Throughput Accounting," Tom explained.

When everyone was back from their break, Tom began again. "I know the material I presented so far is new for most of you, but I want to expand on what I've explained so far. Back in the 1980s a man named Dr. Eliyahu Goldratt introduced the world to what he referred to as his Five Focusing Steps." Tom flashed another overhead on his laptop screen (Figure 6.4) and said, "Here are the five steps that Goldratt presented to the world," Tom explained.

- Step 1: *Identify* the system constraint.

- Step 2: Decide how to *exploit* the system constraint.

- Step 3: *Subordinate* everything else to the system constraint.

- Step 4: If necessary, *elevate* the system constraint.

- Step 5: When the constraint is broken, return to Step 1, but don't let inertia create a new constraint.

FIGURE 6.4
Goldratt's Five Focusing Steps.

Tom began again, "I want everyone to think about how these five steps apply to both the piping system and the simple four-step process we just discussed. In both examples, we were able to identify the system constraint, or that step that limits the output of the remaining steps. You were able to come up with a way to exploit the identified constraint, by increasing the diameter of Section E of the piping system and reducing the cycle time of Step 3 of the 4-step process. You were also able to decide how to subordinate the other steps to the system constraint. In the case of the piping system the subordination step was automatic because the throughput of water was controlled by the smallest diameter pipe. In the case of the 4-step process, you forced Steps 1 and 2 to operate at the same rate as the constraint, which is the essence of subordination," Tom explained.

Tom continued, "Step 4 of Goldratt's Five Focusing Steps tell us that if it is necessary, we should elevate the system constraint. What this means, in reality, is that if we need to reduce the cycle time of the constraining step, we might have to spend some money to improve the capacity of the system constraint. But having said this, normally we will be able to 'break' the constraint of the system by doing things like reducing excess waste within the constraint. This includes things like removing wait times or even transferring some of the work from the constraint to a non-constraint step in the process." "Breaking the constraint simply means that we will have improved its capacity to the point where another step in our process becomes the new system constraint. And when this happens, we need to immediately move our improvement efforts to the new constraint. Remember in the piping diagram, Section E was the original system constraint, but when we increased its diameter, the next smallest diameter pipe became the new system constraint, which was Section B of the piping system. Any questions so far?" he asked the group.

Nancy Watson, the Accounting Manager, raised her hand and said, "I'm a little confused about the subordination step?" "What are you confused about Nancy?" Tom asked. "I remember the argument you made earlier about the negative impact of trying to drive efficiencies higher, but could you explain this step a different way with regards to the negative impact of non-constraints producing to capacity?" she asked. "I'd be happy to Nancy," he replied. "Let's take another look at a different process example," Tom suggested as he flashed Figure 6.5 onto his screen.

"Here we see that Step 3 is the system constraint, because it has the longest cycle time," Tom explained. "Nancy, what happens to this process if

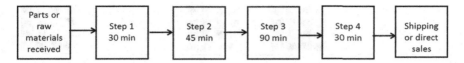

FIGURE 6.5
Simple four-step process.

you are measuring efficiencies and trying to drive this metric higher and higher?" Tom asked. "I'm not sure I understand your question Tom?" she replied in a question like manner. "What I mean is that from a physical perspective, what happens to the flow of product through this system?" he asked Nancy. "In other words, considering the capacity of Steps 1 and 2, which are obviously higher than Step 3, what would this process look like after eight hours, in terms of work-in-process inventory?" Tom added.

"Well, since both Steps 1 and 2 can produce product at a faster rate than Step 3, I would guess that work-in-process inventory would accumulate in front of Step 3," She replied. "That's exactly what would happen Nancy and it would look something like this," Tom said as he flashed another drawing on his screen (Figure 6.6).

"Alright, I understand this, but what's so negative about having WIP in the process?" Nancy asked. "Let's now look at this same process, after three 8-hour shifts of work," he explained as he inserted a new slide onto his screen (Figure 6.7). "It should be obvious that the longer the non-constraints continue to produce at their maximum capacity, the amount of WIP within this process will continue to increase," Tom said.

"I understand that Tom, but what's so bad about having excess WIP within your process?" she asked. Just then, Matt raised his hand and said,

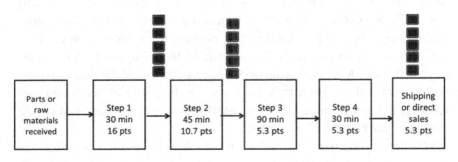

FIGURE 6.6
Process with excessive WIP.

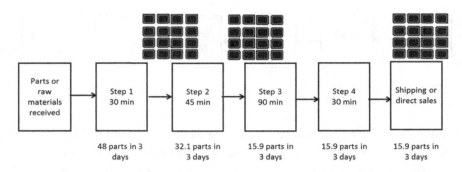

FIGURE 6.7
Process WIP after 3, 8-hour shifts.

"Tom, can I take a shot at answering Nancy's question?" "You sure can Matt," Tom replied. "One of the most important reasons for avoiding excessive amounts of WIP in any process, is what it does to the overall cycle time of individual parts. That is, each of the individual parts in front of Steps 2 and 3, just sit there and wait to be processed until Step 3 completes a part and passes it on to Step 4. The ultimate effect of this is that it needlessly ties up cash that can be used elsewhere in our company," Matt explained. "Alright, I see your point Matt, excessive WIP in any process negatively impacts things like on-time delivery and our cash flow," Nancy said. "Thank you for your explanation Matt," she added. "Good explanation Matt, but I plan on getting into this question in more detail shortly," Tom said.

Tom then suggested that the group take another brief break while he prepares for his next subject to be discussed. Once again, Matt stayed behind and asked, "So, Tom, what are we going to discuss next?" "Now that we've discussed the basics of the Theory of Constraints, I want to turn our attention to Theory of Constraints' version of accounting known as Throughput Accounting," Tom explained. "Matt, I do have a question for you," Tom said. "As a company, what level of experience does Simpson Water Heaters have with Lean Manufacturing or Six Sigma?" he asked. "Based upon my research since I got here, they have tried both Lean and Six Sigma, but apparently not with much success," Matt responded. "Alright, just checking for future reference," Tom said.

When everyone had returned from their break, Tom began again. "In any improvement initiative, the person responsible for the financial well-being of your business plays a pivotal role in assuring that the initiative stays focused on the primary goal of most companies which is to make money now and in the future. Within the confines of an improvement methodology known as the Theory of Constraints, I'm going to present an alternate form of accounting, known as Throughput Accounting (TA), that is intended to be used for real-time financial decisions rather than basing decisions on what happened last month."

Many businesses will emphatically state that the primary goal of their business is to make money and yet they spend the largest portion of their time trying to save money, which is what I am sure I will see here at "Simpson Water Heaters," Tom explained. Tom continued, "The key to profitability is by focusing on that part of the system that controls and drives revenue higher and higher, rather than through cost-cutting. It matters not if you are a service provider, a small business owner, a distributor, or a manufacturer. What you need is a way to sell more product which increases revenue and, ultimately, profitability. In this session I will systematically compare two accounting methods and demonstrate the superiority of Throughput Accounting in terms of profitability improvement."

"Much of what I'm going to explain in this session is taken from the book, *Reaching the Goal* – by John Ricketts, and I highly recommend that you purchase and read this book!" Tom exclaimed. "Because traditional Cost Accounting is so complicated, in this discussion, and because most of you are familiar with Cost Accounting, I won't go into great detail, but I will cover the highlights of it so that a comparison to Throughput Accounting can be made. Before I start, have any of you ever heard of Throughput Accounting?" Tom asked the group. All of them, except Matt, shook their heads as if to say no, so he began his discussion. "If you have any questions as I present this, stop me and ask them," Tom said.

"The figure (Figure 6.8) on the screen illustrates selected elements of Cost Accounting (CA). When Cost Accounting arose in the early 1900s,

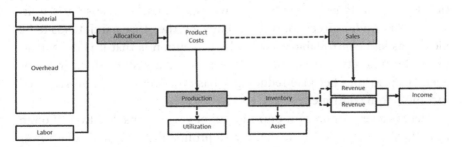

FIGURE 6.8
Selected elements of Cost Accounting.

labor costs dominated manufacturing and workers were paid by how many parts they produced. Back then, it was absolutely reasonable to allocate overhead expenses to products on the basis of direct labor costs for purposes of preparing financial statements. But since automation now dominates manufacturing, and workers are paid by the hour, allocation of large overhead expenses on the basis of small labor costs has created some very real distortions," Tom explained.

Tom continued, "When re-aggregated at the enterprise level, product cost distortions do not affect financial statements very much. Yet, if prices are computed as product cost, plus standard gross margin, which is the prevailing method used in Cost Accounting, product cost distortions carry into product pricing. The net effect is that some products appear to be profitable when they aren't and some products that appear unprofitable really are," Tom explained. "Any questions so far?" he asked. Since there weren't any, he continued.

"A second problem with Cost Accounting is that it encourages factories to produce excess inventory. To refer back to Nancy's earlier question about why having excessive WIP is a bad thing, this happens because of Cost Accounting's push for higher levels of efficiencies in non-constraints. Inventory accumulation can be driven by the counterintuitive effect it has on earnings. Rather than being expensed on the income statement in the period they were incurred, the cost of inventory goes on the balance sheet as an *asset*. Consequently, an inventory profit may be reported, which a business can use to smooth reported earnings, even though it has absolutely nothing to do with real income. If that inventory can't be sold, then inventory on the balance sheet turns into depreciation expense on the income statement and an inventory loss results," Tom explained. "Any questions?" he asked, but there weren't any.

"A third problem with Cost Accounting concerns management priorities. Operating Expense tends to be managed closely because it is well-known and under direct control. Revenue, on the other hand, tends to be viewed as less controllable because the perception is that it is dependent upon the markets and customers. Inventory is a distant third in management priorities because reducing it has an adverse effect on reported income," Tom continued.

"Here is a very important point for all of you to consider. Even though most businesses practice it, the key to profitability is not through how much money you can save! The key to profitability is through how much money you can make! And these two approaches are radically different! Let's now look at a different accounting method referred to as Throughput Accounting (TA) in order to answer this question," Tom said. "And again, if you have questions about the material I am presenting, stop me and ask away," Tom added.

"Throughput Accounting (TA) addresses all of the problems associated with Cost Accounting (CA) that we just saw, by not using product costs. Instead Throughput Accounting eliminates incentives for excess inventory. It's important for all of you to understand that Throughput Accounting cannot be used in place of conventional financial reporting, simply because publicly traded companies, like Simpson Water Heaters, are required by law to comply with GAAP requirements. But having said this, Throughput Accounting does provide a way to make much better 'real time' financial decisions. Throughput Accounting will tell you which products combine to deliver the most profitable mix of products, and trust me, Throughput Accounting's mix will be different than what traditional Cost Accounting would give you," he explained. "Are you telling us that by using Throughput Accounting, the mix of products will change the level of profitability that is different than Cost Accounting?" Nancy asked. "Yes, and I will give you an example of that shortly," Tom responded.

Tom began again, "Throughput Accounting uses three basic financial measures, which are, Throughput (T), Inventory or Investment (I), and Operating Expense (OE). So, let's look at each of these in a bit more detail. Throughput (T) is simply the rate at which your system generates money through sales of products or services, or interest generated. If you produce something, but don't sell it, it's not Throughput, it's just Inventory. Throughput is obtained after subtracting the Totally Variable Costs (TVC). That is, the cost of raw materials, or those things that vary with the sale of a single unit of product or service from your revenue. Are you following me?"

Tom asked, and they all nodded their heads in agreement.

"The next basic financial measure is Inventory or Investment (I) and it represents all of the money that the business has invested in things that it intends to sell. Primarily it includes the dollars tied up in WIP and Finished Product Inventory. The third measure is Operating Expense (OE) and it represents all the money the system spends to turn Inventory into Throughput, and it includes all labor costs. It also includes rent, plus selling, General and Administrative (SG & A) costs. This point of including all labor costs is a huge departure from traditional Cost Accounting. Are you still with me?" he asked and again they all nodded in the affirmative.

Tom continued his explanation of Throughput Accounting, "Throughput is maximized by selling goods or services with the largest difference between price (revenue) and Totally Variable Cost (TVC) and by minimizing the elapsed time between spending money to produce product and receiving money from sales. It's important to understand that Throughput Accounting does not use labor costs to allocate Operating Expense. Unlike traditional Cost Accounting, direct labor is not treated as a variable cost."

Nancy immediately asked why, and Tom immediately responded, "Because just like Simpson Water Heaters, businesses do not adjust their workforce every time demand varies," Tom replied and Nancy understood his reply.

Tom continued, "From these three basic elements of Throughput Accounting, namely T, I, and OE, we can calculate several other key metrics as shown on this screen:

- Net Profit = Throughput – Operating Expense or NP = T – OE
- Return on Investment = Net Profit ÷ Inventory or ROI = NP/I
- Productivity = Throughput ÷ Operating Expense or P = T/OE
- Inventory Turns = Throughput ÷ Inventory or i = T/I"

"In all of my years in Finance, I have never even heard of Throughput Accounting Tom," Nancy said. "And the funny thing is, it all looks so simple," Nancy added. "Okay, let's continue," Tom said. "An ideal decision using Throughput Accounting would be one that increases T, and either decreases or does not change both I and OE, while a good decision increases NP, ROI, P, and i. It's very important to remember that Net Profit is net operating profit before interest and taxes. Under Throughput Accounting, there are no product costs, but instead there are constraint measures that should also be tracked as follows," and he flashed another slide onto his screen.

- Throughput per Constraint Unit: T/CU = (Revenue – Totally Variable Cost)/units
- Constraint Utilization: U = time spent producing/time available to produce

Tom then explained, "The way to maximize T is to maximize these constraint measures. Constraint utilization is very important because every hour lost on the constraint, is an hour lost for the entire business that you can't get back. On the other hand, utilization of non-constraints is not tracked, simply because it encourages excess inventory." "Like our plant does," Matt added. Tom responded, "Yes, just like you guys have been doing."

"So, typical decisions based on the metric, T/CU include things like prioritizing use of the constraint. For example, choosing the best product mix; deciding whether to increase the constraint's capacity through investment; selecting products to introduce or discontinue and pricing products based on the opportunity cost of using the constraint," Tom explained. "Therefore, for normal product decisions, T/CU is used to determine the best mix that results in maximizing Throughput. If, for example, producing less of one product in order to produce more of another product would increase Throughput, then that is a good decision. But for major decisions that might shift the constraint or forfeit some Throughput on current products, then Throughput Accounting uses the following decision-support measures," and he displayed the following on his screen.

- Change in Net Profit: $\Delta NP = \Delta T - \Delta OE$. In this case, the Δ symbol stands for the difference or change in or a comparison between alternatives. Likewise, to show the impact of these investment decisions, the metric Payback: $PB = \Delta NP / \Delta I$ should be used.
- To minimize unfavorable deviations from plans, Throughput Accounting advocates these control measures that should be minimized:
  - Throughput Dollar Days: TDD = Selling price of late order x days late
  - Inventory Dollar Days: IDD = Selling price of excess inventory x days unsold

Tom then explained, "Throughput Dollar Days measures something that should have been done but was not, like shipping orders on time, while Inventory Dollar Days measures something that should not have been done but was, like creating unnecessary inventory." "Are you guys still with me?" Tom asked, and again, they all nodded their heads in the affirmative.

"Tom, this is all starting to make perfect sense to me," Matt said. "And I really like the way you are presenting all of this," he added.

TABLE 6.1

Manufacturing Requirements

	A	B	C	Have	Need
Products					
Demand	100	100	100		
Price	$105	$100	$95		
Raw Material	$45	$50	$55		
Step 1 Time	3	6	9	2,400 minutes	1,800 minutes
Step 2 Time	15	12	9	2,400 minutes	3,600 minutes
Step 3 Time	2	2	2	800 minutes	600 minutes
Total Time	20	20	20		

Tom responded and said, "Well, most of what I presented today is from John Ricketts classic book [1], *Reaching the Goal – How Managers Improve a Services Business Using Goldratt's Theory of Constraints* and, as I said earlier, I strongly encourage all of you to get this book and read it. Ironically, as you can see in the title, it was written to apply to service companies, but it equally applies to production-based companies like Simpson Water Heaters."

"Throughput Accounting is used to identify constraints, monitor performance, control production, and determine the impact of your decisions," and with that, Tom presented a new table on his screen (Table 6.1). "The table you see here is a manufacturing situation consisting of just three parts, with each part requiring the same three steps. Each product requires a different number of minutes per step, but the total time required for each part is the same. Labor costs per minute are the same across all steps," Tom explained.

Continuing Tom explained, "As you can see, Part A clearly has the highest price and the lowest raw material cost per part while part C has the lowest price and highest raw material cost per part. Because the same workers will be used to produce any product mix, it would seem that the best mix would be to produce as much of part A as demanded, then B, then C. Following this priority order, the factory will produce 100 units of A, 75 of B, and none of C. Note that Step 2 limits enterprise production regardless of whether it's actually recognized as the constraint. Operating Expense includes rent, energy and labor." "Let's look at an example comparing Cost Accounting (Figure 6.2) to Throughput Accounting's (Figure 6.3) product mix decision," Tom said.

TABLE 6.2

Cost Accounting Product Mix

Products	A	B	C	Have	Need
Demand	100	100	100		
Price	$105	$100	$95		
Raw Material	$45	$50	$55		
Step 1 Time	3	6	9	2,400 minutes	1,800 minutes
Step 2 Time	15	12	9	2,400 minutes	3,600 minutes
Step 3 Time	2	2	2	800 minutes	600 minutes
Total Time	20	20	20		

	Products			
Cost Accounting	A	B	C	Total
Product Cost	$100	$111	0	
Mix	100	75	0	
Step 2 Used	1,500	900	0	2,400
Revenue	$10,500	$7,500	0	$18,000
Raw Material	$4,500	$3,750	0	$8,250
Gross Margin	$6,000	$3,750	0	$9,750
Operating Expense	$5,455	$4,545	0	$10,000
Net Profit	$545	($795)	0	($250)

Tom continued, "When Cost Accounting allocates operating expense to products based on their raw material costs, the resulting product costs confirm the expected priority: A has a lower product cost than B. Unfortunately, with this product mix, this business generates a net loss of $250. Because Part A appears to be profitable while Part B generates a loss, it's tempting to conclude that producing none of B would stop the loss. However, the OE covered by B would then have to be covered entirely by A, which would yield an even larger loss. If additional work were started, in an effort to keep the workers at Steps 1 and 3 fully utilized, or to maximize their efficiency, work-in-process inventory would grow. The inevitable conclusion, using Cost Accounting, is that this business is not profitable!" Tom explained. "Let's now look at this same company using Throughput Accounting and see if the results tell us the same things or not," Tom said as he flashed a new table onto his screen. "As you can see in this table, Throughput Accounting provides an entirely different perspective when looking at this business and its potential product mix," Tom explained.

Tom then explained, "Throughput Accounting ranks product profitability according to Throughput on the constraint per minute (T/CU/t). And it does not allocate OE to products. So, based upon this, Product A yields $4 per minute on the constraint, B yields $4.17, and C yields $4.44. Throughput Accounting says the priority should be to produce as much of C as capacity will allow, then B, then A, which is the exact opposite priority of Cost Accounting. Because Step 2 is the constraint, producing 100 units of C, 100 of B, and 20 of A is all that can be done. But the good news is, with this product mix from Throughput Accounting, instead of a $250 loss when using Cost Accounting, this business now generates a net profit of $200. The only difference being the product mix!" "What?" Nancy exclaimed. "Could it be that we have been using the wrong product mix here in our plant?" Nancy asked. "It certainly appears that we might have been!" Matt added.

Tom continued, "Effective use of Throughput Accounting requires different information than from Cost Accounting, so new report formats must be developed and implemented. For example, a Throughput Accounting earnings statement shows T, I, and OE relative to the constraint, while conventional Cost Accounting reports are oblivious to the constraint. Just as Cost Accounting and Throughput Accounting rank product profitability differently, they may also rank customer profitability quite differently. Several Throughput Accounting outcomes are worth emphasizing,"

TABLE 6.3

Throughput Accounting Product Mix

Products	A	B	C	Have	Need
Demand	100	100	100		
Price	$105	$100	$95		
Raw Material	$45	$50	$55		
Step 1 Time	3	6	9	2,400 minutes	1,800 minutes
Step 2 Time	15	12	9	2,400 minutes	3,600 minutes
Step 3 Time	2	2	2	800 minutes	600 minutes
Total Time	20	20	20		

	Products			
Throughput Accounting	A	B	C	Total
T/CL	$60	$50	$40	
T/CU/t	$4.00	$4.17	$4.44	
Mix	20	100	100	
Step 2 Used	300	1,200	900	2,400
Revenue	$2,100	$10,000	$9,500	$21,600
Raw Material (TVC)	$900	$5,000	$5,500	$11,400
Throughput (T)	$1,200	$5,000	$4,000	$10,200
Operating Expense (OE)				$10,000
Net Profit (NP)				$200

Tom explained as he flashed another slide on his screen (Figure 6.9). Financial measures reverse management priorities from OE, T, and I for Cost Accounting to T, I, and OE for Throughput Accounting.

- Performance measures for Throughput Accounting are not distorted by cost allocations for Cost Accounting.
- Constraint measures eliminate conflict between local measures, like machine utilization or operator efficiency and global measures or performance of the business.
- Control measures remove the incentive to build excess inventory and replace it with the incentive to deliver products on time.

Tom began again, "Let's now review the primary components of Throughput Accounting, starting with Throughput. Throughput at your company is achieved by processing parts, selling or delivering them to customers and receiving payment for all goods you sold. Again, inventory is not Throughput! Inventory or Investment (I) is primarily the amount of WIP and finished goods inventory, but it also includes all purchased parts for sales or the equipment, buildings and other assets required to produce parts, if you're a manufacturer. The real key to reducing 'I' is to stop the practice of pushing orders through your processes and replace it with pulling orders through your processes. Use the concept of nothing comes into your process until something exits the constraint or synchronizing flow. Too much WIP at one time leads to extending the productive cycle time of every part, causing late deliveries of parts and unhappy customers," Tom explained.

- Financial measures reverse management priorities from OE, T, and I for Cost Accounting to T, I, and OE for Throughput Accounting.

- Performance measures for Throughput Accounting are not distorted by cost allocations for Cost Accounting.

- Constraint measures eliminate conflict between local measures, like machine utilization or operator efficiency and global measures or performance of the business.

- Control measures remove the incentive to build excess inventory and replace it with the incentive to deliver products on time.

FIGURE 6.9
Throughput Accounting outcomes

Tom continued, "And finally, Operating Expense is all the money the system spends in order to turn Inventory into Throughput including all labor costs. The key for your company to reduce labor costs is by improving Throughput at a much faster rate by removing waste and variation within the constraint. In doing so, this will reduce the dependence on overtime to play catch-up and reduce overall dollars spent on overtime. It will also improve the morale of the workforce because you have eliminated the fear of layoffs. Think about it, if you can generate additional Throughput with the same Operating Expense, you will return much more to your company's bottom line," Tom explained.

"So, there's your comparison of these two markedly different accounting methods. It should be clear to you that, if you continue using traditional Cost Accounting to make your key financial decisions, like product mix, your company could be missing an opportunity to make more money. And since the goal of most companies is to make money now, and in the future, doesn't it make sense to use Throughput Accounting to make your real time financial decisions?" Tom said as he finished his presentation on accounting methods. "So, what do you guys think?" Tom asked.

Nancy was the first to comment, "I am truly amazed at what we heard today! I just never dreamed that with such a simple set of metrics, profit numbers could be enhanced dramatically just by changing the mix!" Nancy then added, "I have been searching for a way to dramatically increase profitability and thanks to the Theory of Constraints, I'm certain we have found our way!" Matt then added, "I know I can speak for everyone here today when I say, thank you Tom for such an enlightening discussion." Tom then added, "Guys, there's a lot more to the Theory of Constraints and as we progress, you'll see new ways of doing business. One thing I want everyone to do, is that I want you to present what you learned today to other key members of your staff!" Tom stated emphatically.

"I do have a question for you Tom," Matt said. "And what question is that Matt?" Tom asked. "When we first started our improvement journey, we began by implementing Six Sigma and we did see improvement in our profits and on-time delivery. We then tried implementing Lean Manufacturing and again, we saw additional improvements using this method," he added. "My question for you is this. Is there a way that we can combine both of these improvement methods with the Theory of Constraints?" Tom responded by asking a question, "What do you think Matt?" "I would think there would be, and I think the outcome would be major improvements in things like profits and on-time delivery," Matt said. Tom responded, "Well Matt, as we go forward, you will see exactly how to combine the best of all three methods." And with that, Tom looked at the clock and said goodbye to everyone in the room. On his way out the door to the airport, he turned to Matt and told them he would be back sometime soon.

REFERENCE

1. John Ricketts, *Reaching the Goal – How Managers Improve a Services Business Using Goldratt's Theory of Constraints*, 2008, Westford, MA: IBM Press.

7

Maximo Health Center Complex's New Beginning

During Tom's flight home from Detroit, he decided that he needed to start planning for his next trip to the Maximo Health Center Complex. While he had already created a list of performance metrics that he would track during his improvement efforts, he decided to take another look at the list to finalize it. His initial list of metrics included the following metrics in Table 7.1.

As he was reviewing his ideas for performance metrics, he thought to himself, "Have I included everything that will tell me how the hospital is doing?" He realized that there would be other performance metrics that would be used during the improvement effort, but what he was trying to do was create a list of those metrics that would, in effect, tell the story of how successful the overall improvement effort had been. As he looked over his list, he felt alright with the metrics he had chosen. He then pulled out his i-Phone, reviewed his schedule, and decided that he would contact Pete

TABLE 7.1

Key Performance Metrics for Each Hospital

Performance Metric	Metric Description
% Profit Margin	Appraisal of the percentage profit for each hospital using Throughput Accounting.
Average Hospital Stay	Appraise the amount of time your patients are staying in your hospital after admission.
Patient Wait Times	Calculate the average length of time patients have to wait to receive treatment or have tests run.
Patient Satisfaction	Calculate how patients felt while being taken care of in each hospital and/or how they felt about the results.
Efficiency % or Utilization	Calculate the percent efficiency for key processes within each hospital, including surgeries and testing.

Hallwell to schedule a visit to begin the improvement effort at Maximo Health Center Complex. And with that, he decided to take a brief snooze on his way to the Pittsburgh Airport.

Tom returned home around 10:00 pm and went directly to bed. The next morning Tom woke up early, showered, and ate breakfast. He dialed Pete's number and after several rings, Pete answered the phone. "Hello, this is Pete Hallwell, how can I help you?" he said as he answered the phone. "Hi Pete, it's Tom here," Tom replied. "I was wondering if I can come in and meet with you about our upcoming improvement effort?" Tom asked. "Yes, absolutely!" Pete replied. "When would you like to come in Tom?" Pete asked. "Are you free tomorrow?" Tom asked. "I'm actually free today, if that works for you Tom?" Pete responded. "That would be great Pete, how soon can I come in?" he asked. "Why don't you jump in your car and come right now?" He replied. "I'll be there shortly Pete," he replied, and he hung up.

Shortly thereafter Tom arrived, and Pete was outside waiting for him. They shook hands and went up to Pete's office. "So, Tom, what is it that you want to talk about?" Pete asked. "Next week I'm supposed to start my consulting gig here and I wanted to give you an idea of what I'd like to do on the first day," Tom explained. "One of the things I want to do is have a general meeting with the people who run each of the hospitals, just to give them an idea of what we'll be doing going forward. So, one thing I need you to do is to invite each member of the hospital to be in your conference room on Monday morning," Tom said. Pete made notes as Tom was explaining what he wanted to do. "What time would you like this first meeting to be Tom?" Pete asked. "I think we need to start at 8:00 am and then plan on it lasting until early afternoon some time," Tom explained.

"What do you plan on covering at this meeting Tom?" Pete asked. "Similar to what I explained to you and your two Accounting employees. I want to explain the basics of the Theory of Constraints and how we can go about combining it with both Lean and Six Sigma. I'll also cover things like Throughput Accounting, Theory of Constraints' version of scheduling, and how to avoid high levels of inventory while totally avoiding stock-outs," he explained. "Wow, that seems like a lot of new ideas to share in one setting!" Pete replied. "Not really Pete, as they're all tied together under the heading of the Theory of Constraints," Tom responded. "Okay, I'll set up the meeting for 8:00 Monday morning Tom," Pete replied. And with that meeting, Tom said, "Okay Pete, I'll see you on Monday."

Tom spent the weekend putting together his slide decks for his Maximo Health Center Complex meeting on Monday. As he was working on his presentation, he thought to himself, "I really need to know more about the individual hospitals that make up the Maximo Health Center Complex." He got on the internet to search for the make-up of Maximo Health Center Complex and found what he needed to know. The list of hospitals and their specialties included the following:

1. Maximo Children's Hospital, specializing in children's ailments.
2. Maximo Women's Hospital, specializing in pregnancies.
3. Maximo Veteran's Hospital, specializing in military veterans.
4. Maximo Oncology Hospital, specializing in cancer treatments.
5. Maximo Surgical Hospital, specializing in surgical operations.
6. Maximo Emergency Hospital, specializing in emergency patients.

As he was reading about each of the hospitals, he found that in addition to each of the individual hospitals, Maximo also owned and operated a variety of clinics throughout the city, which included facilities like dental, allergy, psychiatric and others. "Not sure where I should start my consulting effort? I guess I'll probably have a much better idea of the intrinsic order after my meeting on Monday?" Tom thought to himself. Tom worked all day on his presentation and finally completed his slide decks.

On Monday morning, Tom arrived at Maximo Health Center Complex's corporate office. He signed in, and the security contacted Pete to let him know that Tom had arrived and was in the lobby. Shortly thereafter Pete arrived, and they both went to the seventh floor conference room. The room as full of people who were there to hear Tom's presentation. Tom set up his equipment, and Pete introduced Tom to the audience.

One by one, they introduced themselves to Tom, along with their positions at Maximo Health Center Complex. "Good morning Tom, I'm Tom Jones, the CEO from Maximo Children's Hospital, and we specialize in all children's ailments," he said. "Hi Tom, I'm Philip Zagst, and I'm the Chief Quality Executive from Maximo Women's Hospital. We are specialists in pregnancy deliveries," Philip explained. "Good morning Tom, I'm Marie Thomas and I'm the CFO at Maximo Veteran's Hospital, specializing in military veteran's ailments," she said. "Hi Tom, I'm Terry Sample, the COO at Maximo Oncology Hospital where we specialize in cancer treatments," he explained. "Good morning Tom, I'm Patricia Smith, the COO at Maximo Surgical Hospital and we specialize in surgical operations," she said. "And I'm Ted Simpson, the COO at Maximo Emergency Hospital, and we specialize in emergency patients," he explained.

And with the introductions complete, Tom began his presentation. "Good morning everyone, I'm happy to meet all of you," Tom said. "Today is a monumental day for Maximo Health Center Complex, simply because you're going to hear about an improvement methodology that most, or all of you, have never seen before. I know you have tried using Lean Manufacturing with some improvements in profitability, but not what you had hoped for. I know that you also attempted to implement Six Sigma without much success. Today I'm going to provide the *missing link* in virtually all improvement initiatives. How many of you have heard of something called the Theory of Constraints?" Tom asked the group. The audience members looked at each other, but none of them raised their hands indicating that they had never heard of the Theory of Constraints.

Tom then said, "It's not surprising to me that you've never heard of this methodology before, simply because it hasn't been used much in the healthcare arena." Tom continued, "Without further delay, that's where

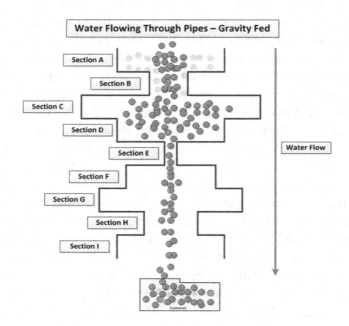

FIGURE 7.1
Piping system with Section E as the constraint.

we're going to start," and he flashed his infamous piping system onto the screen (Figure 7.1). "What you see here is a simple piping system used to deliver water. Each section of the piping system has a different diameter with water entering into Section A, then flows into Section B and continued downward until it enters the receptacle at the base of this system. The demand for water has increased and you have been asked to increase the volume of water flowing through this system. My question to you as a group is what would you do and why would you do it?" he asked.

The group studied the drawing until Philip Zagst, the Chief Quality Executive, said, "I think the only way to increase the amount of water flow would be to increase the diameter of Section E of the piping system. I say this, because, since it is the smallest diameter pipe, this section limits the flow of water through the entire piping system." "That is absolutely correct Philip, the water flow is being constrained because of Section E's small diameter pipe," Tom replied. "Does everyone see this?" Tom asked the group, and they all indicated that they did.

"Let's say we did increase the diameter of Section E's pipe. What do you think would happen?" he asked the group. Marie Thomas, the CFO at Maximo Veteran's Hospital, raised her hand and said, "Well based upon the diameters of the different pipes in this system, I would think that the flow of water would now be limited by Section B, because it would now have the smallest diameter pipe in this system?" "You are absolutely correct Marie and it would now look like this," he said and flashed a revised piping system drawing on the screen (Figure 7.2).

"What you see here is the revised piping system, just as Marie described," Tom explained. "Here's another question for you," Tom said. "Would changing the diameter of any other pipe have resulted in an increased flow of water through this system" he asked the group. In unison, they all said no, only by increasing the diameter of Section E would have resulted in increased flow of water. "What you have just learned is the basic concept of a system constraint," Tom explained. "So, you're probably wondering, how does a piping system apply to our hospitals?" Tom stated and with that, he loaded his next slide onto the screen (Figure 7.3).

"What you see on the screen, is a simple example of the treatment of a patient for some form of cancer," Tom explained. "The patient arrives at the hospital, signs in and is escorted to the treatment area which takes approximately 10 minutes. The patient then waits in line to receive the specific treatment which takes roughly 30 minutes. The patient then receives

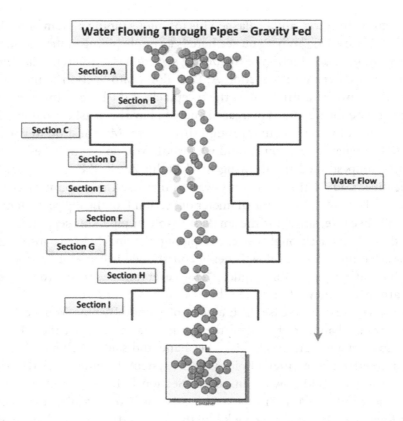

FIGURE 7.2
Piping system with Section B as the new constraint.

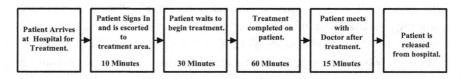

FIGURE 7.3
Flow of patients for cancer treatment.

the specific treatment which in this example takes 60 minutes. And finally, after the patient receives his or her treatment, they then meet with the doctor for about 15 minutes. After meeting with the doctor, the patient is released." "So, here's my question for you. If you wanted to increase the number of patients this hospital could see and treat, what would you do and why would you do it?" Tom asked.

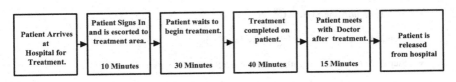

FIGURE 7.4
Patient flow after improvement.

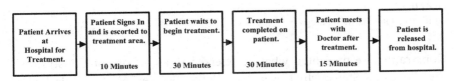

FIGURE 7.5
New oncology treatment times.

Terry Sample, the COO at Maximo Oncology Hospital, immediately raised his hand and said, "Based upon what we just learned from the piping system, the constraint is when the patient receives treatment. I say this because this step has the longest cycle time at 60 minutes." "Correct Terry, so if you wanted to increase the number of patients you were to treat, what would you have to do?" Tom asked. "Clearly, you would have to reduce the time for this step," Terry replied. "Correct again Terry," Tom said. "Let's say you were able to reduce this step by 20 minutes, where would your new constraint be located then?" He asked as he flashed a new figure on his screen (Figure 7.4).

Terry responded and said, "Clearly this step would still be the constraint because it still takes the longest time to complete. But the good news is, we would still be able to see more patients." "That is absolutely correct Terry!" Tom exclaimed. "And what would happen if we were able to remove 10 more minutes from this step Terry?" Tom asked as he flashed the new drawing on his screen (Figure 7.5).

"If this were to happen, the new constraint would be patients waiting to begin treatment," Terry replied. "Actually, you would end up with a duel constraint," Tom interjected. "But how would it be possible to reduce the treatment time down to 30 minutes, if it now takes 60 minutes to complete?" Terry asked. "Good question Terry, and I'll answer that question in a few minutes," Tom responded. "The Theory of Constraints was created by a man named Dr. Eliyahu Goldratt. He wasn't a medical doctor, but rather a PhD type doctor. When he first developed the Theory of

- Step 1: *Identify* the System Constraint.

- Step 2: Decide how to *exploit* the System Constraint.

- Step 3: *Subordinate* everything else to the System Constraint.

- Step 4: If necessary, *elevate* the System Constraint.

- Step 5: When the constraint is *broken*, return to Step 1 to locate the new constraint.

FIGURE 7.6
Goldratt's Five Focusing Steps.

Constraints, he presented what he referred to as Theory of Constraints' Five Focusing Steps, which were as follows (Figure 7.6)," as he flashed a new overhead on his screen.

"So, based upon our example, you have identified the System Constraint and have come up with a way to exploit it to the point where you're able to treat more patients," Tom explained. "So, let's now look at Step 3, subordinate everything else to the System Constraint," Tom added. "Thinking back to our original drawing of this process (Figure 7.3), how fast do you think the steps in front of the constraint should be running?" has asked the group. Ted Russell, the Purchasing Manager, responded and said, "They should be running at maximum speed so that more patients can be treated." "Does everyone agree with what Ted has just said?" Tom asked the group. Three people in the audience said yes that they agree, while the others remained silent.

"Let's take a look at what might happen if the first two steps were to run at maximum capacity," Tom said as he flashed a new overhead onto the screen (Figure 7.7) and said, "What you see here is the negative impact of not 'subordinating Steps 1 and 2' to the system constraint." "Because the system constraint controls the flow of patients, by running the first two steps to their maximum, we end up with a 'stack-up' of patients in front of the system constraint. We haven't treated any more patients, but we have filled up our waiting room with more patients. This is the end result of not subordinating everything to the system constraint," Tom explained. "Does everyone see my point here?" he asked, and it seemed like they all did.

"Now let me get back to the question Terry asked, which was 'How would it be possible to reduce the treatment time down to 30 minutes?'" Tom said. "Goldratt's fourth step says, 'If necessary, elevate the system constraint,'" Tom explained. "During the first two steps, very little if any money needs

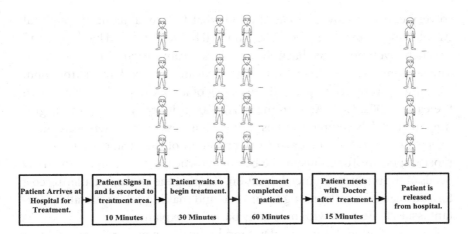

FIGURE 7.7
Steps 1 and 2 running at maximum capacity.

to be spent to improve the capacity. I say this because most of the time you will find excessive waste in your processes and you will be able to reduce the cycle time. But let's say you have removed all of the waste that you can, and the same step is still not fast enough to see and treat more patients. Goldratt's Step 4 says, if necessary, elevate the system constraint," Tom explained.

"In our example, we had removed so much time from our system constraint, that Terry didn't think it would be possible to reduce the time down to 30 minutes," Tom said. "But what if we added another treatment area, so that we virtually cut the treatment time in half. This would be the equivalent of cutting the treatment time from 60 minutes down to 30 minutes," Tom explained. "You're probably all thinking that this would cost too much for the hospital to do this, but after you hear about the Theory of Constraints version of accounting, known as Throughput Accounting, I think you'll see that the belief that it would cost too much to add another treatment area, is not correct," Tom explained.

Tom began again, "Goldratt's Step 5 tells you that once the constraint has been broken, return to Step 1 and identify the new system constraint. I have been using the Theory of Constraints for a number of years now and the results achieved have been simply amazing. This concludes the first part of my presentation, so let's take a fifteen-minute break and when you return, you'll learn about Throughput Accounting," Tom said. Pete approached Tom and said, "Tom, what you presented so far today was so very easy to follow and based upon what I learned about Throughput Accounting from you, this next session will be well accepted by the group."

When everyone was back from break, Tom began his session on Throughput Accounting. "The way I want to explain Throughput Accounting is by relating a fictitious story of a sock maker," he began. "In the early 1900s, Cost Accounting (CA) was in its early stages and beginning to be widely accepted and used. For a business owner, there were many things to consider in the day-to-day operation of the business. One of the most important functions of the business owner was tending to the daily needs of the business financial situation. Keeping the books, calculating cost for raw materials, calculating labor cost, and making sales were all important issues to be dealt with on a daily basis," he explained.

He began again, "It was understood by business owners that, in order to stay in business and make money, the cost they paid for the products or services rendered had to be less than the selling price of their products or services. If it wasn't, then they would quickly go out of business. Then and now, the needs of businesses haven't changed much, but other things have changed."

"The ideas and concepts about what was important to measure, and how to measure them, were starting to form and were being passed from one generation to the next. This was considered important information that you needed to know, in order to be successful. Without this understanding, it was assumed that you would fail. Back then, the business structure and methods were different than they are today. The labor force was not nearly as reliable, and most workers did not work 40 hours a week. When they did work, they were not paid an hourly wage, but instead were paid using the piece-rate pay system," Tom explained.

"As an example, suppose you owned a knitting business, and the product you made and sold was socks. The employees in your business would knit socks as their job. With the piece-rate pay system, you paid the employees based on the number of socks they knitted in a day, or a week, or whatever unit of time you used. If an employee knitted ten pairs of socks in a day, and you paid a piece rate of $1.00 for each pair knitted, then you owed that employee $10.00. However, if the employee didn't show up for work and didn't knit any socks, then you owed the worker nothing. In this type of work environment, labor was truly a variable cost and deserved to be allocated as a cost to the product. It just made sense in a piece-rate pay system. The more socks the employees knitted, the more money they could make. Also, as the business owner, your labor costs were very precisely controlled. As I mentioned, if employees didn't make any socks, then you didn't have to pay them," Tom continued.

"In time, metrics for calculating labor costs changed and the labor rates changed as well. Many employees were now paid a daily rate, instead of a piece rate. Labor costs had now shifted from a truly variable cost per unit, to a fixed cost per day. In other words, the employees got that same amount of money per day, no matter how many pairs of socks they knitted or didn't knit. As time went by, the employee labor rates shifted again. This time, labor rates shifted from a daily rate to an hourly rate. With the new hourly rate came the more standardized work week of forty hours, or eight hours a day, five days a week. With the hourly rate, the labor costs now became fixed," he explained.

Before Tom continued, he scanned the audience to make sure everyone was following what he had to say. When he was comfortable that they were, he began again, "With these changes, it became apparent to the sock-knitting business owner that, in order to get the biggest bang for the labor buck, the owner needed to produce as many pairs of socks as he could in a day, in order to offset the rising labor costs. The most obvious way to do that was to keep all of your sock knitters busy all of the time making socks. In other words, efficiency was a key ingredient, and needed to be increased. If the owner could make more pairs of socks in the same amount of time, then his labor cost per pair of socks would go down. This was the solution the business owner was looking for, *reducing his costs*. This had to be the answer, or so he thought."

Tom continued with his story, "With these new-found levels of high efficiency came another problem. The owner quickly noticed that he had to buy more and more raw materials just to keep his employees working at such high efficiency levels. The raw materials were expensive, but he had to have them. The owner knew that his past success was directly linked to his ability to maintain such high efficiencies and keep his cost low. More and more raw materials were brought in and more and more socks were made. The socks were now being made much faster than he could sell them. What he needed now was more warehouse space to store all of those wonderfully cheap socks! So, at great expense, the owner built another warehouse to store more and more cheap socks. The owner had lots and lots of inventory of very cheap socks. According to his numbers, the socks now were costing next to nothing to make. He was saving lots of money, or so he thought."

Tom continued, "Soon the creditors started to show up wanting their money. The owner was getting behind on his bills to his raw material suppliers. He had warehouses full of very cheap socks, but he wasn't selling his socks at the same rate he was making them. He was just making more socks. He rationalized that he had to keep the costs down, and in order to do that, he had to have the efficiency numbers high. The business owner soon realized that he had to save even more money. He had to cut his costs even more, so he had to lay people off to reduce his workforce to save even more money. He wondered how he ever get into a situation like this? His business was highly efficient and his cost per pair of socks was very low. He had saved the maximum amount of money he could, and yet he was going out of business!"

"Reality had changed, and labor costing had changed (labor shifted from a variable cost to a fixed cost), but the Cost Accounting rules had not changed. The owner was still trying to treat his labor cost as a variable cost. Even today, many businesses still try to treat their labor cost as a variable cost and allocate the labor cost to individual products or services. When the labor costs are allocated to a product or service, then companies try and take the next step—they work hard to improve efficiency and drive down the labor costs per part, or unit of service," Tom explained.

Tom stopped and said, "This erroneous thought process is ingrained in many business owner's minds, and they believe that this action will somehow reduce their labor costs. And if you could reduce labor costs, then you are making more profit. But take just a moment and reflect back on the consequences of the sock maker's experience with cost savings and the high efficiency model. Are these end results anywhere close to what the business owner really wanted to have happen?" Tom asked in general.

Tom continued, "The efficiency model, when measured and implemented at the wrong system location, will have devastating effects on your perceived results. The end results will actually be the opposite of what you expected or wanted to happen. I wonder why, with all of the technology improvements accomplished throughout the years, it is still acceptable to use Cost Accounting rules from the early 1900s? So, let's look more into the 'rules' of Cost Accounting."

He began again, "The primary focus of Cost Accounting is per part or per unit cost reductions. Because perceived cost reductions are viewed so favorably, is it any wonder why there is so much emphasis on efficiency? And yet cost reductions don't seem to be the answer. There have been many highly efficient companies that have come close to going out of business or have actually gone out of business. Have you ever heard of a company that has saved themselves into prosperity? Think about it, any perceived savings that the sock maker thought he was getting, were quickly eroded by buying more raw materials. In fact, it ended up costing the sock maker much more money than he realized and not saving him anything! He was doing all of the recommended practices and yet he was failing."

"Many companies will emphatically state that the primary goal of their company is to make money, and yet they spend the largest portion of their time trying to save money. It would appear they've forgotten what their goal really is. The strategy you employ to make money is vastly different than the strategy you would employ to save money. For most companies, the assumption is that saving money is equal to making money. That is, if you somehow save some money, it's the same as making money, and this is simply not true!" Tom emphasized.

These two concepts are divergent in their thinking with each taking you in a different direction with different end results. If the real goal of your company is to save money, then the very best way to accomplish your goal is to go out of business. This action will save you the maximum amount of money. However, if the goal of your company is to make money, then a different strategy must be employed which is maximizing through-put through the system. Let's now look at a different form of accounting known as Throughput Accounting, Tom explained. "Any questions so far?" he asked. There weren't any questions, so he continued on with his presentation.

"Suppose we consider again the same example using the sock maker. Suppose the sock maker wants to make three times as many socks as he is making now. What would he have to do? Using the piece-rate pay system, he would have to hire three times as many employees to be sock makers and pay them a piece rate of $1.00 per pair. So, in order to make three times as many pairs of socks, the labor rate must go up and he then has to hire three times as many people. In the piece-rate world, getting three times as much through the system will cost him three times as much in labor," Tom explained.

"Now let's suppose that our sock maker is paying an hourly wage, rather than a piece rate. Further suppose he figures out a way to make three more pairs of socks, per worker, per day. By being able to make three times as much, how much do his labor costs go up? They do not go up at all! He still pays the workers an hourly rate, whether they make one pair of socks or ten pairs of socks. He only has to pay the employees once, not a rate based on the number of socks made. His only increase in cost comes from buying more raw materials to make the socks. So, why does modern day Cost Accounting still try to allocate a labor cost per unit of work, and then claim that increased efficiency drives down the cost per part? The fact is, it does no such thing! In today's reality, labor costs are fixed, not variable!" Tom continued his explanation.

"Throughput Accounting is not a frontal attack on Cost Accounting, it is just a different way to view the accounting measures, solve issues, and manage the company at a much higher success and profitability level. It's an update of the accounting rules, if you will, that is much more in line with current business reality. It is my contention that understanding Throughput Accounting will be your company's lever to success," Tom interjected. "The bottom line is that Throughput Accounting is a much better way to make real time financial decisions!" Tom added.

"Throughput Accounting uses primarily three performance metrics, namely Throughput (T), Investment/Inventory (I), and Operating Expense (OE). These metrics are a simplified methodology that removes all of the mystery of accounting and rolls it into three simple measures," Tom explained and flashed a new overhead on his screen (Figure 7.8).

Tom then said, "When you read and understand these definitions, it seems likely that all the money within your company can be categorized to fit within one of these three measures." "Any questions?" Tom asked.

There weren't any questions, so Tom continued, "In thinking about Throughput Accounting (TA) it is important to consider the following thoughts. Throughput Accounting (TA) is neither costing nor Cost Accounting (CA). Instead, Throughput Accounting is focused on cash, without the need for allocation to a specific product or service. This concept includes the variable and fixed expenses for a product or service. The only slight variation would be the calculation for Total Variable Cost (TVC). In this case the Totally Variable Cost is a cost that is truly variable to a product or service, such as raw materials, paying a sales commission, or shipping charges. The sum total of these costs becomes the product TVC."

Tom continued, "Totally Variable Cost is only the cost associated with each product or service. Some would argue that labor should also be added as a variable cost per product or service, but this is not true! Labor is no longer a variable cost, it's a fixed cost. With the hourly labor

1. *Throughput* is the rate at which inventory is converted into sales. If you make lots of products and put them in a warehouse, that is not throughput, it's inventory. The products or services only count as throughput if they are sold to the customer and fresh money comes back into the business system.

2. *Investment/Inventory* is the money an organization invests in items that it intends to sell. This category would include inventory, both raw materials and finished goods. This includes buildings, machines, and other equipment used to make products for sale, knowing that any or all of these investments could at some point in time, be sold for cash.

3. *Operating Expense* is all of the money spent generating the Throughput. This includes, rent, electricity, phone, benefits, and wages. It is any money spent that does not fit within one of the first two TA categories.

FIGURE 7.8
Three performance metrics of Throughput Accounting.

measures, you pay employees for vacation, holidays and sick leave. The employees cost you exactly the same amount of money whether they are at work or not. Using this example, labor is an Operating Expense, and not a variable cost associated with products, and this is a key point to remember."

"The following definitions apply to Throughput Accounting, Tom explained as he loaded a new overhead on his screen (Figure 7.9)," Tom explained.

Tom continued, "Some would argue that Throughput Accounting falls short because it is not able to pigeon-hole all of the categories of Cost Accounting into Throughput Accounting categories. Things like interest payments on loans, or payment of stock-holder dividends, or depreciation of machines or facilities. However, this argument appears to be invalid. Ask yourself, which one of those specific categories can't be placed into one of the Throughput Accounting categories?"

- Throughput (T) = Product Selling Price (SP) – the Total Variable Cost (TVC). Or T = SP – TVC

- Net Profit (NP) = Throughput (T) minus Operational Expense (OE). Or NP = T – OE

- Return on Investment (ROI) = Net Profit (NP) divided by Inventory (I). Or ROI = NP/I

- Productivity (P) = Throughput (T) divided by Operating Expense (OE). Or P = T/OE

- Inventory Turns (IT) = Throughput (T) divided by Inventory Value (IV). Or IT = T/I

FIGURE 7.9
TA definitions.

"The baseline Throughput Accounting concept is really very simple. It you have to write a check to somebody else, it's either an Investment (I) or an Operating Expense (OE). It's an Investment if it is something you can sell for money at some point in time. It's an Operating Expense if you can't. Put this debt in the category that makes the most sense. On the other hand, if somebody is writing a check to you, and you get to make a deposit, then it's probably Throughput (T). Cost Accounting rules have made it much more complicated and difficult than it needs to be. When you make it that complex and difficult, and intently argue about the semantics, the stranglehold that Cost Accounting has on your thinking becomes even more obvious," Tom explained.

"Throughput Accounting is really focused on providing the necessary information that allows decision makers to make better decisions. If the goal of the company is truly to make money, then any decisions being considered should get the company closer to the goal and not further away. Effective decision-making is well suited to an effective T, I, and OE analysis. This analysis can show the impact of any local decisions on the bottom line of the company. Ideally good business decisions will cause three things to happen," Tom explained as he loaded another slide on his screen (Figure 7.10).

After explaining these three points, Tom suggested that the group take a small break.

When everyone was back from their break, Tom began again, "The decision-making process becomes much easier when these three factors are considered. The movement either up or down, of these three measures should provide sufficient information for good strategy and much better decisions. Any good decision should be based on global impacts to the company and not just a single unit or process in isolation. If your thinking

1. *Throughput* (T) to increase.

2. *Investment/Inventory* to decrease or stay the same. It is also possible that investment can go up, as long as the effect on T is exponential. In other words, sometime a very well-placed investment can cause the T to skyrocket.

3. *Operating Expenses decrease or stay the same.* It is not always necessary to decrease Operating Expense to have a dramatic effect. Consider the situation where the T actually doubles, and you didn't have to hire anyone new to do it, nor did you have to lay anyone off.

FIGURE 7.10
Three outcomes good business decision will cause.

is limited to the lowest level of the organization, and you are focused on the wrong area, then the positive impact will never be seen or felt by the entire organization."

Tom continued, "If we compare these two accounting methods at the highest level, then Cost Accounting is all about the actions you take to try and save money, while Throughput Accounting is all about the action you take to make money. Once you've made the cost reductions and you still need more, what do you do next? Where else can you reduce costs? On the other hand, making money, at least in theory, is infinite. What is the limit on how much money your company can make now?" and Tom loaded a new overhead onto his screen (Figure 7.11).

This figure compares the top-level priorities of these two accounting approaches. With these differences in priorities, it is easy to see why Cost Accounting is focused on saving money, while Throughput Accounting is focused on making money. So, consider the real goal of your company before you decide which path to take.

"You can pick up the newspaper or watch TV almost any day of the week and see the effects of these priorities. You can read about or hear about company XYZ that is going to lay off 500 employees, in order to reduce costs and become more efficient and align themselves to be more vertical with the customer and . . . blah, blah, blah! What these companies are really saying is they have forgotten how to make money or maybe they really never learned how to make money. They are so focused on saving money that they have forgotten what the real goal of the company is, which is clearly making money!" Tom explained.

Priority	Common Practice	Common Sense
1.	OE	T
2.	T	I
3.	I	OE
	Cost World Thinking	Throughput World Thinking

FIGURE 7.11
Comparison of cost and Throughput Accounting.

"So, how did all of this come about? Why are things happening the way they are? If all of this Cost Accounting and saving money is so good, then how come so many companies seem to be in financial trouble or worse yet, going bankrupt! There are many reasons, and some could be debated for months, but no matter how many reasons there may be, all of them are not equal. Some reasons are bigger players than others, and as such, have had a far greater impact." Tom explained.

"Let's now look at the cost model associated with both the Cost Accounting and Throughput Accounting concepts. It provides an interesting history about why things are the way they are," Tom said and loaded another overhead on his screen (Figure 7.12). "This overhead defines the cost model concept for both Cost Accounting and Throughput Accounting. The product depicted in this overhead is exactly the same for both models. It indicates the same selling price, same manufacturing process, same everything. In the Cost Accounting model, you'll notice the layers of allocated cost that are applied to each product, as some percentage of the cost, or allocated rate. The sum total of all of these costs, whatever it may be, equal what Cost Accounting considers to be the cost to manufacture. Let's look at each layer," Tom said.

"Raw Materials represents the total cost of all the raw materials used in the product you produce. An average raw material cost for most companies might be around 40%, but some can, and will, go much higher. Labor Costs are the allocated labor cost per parts. It is usually calculated based

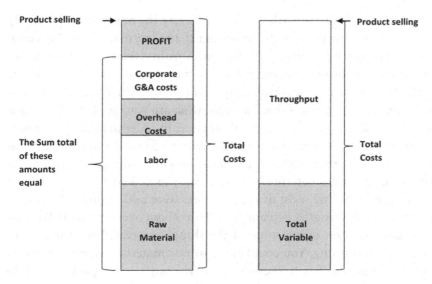

FIGURE 7.12
Different layers of CA and TA.

on some type of total parts per hour, or day, or production batch, or order, or some other value. Then the total labor cost is divided by the number of parts produced to arrive at the percent of labor to be allocated to each part," Tom explained.

Since everyone seemed to be following him, he continued, "Overhead Costs, represent the allocated percentage per part to pay for all of the overhead costs. These include items like the management staff, administrative jobs, training and so on. Usually these types of overhead assignments, cover many types of parts, but also no part in particular. Human Resources or even Finance are examples of organizations that fit in the overhead category. You need to have some place to charge and collect your overhead costs. Corporate General and Administrative is the allocated cost that pays for all of the corporate staff and everything they provide. Profit is the location where you add the percentage of profit you want to receive for your product while the Selling Price (SP) is the selling price for your product or service, once you've gone through and added together all of the manufacturing cost categories and the percentage of profit."

Tom continued his explanation, "There very well could be more layers in your company, but in the end, the hope is that when you add up all of the costs and sell to the market, or consumer, or the next guy in the supply chain, your selling price is always greater than your manufacturing costs. If it is, then you have made a profit. But in reality, the selling price is not determined by the manufacturer, but rather by the customer. If the price is too high, customers simply won't buy your product or use your service and will look elsewhere. So, if that happens, what are your options? Somehow you have to lower your cost and selling price, in order to make your product or service more attractive to the consumer. So how do you do that? You could cut your profit margins, but most organizations do not like to do that. If you can't do that, then what else can you look for?"

Tom could see that most of the attendees were taking prolific notes, so he continued his lengthy explanation, "How about overhead cost? You can slow down or stop doing some of the things associated with overhead, for example, training. You could cut your raw materials expense. Perhaps you could find a different a vendor, or maybe buy cheaper parts. If you do that, then what about the quality risk? How about cutting labor costs? If you could just get more efficient, then your labor costs would go down. If labor costs go down, then you can make more profit – correct? I think that by now you understand the cycle of chaos that takes place when you focus on efficiency. Disaster usually follows in short order and such is life in the cost model cycle."

"In your company, if you do not pay your employees using the piece-rate pay system, then the assumption of using allocated labor costs, or any costs, is invalid! Why is the stigma of allocated costs so strong in Cost Accounting? The assumption that higher efficiency will reduce the cost per part is also invalid. In today's reality of the per hour rate, the cost remains the same," Tom explained.

"The Throughput Accounting cost model contains only Total Variable Cost (TVC) and Throughput (T). The calculation is simple: Throughput equals Selling Price minus Totally Variable Costs or $T = SP - TVC$. Throughput, in essence, equals the dollars remaining from selling the product or delivering your service, after you have subtracted the TVC cost and received payments. Nothing is allocated, nothing is assumed, it's just a simple cash calculation from the sale," Tom explained. "I hope after our discussion today you have a good idea of why Throughput Accounting is a superior accounting method for making real-time financial decisions. There is more to Throughput Accounting than what I presented today, but for now, I'm open for questions," Tom said.

Pete raised his hand and asked, "It seems apparent to me that our company should be using Throughput Accounting to make our financial decisions going forward. My questions is actually a simple one and that is why in the world have we not heard about this method before today?" "That's a great question Pete, and I wish I had a good answer for you," Tom replied. "Cost Accounting has had a 'death grip' on companies for many years, but I promise you, if you begin using Throughput Accounting to make your financial decisions, your profitability will improve dramatically. The key takeaway from today's session is that there is a huge difference between trying to improve profitability by saving money, compared to making money. In future sessions, we will use your own companies to demonstrate why this difference matters," Tom explained.

"Pete, I know we had planned on covering other subjects in today's session, but because of the length of time spent comparing these two accounting systems, I think we need to schedule the other subjects for another day," Tom suggested. "That works for me Tom, how soon would you like to schedule the next session?" Pete asked. "How about Thursday of this week?" Tom suggested. "I think we can arrange that Tom," Pete replied and told Tom he would call him with the details of when the next session would be. And with that, the session ended, but before Tom left, he had a proposal for Pete.

"Pete, I know you at Maximo have spent a lot of money training people on both Lean and Six Sigma and if you're like many other companies who have done the same thing, you didn't see an acceptable return on your investment. Next week, I'm planning on traveling to Detroit to present something I refer to as the Ultimate Improvement Cycle, which is the integration of Lean, Six Sigma, and the Theory of Constraints. I think it's something that would be of profound interest to you at Maximo. I'd like to invite you to come to Detroit to sit in on this session, because eventually we need to implement this at Maximo," Tom explained. "I would love to attend this session, but I have one request," Pete replied. "And that is?" Tom asked. "I'd like to bring a couple other people with me who will ultimately be responsible for implementing this within our Hospital Complex," Pete said. "I'm sure that will be fine. The session will hopefully start at 8:00 am and will last all day. I'll send you the address tomorrow, as well as the date and time for the session," Tom replied and then he left.

When he returned home, he called Matt and let him know what he had planned, and Matt was perfectly fine with the date and time, which was the following Monday, as well as having several of Maximo's personnel join them for this training session. Tom then emailed Pete and let him know that everything was set, and he attached the location of the training session as well as the date and time.

8

Simpson Water Heaters' Next Meeting

The last time Tom was at Simpson Water Heaters, he had delivered the basics of the Theory of Constraints as well as Throughput Accounting and things went well during his presentation. Prior to him leaving, Matt Maloney, Simpson's Plant Manager, had asked him if there was a way to combine Lean, Six Sigma, and the Theory of Constraints. Tom had explained to him that there was and that he would return to Simpson Water Heaters to discuss that very subject. On his way home from Maximo Health Center Complex, Tom decided to give Matt a call and confirm the meeting on his combination of improvement initiatives, as well as Maximo's people attending.

After Tom hung up from his call with Matt, he called the airlines and was able to make flight arrangements for Sunday evening to Detroit. He texted Matt and let him know he would be coming to make his presentation on Monday and that he should set it up for 8:00 am. Matt responded back to Tom to confirm the time. Tom decided to work on his presentation the rest of the day on how best to combine the three improvement initiatives. He let his wife know that he would be flying to Detroit Sunday evening to make his presentation the following day. Tom's flight was at 7:00 pm, so at 5:30 pm on Sunday, he left for the airport. He checked in and boarded the airplane. The flight to Detroit was uneventful, and after they landed, he picked up his rental car and drove to his hotel.

The next morning Tom woke up around 6:00 am, got dressed, and had breakfast. He then drove to Simpson Water Heaters and arrived around 7:45 am. In addition, the three representatives from Maximo Health Center Complex had arrived and Pete introduced his two counterparts to Tom. "This is Jimmy Thompson and he's a Lean Six Sigma Blackbelt. This is Susie Wong and she is also a Blackbelt." Matt met them all in the lobby, and they all walked to the conference room. Matt then said, "Tom, I don't think I've ever looked more forward to hearing a presentation on how to combine these three methodologies." Tom responded and said, "I think you'll find this to be not only interesting, but helpful to your company."

At 8:00, everyone was seated, and Tom began his presentation. "One question I always ask, when consulting for a new company is, 'How's your improvement effort working for you?' The majority of companies that I have worked with had invested lots of money in training, but they weren't seeing enough profit hitting the bottom line to justify the money they had spent. Like any other investment, they expected a rapid and suitable Return on Investment (ROI), but it just wasn't happening the way they imagined or at least hoped that it would. Like Simpson Water Heaters, some had invested in Six Sigma and had trained many of their employees to become Green Belts and/or Black Belts? Some may have even gone out and hired a Master Black Belt?" Tom explained.

Tom continued, "Some of the companies I have helped, have invested a large sum of money training people on Lean Manufacturing, while others had tried going the Lean Six Sigma route. So, if you were one of the companies, the question you may have asked yourself was probably something like, 'Why aren't we seeing a better return on our investment?' You knew improvements were happening, because you were seeing all of the improvement reports, but you just weren't seeing these same improvements positively impacting your bottom line at a high enough rate, again to justify all of the money you had spent on training. 'Is that the case here at Simpson Water Heaters?'" he asked. Matt replied, "Yes, absolutely it is."

Tom then said, "In my position with Tires for All, I too experienced this same dilemma. We had tried both Lean and Six Sigma, and although we did see improvements to our profitability, the level of improvement was not good enough to satisfy our Board of Directors. And then I had an epiphany of sorts. At Tires for All we had hired a consultant to help us and in so doing, it absolutely changed the course of history for Tires for All and for myself. What I discovered was that it was all about having the correct *focus* and *leverage*. By knowing where to focus my improvement efforts absolutely transformed me. The key to my epiphany was that I discovered something called The Theory of Constraints, that you heard about in my last visit."

Tom continued, "The Theory of Constraints explains that within any company, including Simpson Water Heaters, there are key leverage points that truly control the rate of money generated by a company.

Sometimes these leverage points are physical bottlenecks, but many times they are just policies that prevent companies from realizing their true profit potential. In my analysis, the successful efforts all had one thing in common, and that was the focal point of their improvement effort. In this session, I'm going to demonstrate to you how to use the power of the Theory of Constraints to truly jump-start your Lean and Six Sigma improvement efforts. But better yet, I'm going to help you turn all of those training $'s into immediate profits, and then illustrate how to sustain your efforts over the long haul."

"If Simpson Water Heaters is like many other companies, there always seems to be a rush to run out and start improvement projects, without really considering the bottom-line impact of the projects selected. Many companies even develop a performance metric that measures the number of on-going projects, and then attempt to drive this metric higher and higher. Instead of developing a strategically focused and manageable plan, many companies try to, in effect, 'solve world hunger!' Many Lean initiatives attempt to drive waste out of the entire value chain, while Six Sigma initiatives attempt to do the same thing with variation. There's nothing wrong with either of these strategies, but they must be focused on the right area within your company to achieve their maximum benefits," Tom explained.

Tom could see that he had a very captive audience, so he continued, "The real problem with failed Lean and Six Sigma initiatives is really two-fold. There are typically too many projects and most of the projects are focused primarily on *cost reduction*. The true economic reality that supersedes and overrides everything else, is that companies have always wanted the most improvement for the least amount of investment. Attacking all processes and problems simultaneously, as part of an enterprise-wide Lean-Six Sigma initiative, quite simply overloads the organization and does not deliver an acceptable ROI. In fact, according to some studies, the failure rates of many Lean-Six Sigma initiatives are hovering around 50%. With failure rates this high, is it any wonder why companies abandon their improvement initiatives and simply back-slide to their old ways?"

"Earlier I said that focusing projects on cost reduction was one of the primary reasons that many Lean-Six Sigma initiatives are failing. Across-the-board cost-cutting initiatives are pretty much standard for many businesses. My belief is that focusing solely on cost reduction is a colossal mistake. So, if this misguided focus isn't right, then what is the right approach? What is it that companies should be doing to maximize

1. What to change?

2. What to change to?

3. How to cause the change to happen?

FIGURE 8.1
Three critical questions.

their profits? Based upon my experiences in a variety of organizations and industries, the disappointing results coming from Lean and Six Sigma are directly linked to failing to adequately answer three questions," and he inserted a new slide (Figure 8.1)

"Take a look at your own company. Are your improvement projects focused on cost reduction? Do you have an army of Green Belts and Black Belts? Do you have so many projects that they are actually bogging down your company? Are your Six Sigma projects typically taking 2–4 months to complete? Are they providing you with real bottom line impact or are they simply a mirage? You will recall from my last visit I demonstrated the basics of the Theory of Constraints using my simple piping diagram. I then showed you a simple four-step process and you were able to correctly identify the constraint within each example. And to reinforce to you that saving money is not the same as making money, I presented Throughput Accounting to you and showed you why it's a superior way to make real time financial decisions. You also learned that focusing on increasing Throughput was critical to becoming more profitable," Tom explained.

"So, the question then became, how do I know where to focus my improvement efforts? Goldratt also developed his own version of a process of on-going improvement and he gave us five simple steps to follow. I explained that these five steps will form the framework for significant and sustainable improvement for your company," he explained as he loaded a new slide on the screen (Figure 8.2).

Tom continued, "OK, so that's your Process of On-Going Improvement (POOGI) introduced by Goldratt back in the 1980s. Once again, think back to my drawings of the piping system and 4-step process and try to imagine your POOGI and how it might apply to your company. Are you following a logical pathway for improvement or are you instinctively moving to the next improvement project? This logical pathway is what I refer to as the Ultimate Improvement Cycle (UIC) and today I'm going give you the details of how this improvement methodology should be implemented in your company."

1. Identify the system constraint.

2. Decide how to exploit the constraint.

3. Subordinate everything else to the above decision.

4. If necessary, elevate the constraint.

5. Return to Step 1, but don't let inertia become the constraint.

FIGURE 8.2
Goldratt's Five Focusing Steps.

"As I just mentioned, there's an improvement methodology that I refer to as *The Ultimate Improvement Cycle* (UIC). One of the most important points I just presented was the need to combine the two most popular improvement methodologies, Lean and Six Sigma, with the Theory of Constraints. And while Lean and Six Sigma are an integral part of this integrated method, both are missing a key ingredient, and that is a focusing mechanism. Theory of Constraints clarifies where you must focus your Lean and Six Sigma initiatives, in order to realize an acceptable return-on-investment (ROI). Of course, that focal point is the system constraint. The system constraint represents the leverage point for your improvement efforts and delivers the Return on Investment needed to justify your training investment," Tom continued.

"During my last visit, I brought forward a different accounting method referred to as Throughput Accounting (TA). I explained that Throughput Accounting was never intended to replace traditional Cost Accounting (CA) because companies are required by law to follow GAAP reporting rules and requirements. Remember I explained that Throughput Accounting was developed to help make easier and more logical real-time financial decisions," Tom added. "I also explained that in order to judge if an organization is moving toward its goal of making more money, I explained that three basic questions need to be answered," and he loaded a new overhead (Figure 8.3).

1. How much money is generated by your company?

2. How much money is invested by your company?

3. How much money do you have to spend to operate your company?

FIGURE 8.3
Three basic questions.

"During my last visit, I explained that Traditional Cost Accounting is not only difficult to understand, but it's all about what you did last month or last quarter. The key point brought forward in my previous visit, was that Cost Accounting teaches you that the pathway to profitability is through cost-cutting, that is saving money, and this belief is simply wrong. The correct pathway to improving profitability is through making money which is completely different than saving money. I explained that in order to have real-time financial decisions, Theory of Constraints pursues profitability by using three simple financial measurements," he explained as he posted a new overhead (Figure 8.4).

"I also explained that from these three basic financial measurements, you are then able to calculate Net Profit (NP) and Return-On-Investment (ROI) as follows," and he loaded a new overhead on his screen (Figure 8.5).

"As explained previously, and without sounding too redundant, the Theory of Constraint's process of on-going improvement is a direct result of always focusing your efforts toward achieving the system's goal. In order to achieve this focus, Goldratt and Cox developed a five-step process toward that end," Tom explained and loaded another overhead (Figure 8.6).

"In the Lean Improvement Cycle, you are primarily interested in removing unnecessary waste from your process, in an effort to improve the flow of products through your processes. You do this by using the following five steps," and he load a new overhead (Figure 8.7).

1. Throughput (T): The rate at which the system generates new money primarily through sales of its products.

2. Inventory or Investment (I): The money the system invests in items it plans to sell.

3. Operating Expense (OE): The money spent on turning (I) into T.

FIGURE 8.4
Three simple financial measurements.

1. Net Profit = Throughput (T) − Operating Expense (OE) or NP = T − OE

2. Return-On-Investment = (Throughput − Operating Expense) ÷ Investment or (T − OE) / I

FIGURE 8.5
Calculations for NP and ROI.

1. Identify the system's constraint(s).

2. Decide how to exploit the system's constraint(s).

3. Subordinate everything else to the above decision.

4. Elevate the system's constraint(s).

5. If in the previous steps a constraint has been broken, return to Step 1, but do not

   allow inertia to cause a system constraint.

FIGURE 8.6
Theory of Constraints' Five Focusing Steps.

1. Define and identify what value is.

2. Identify the entire value stream.

3. Make value flow without interruptions.

4. Let customers pull value from the producer.

5. Relentlessly pursue perfection, making our processes less and less wasteful.

FIGURE 8.7
Lean's five steps.

"A true lean implementation will definitely produce a better process, as long as it is done correctly and if it is applied in the right location, but this is sometimes a big if," Tom added.

Tom continued, "In the Six Sigma Improvement Process, you are primarily interested in identifying variation, then reducing it, and finally controlling it. The steps for Six Sigma are as defined by the acronym DMAIC as follows," as he loaded another overhead (Figure 8.8).

Tom then suggested that they take a short break and that when they return, he would demonstrate how to combine these three improvement strategies.

1. Define problems and requirements and set goals.

2. Measure the key steps and validate and refine the problems identified in Step 1.

3. Analyze the pertinent data to develop or validate our causal hypotheses.

4. Improve the process by testing solutions and removing root causes.

5. Control our processes by establishing standard measures.

FIGURE 8.8
Six Sigma's five steps.

"Are there any questions or comments before we take a break?" Tom asked. Matt raised his hand and said, "I don't know about everyone else, but I don't think we need a break just yet?" he said in a question format. Tom then said, "By a show of hands, how many of you want to delay your break?" Everyone in the room wanted to delay the break, so Tom continued.

"So, by now you must be wondering why we are going to such great lengths to explain these three, very separate and, to this point, mostly stand-alone initiatives? What does the Theory of Constraints have to do with either Lean or Six Sigma or vice versa? The answer to this question is quite simply, everything!!! The key to successful Lean, Six Sigma and Theory of Constraints implementations, in terms of maximizing throughput and return on investment, is to ensure that your company's efforts are focused on the right area of your business, and the Theory of Constraints provides this focus. The right area of focus is always the system constraint! While Theory of Constraints provides the needed focus, Six Sigma and Lean provide the tools needed to reduce waste and variation. In effect, Lean, Six Sigma, and Theory of Constraints form what I call The Ultimate Improvement Cycle!" Tom explained.

"It's quite likely that there could be some disparaging and reproachful comments from both the Lean and Six Sigma camps, and there will no doubt be attempts to discredit this approach. Zealots of any kind seem to always assume a defensive posture when their beliefs are being challenged. But the fact is, we're not challenging the validity of Lean or Six Sigma or the Theory of Constraints. We're simply presenting a better approach for all three initiatives. All three initiatives are vital pieces to the improvement pie and this combination of the three is a better approach to improvement than each being pursued in isolation as stand-alone initiatives," Tom explained.

Tom continued, "So just what would happen if you were to combine the best of all three of these improvement initiatives into a single improvement process? Just what might this amalgamation look like? Logic would say that you would have an improvement process that reduces waste and variation, but primarily focusing in the operation that is constraining throughput. That is exactly what we have! The figure on the screen (Figure 8.9) is a depiction of how to combine these three separate, but absolutely dependent improvement methodologies."

Tom then explained, "As I said earlier, this graphic is what I refer to as the Ultimate Improvement Cycle (UIC) which combines the power of Lean, Six Sigma, and Theory of Constraints improvement cycles to form

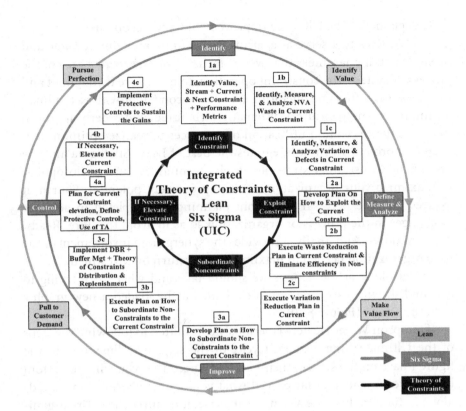

FIGURE 8.9
The UIC methodology.

a more powerful and profitable improvement strategy. This improvement cycle weaves together the DNA of Lean and Six Sigma with the focusing power of the Theory of Constraints to deliver a powerful and compelling improvement methodology that will generate amazing results that your company hasn't seen before. All of the strategies, principles, tools, techniques and methods contained within all three improvement initiatives, are synergistically blended and then time-released to yield improvements that far exceed those obtained from doing these three initiatives in isolation from each other."

"There are four distinct phases of the Ultimate Improvement Cycle which are, *analyze, stabilize, flow,* and *control*. Each phase is critical to the optimization of revenue and profits. Don't jump from one to the other, simply follow them in sequential order," Tom said as he scanned the audience for questions or comments, but again there weren't any, so he continued.

He explained, "The Ultimate Improvement Cycle accomplishes five primary objectives that serve as a spring-board to maximizing revenue and profits. First, it guarantees that we are focusing on the correct area of the process or system, the constraint operation, to maximize throughput and minimize inventory and operating expense. Second, it provides a roadmap for improvement to ensure a systematic, structured, and orderly approach to assure the maximum utilization of resources to realize optimum revenue and profits. Third, it integrates the best of Lean, Six Sigma and the Theory of Constraints strategies, tools, techniques, and philosophies, to maximize your organization's full improvement potential. Fourth, it assures that the necessary, up-front planning is completed in advance of changes to the process or organization so as to avoid the 'Fire, Ready, Aim!' mindset. And finally, it provides the synergy and involvement of the total organization needed to maximize your return on investment."

"So, let's look at the actions we should take and what we're trying to accomplish with each one," Tom explained as he loaded a new graphic onto the screen (Figure 8.10).

"If Simpson Water Heaters is seriously committed to following the steps of the Ultimate Improvement Cycle, in the sequence illustrated in the figure I have on the screen, then I am convinced that you will see bottom line improvements that far exceed what you've experienced using stand-alone initiatives. Just like any new initiative, it requires the entire organization's focus, discipline, determination, and a little bit of patience. This is new territory for Simpson Water Heaters, so follow the path of least resistance that I have provided for you…it truly does work!" Tom explained and he then recommended another break.

When everyone returned from the break, Tom continued his discussion on the Ultimate Improvement Cycle. "Referring to the overhead on the screen, you may be wondering, 'So just how do we accomplish each of the steps in the Ultimate Improvement Cycle?' We do so by using all of the tools and actions that we would use if we were implementing Lean and Six Sigma as stand-alone improvement initiatives, but this time we focus most, if not all, of our efforts primarily on the constraint operation. The figure on the screen lays out the tools and actions we will use and perform at each step of the Ultimate Improvement Cycle and as you can see there are no new or exotic tools that I am introducing. In creating the Ultimate Improvement Cycle one of my objectives was to keep things simple, and I

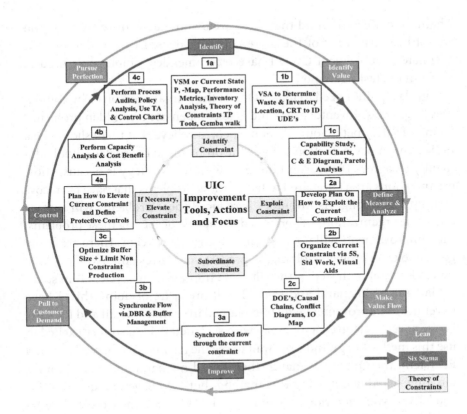

FIGURE 8.10
UIC improvement tools, actions, and focus.

think you'll agree that the tools I've laid out to use are all of the basic and time-tested tools that have been around for years."

"For example, in Step 1a we will be creating a simple current state Value Stream Map to analyze things like where the excess inventory is, what the individual processing times are, cycle times and the overall lead time within the process. We will use this tool to identify both the current and next constraint. We will also be looking at the current process and information flow and performance metrics to make certain that the metrics stimulate the right behaviors and that they will in fact track the true impact of our improvement efforts," he explained.

He continued, "Likewise in Steps 1b and 1c we will be analyzing our process by using simple tools like Pareto Charts, Run Charts, Spaghetti Diagrams, Time and Motion Studies, Cause & Effect Diagrams, Causal

Chains, etc. Keep in mind that these are by no means the only tools you can utilize, just some of the more common ones. In each phase of the Ultimate Improvement Cycle I have recommended simple tools used to perform the tasks at hand."

"One last point I need to make. One of the primary reasons why companies have excess inventory on hand is to compensate for hidden problems, a kind of safety net if you will. Some people believe that there should be a radical inventory reduction to force the problems to the surface, but I adamantly disagree. The reason I disagree with this strategy is because most organizations aren't prepared to tackle these problems that have been covered up for so long. As inventory is reduced these problems will surface and if the organization isn't prepared or capable of solving these problems, then improvements will not happen, and chaos will reign. There are many good books on problem-solving, so prepare yourselves now. Now let's look more closely at each step in the Ultimate Improvement Cycle," Tom said.

Matt raised his hand and said, "In all my years of doing this, I have never heard improvement efforts explained in so much detail and for sure, I have never been given a roadmap with such detail. I am so very excited to use this methodology and can't wait to see the results we achieve." Cynthia Eberstein, the Quality Manager, then raised his hand and said, "Tom, I too am excited about using this method, but I do have one question for you." "And your question is?" Tom asked. "What are the expected deliverables we should be expected to deliver?" Cynthia asked. Without hesitation, Tom responded and said, "It's ironic that you would ask that question Cynthia, because the next part of my presentation will be focused on the expected deliverables from the Ultimate Improvement Cycle."

"In this part of my session, I'm going to lay out each of the expected deliverables when implementing the Ultimate Improvement Cycle." And with that, Tom flashed a new figure on the screen. "In this figure (Figure 8.11) I have laid out the expected deliverables for each step of the Ultimate Improvement Cycle that Cynthia just asked about. I'm sure you will have questions as we progress around this figure, so speak up when you do," Tom encouraged everyone.

Tom began again, "As I said earlier, when I created this methodology, I wanted to keep everything simple, so as you can see, the wording is very descriptive, but very simple. In Step 1a, using things like Value Steam Maps, or simple Process Maps, or even Gemba walks, you should come away with a complete picture of the system you're attempting to improve,

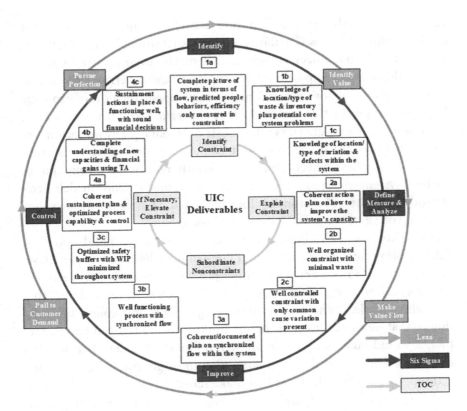

FIGURE 8.11
Expected deliverables from the UIC.

in terms of flow and predicted people behaviors. In addition, you need to make sure that efficiency is now only truly measured and acted upon in the step that is constraining system throughput. This, of course, assumes that you have correctly identified the system constraint."

Tom continued, "In Step 1b, you are attempting to gain knowledge of both the location and type of waste within your system, plus the location of inventory, plus any potential core problems that exist within the system you're attempting to improve. These problems could be a variety of different types of problems, including things like high levels of work-in-process inventory, high levels of waste, or even excessive amounts of equipment downtime."

Continuing Tom said, "In Step 1c, we are interested in understanding both the location and type of variation we are experiencing, as well as any recurring defects that exist within the system being improved. Here, you will be running Process Capability studies, performing Pareto Analyses, creating Cause and Effect Diagrams and maybe even creating Control Charts. This is a very important step, simply because recurring defects that result in either scrap or rework can seriously impede the flow of products through your production system. We are concerned with defects ahead of the constraint that might starve the constraints, but equally important are defects that occur after the constraint as they leave the system constraint. In both cases, these defects could significantly reduce the throughput of the total system which could result in missed shipments and late deliveries of products to the end customer," Tom explained. "Are there any questions on what you've heard so far?" Tom asked the group.

Greg Thompson, the Production Manager raised his hand and said, "This make perfect sense to me, but if I remember what you said earlier, we aren't supposed to take action on things just yet. Is that correct?" he asked. "Great question Greg," Tom responded. "The answer is, yes and no," Tom said with a smile. "What we are attempting to do is only collect information so that we can develop a coherent improvement plan. But having said that, it would make no sense at all, if you found a problem that was fixable immediately, and then wait for a plan to be generated before taking action," Tom explained. "Does that make sense to you Greg?" Tom asked, and Greg responded with his head bobbing up and down indicating that it did. "Are there any other questions?" he asked that group, and when there weren't any, he continued his presentation on deliverables.

In Step 2a, we will use all of the information collected in Steps 1a, 1b, and 1c to develop a coherent system action plan on how we intend to improve the quality and capacity of the system being improved. In effect, we will be using Goldratt's second step, 'exploiting' the system constraint. You should now know where the system constraint is located, the performance metrics that are in place which stimulate the expected people behaviors, the location of excessive waste and variation, and you should no longer be measuring efficiencies in non-constraints. Let me say this about measuring efficiencies. You may have a corporate edict to continue measuring efficiencies in non-constraints, but the only efficiency result that truly matters is the efficiency of system constraint. Here we are applying Goldratt's third step, 'subordination,' Tom explained.

"My recommendation is that this plan should be developed as a team and not just by a single person. The plan should clearly identify specific actions to be taken," he explained. Tom continued, "In Steps 2b and 2c your deliverable should be a well-organized constraint with minimal amounts of waste. You will be effectively executing both your waste and variation reduction plan focused on the system constraint. In addition, after implementing your improvement plan, you should only have common cause variation within the system being controlled using things like Control Charts to maintain control," Tom explained.

"Continuing on, Step 3a's deliverable is a coherent, well documented plan on synchronizing flow throughout and within your system. Here your plan will be focused on how to subordinate non-constraints to the current system constraint. When implemented, this plan will result in a well-functioning process with synchronized flow, using both Drum Buffer Rope coupled with Buffer Management, which is the hallmark of Step 3b. In Step 3c, you will have also optimized your buffer size and will have limited your non-constraint production by never out-pacing the drum or system constraint. I can't emphasize enough how important this step is! Any questions here?" he asked. Once again, Greg raised his hand and asked, "What the hell is Drum Buffer Rope?" Tom replied and said, "Drum Buffer Rope is Theory of Constraints' version of a scheduling system, which I will explain on my next visit."

Matt Maloney raised his hand and asked, "How long should it have taken to get this far along on the Ultimate Improvement Cycle?" "Being a Plant Manager, a question related to time doesn't surprise me at all," Tom thought to himself. "Matt, he responded," while there isn't a specific amount of time expected to complete these first three major steps, I would tell you not to apply a time limit. Think about what you're attempting to do here. Obviously if your process is already functioning well, then you might expect to complete this rotation fairly quickly. On the other hand, if your current system is delivering poor results, which is the case here at Simpson Water Heaters, then it will take much longer. The key point here is, don't rush through this process!" Tom explained.

After answering Matt's question, Tom continued, "Having completed the first three major steps of the Ultimate Improvement Cycle, you will have significantly improved your production system. In fact, if you've done your work correctly, you may have already 'broken' your current constraint, but if you haven't, then you must develop a plan on how to 'elevate' the constraint. Remember back in Step 1a, I told you to identify both the current and next constraint? I did this in anticipation that the current constraint would eventually be broken and a new one would immediately appear, so be ready to move to it," Tom explained.

Tom continued, "In addition, we want to make sure that all of our improvements will remain in effect, so I instruct you to define protective controls to guarantee this state will continue. Having said this, your deliverable in Step 3a is the development of a coherent sustainment plan which will include protective control devices such as Control Charts. Wouldn't it be a shame that after all of your hard work to bring your process under control that you might take actions that remove your control?"

"So, the deliverables for Steps 4a, 4b, and 4c would all be aimed at sustaining the gains you have already made. Your actions would include things like performing routine process audits and maintaining Process Control Charts. Another important deliverable in this step is at least a basic understanding of Throughput Accounting by the shop floor employees, so that sound financial decisions can be made in real time. In addition, it is very important that the operators running the machines understand how Control Charts are maintained so that process control can be a way of life on the shop floor," Tom explained.

Tom began again, "This completes the first rotation of the Ultimate Improvement Cycle, but we're not finished yet. We must make sure that everyone is prepared for the next constraint which will appear almost immediately, when the current constraint is broken, and it will be. By preparation, I mean that all of the sustainment tools we developed, as we progressed around the Ultimate Improvement Cycle, must be maintained if our improvements are to be sustained. This completes my presentation, so I want to open the floor for questions, comments and concerns," Tom stated.

Matt was the first one to comment, "I have been involved in manufacturing for most of my career and I've been to many training sessions on a variety of subjects. Having said this, I have never been in a training session that was as complete as this one. So, Tom I just want to say thank you for what you presented today. As I look into the future, I see very positive things happening at Simpson Water Heaters! I truly believe that our profit margins will turn positive and that the Board of Directors will be very happy with our new direction. Why do I say that? I say that because I know that, if we follow the steps outlined in the Ultimate Improvement Cycle, we will have record profit margins and a plethora of satisfied customers. I see our on-time delivery becoming one of the best in the business!"

Greg was the next one to speak and said, "I too have a positive outlook for the future of Simson Water Heaters! One of the keys to our success will be how well we embrace the concepts of Throughput Accounting. By using this method, I can see a vast improvement in our real time financial decisions. I also believe our cash on hand will be significantly improved, simply because we won't be tying up our cash on excessive amounts of inventory."

Nancy Watson, the company's Accounting Manager, then spoke up and said, "I'm excited for a variety of reasons. First, I always worry about having to lay people off, but with the Theory of Constraints in place, our future growth will mean that we need all of our hourly workers to satisfy our future demand. I can also see our equipment downtime improving dramatically and our process flow improving intensely! I can honestly say I have never been this excited about the future of Simpson Water Heaters!"

"Any other comments, questions or concerns?" Tom asked.

Cynthia Eberstein, Simpson's Quality Manager, was the next to speak, "I am so happy that our path to improvement took the route that it did. Think about it, we first tried Six Sigma and learned valuable tools and techniques. We then employed Lean Manufacturing and learned all about waste and value. But as good as these two methods are, their full potential won't be realized until we combine them both with the Theory of Constraints! Using the Ultimate Improvement Cycle is the key to improvement and I'm excited to get all of the Green Belts and Black Belts leading the charge to our future. I can absolutely say that Simpson Water Heaters will be the leader in the water heater industry!"

Pete Hallwell from Maximo then commented and said, "I am excited to return to Maximo with our new-found knowledge of this amazing improvement initiative. I can see so many areas where this integrated methodology will apply. Areas like treatment clinics, emergency departments, and the list goes on and on, so thank you so much for inviting us to be a part of this experience." When there were no more comments, Tom addressed the group. "I appreciate all of your glowing comments about what you heard today, but I want to tell you that there is much more to the Theory of Constraints that you haven't heard about yet.

On my next trip, I'll teach you about the Theory of Constraints scheduling system, which I mentioned earlier, Drum Buffer Rope. I will also explain the Theory of Constraint's Parts Replenishment Solution. You will hear all about how you will be able to reduce your part's inventory by fifty percent while at the same time, reducing your stock-outs to near zero! I also want to teach you how to develop something called the Goal Tree, which is a tool you can use to plan your future strategically, and I think when you see it, you'll fall in love with it. I think it's time to call it a day, so thank you again for taking the time to listen to what I had to say today."

When everyone had departed the conference room, Matt and Tom began another discussion about when Tom would be coming back. Matt indicated he was excited to learn about Drum Buffer Rope, the Theory of Constraint's Parts Replenishment Solution, and The Goal Tree. And with that, Tom left for the airport.

9

The Next Step at Maximo Health Center Complex

It was Thursday morning and Tom was on his way to Maximo Health Center Complex to present a couple of different subjects, namely the Theory of Constraints Replenishment Solution and the Goal Tree. He made a quick call to Pete, to let him know he would be there shortly. Upon arrival there, he saw Pete standing outside waiting for him. Tom parked his car and walked up the stairs where he met Pete. The two of them shook hands and took the elevator to the seventh floor conference room. On the way to the seventh floor, Pete said, "Tom, thank you so much for inviting Jimmy Thompson, Susie Wong and me to attend your session in Detroit. The three of us discussed it the next day and we can't wait to get started on our own implementation." He then added, "Your presentation of how to combine Lean, Six Sigma, and the Theory of Constraints made it sound so simple to implement!" The attendees for his session today were already seated, so Pete introduced Tom and he began.

Tom began, "Before I begin, what I'm about to present is based upon a typical manufacturing company and not healthcare. But as I present this information, I want you all to think about how it might apply to your own hospitals and medical facilities. The fact of the matter is, it matters not what type of company you are working in, because everything you will hear today applies equally to medical or manufacturing companies or any other type of company." With that introduction, Tom began.

"Most, if not all, businesses are linked one way or another to some kind of supply chain. They need parts or raw materials or medical supplies from somebody else, in order to do what they do and pass it on to the next system in line until it finally arrives at the end consumer. Depending on what you make or what service you deliver, and how fast you make or deliver it, the supply chain can be your best friend or worst enemy. If it works well, it's your best friend. If it doesn't work well, it's your worst enemy. And of course, we all want it to be our best friend," Tom explained.

Tom continued, "The fundamental problem with most supply-chain systems is that they have remained stagnant in their thinking through time, while business reality has flexed in a cycle of constant change, sometimes at an exponential rate. There are many new supply-chain software applications, with each proposing that it will solve the problems associated with the supply chain. These new software applications have come about mostly because of advances in computer technology, but few have solved the real issues of the supply chain. While it is true that these systems can provide an enormous amount of information very fast, sometimes system speed is less important than having access to the correct information. What difference does it make how fast you get the information, if it's the wrong information?"

"The new business reality has caused a need for change in supply-chain systems, but most systems simply have not changed. Businesses now are required to build products or deliver services more cheaply, with higher quality, and with faster delivery of products and services. These are the new rules of competition," Tom explained. He continued, "You either play by the rules or you must get out of the way. The rules in business have changed, and yet many businesses insist on doing business the same 'old' way. How come?" he asked rhetorically.

"Usually, the most common answer given is, 'Because that's the way we've always done it,' he explained, and he noticed everyone moving their heads in agreement." Tom continued, "The old system and the old rules may have worked in the past, but times are changing. If your supply-chain system has not changed to align with the new rules, then the gap between supply-chain output and system needs will continue to grow. If the supply-chain system is not changed to meet future needs, then there is very little hope of getting different results, and such was the case at Tires for All," Tom explained.

Tom scanned the room to see if everyone was understanding what he had explained so far and then continued. "Many supply-chain systems were designed to solve a problem. And the problem they were trying to solve was the needed availability of parts, raw materials, supplies, or inventory. In other words, the right parts or materials or supplies, in the right location, at the right time. These systems were designed to hold inventory in check. That is to say, don't buy too much, but also don't allow stock-out situations to occur. Then and now, managing the supply chain is a tough job and there are many variables that can require constant attention. You don't want to run out of parts or materials, and yet, sometimes you still run out of them. You don't want excess inventory, and yet sometimes you have too much inventory. This constant negative cycle of sometimes too much and sometimes too little has continued through time. The supply problems encountered years ago are still the problems being encountered today," Tom explained.

"For many companies the supply chain/inventory system of choice is one referred to as the Minimum/Maximum (MIN/MAX) system. Parts or inventory levels are evaluated based on need and usage, and some type of maximum and minimum levels are established for each item. The traditional rules and measures for these systems are usually quite simple," and with that Tom loaded a new overhead on the screen (Figure 9.1).

"Is this what rules you're using here at Maximo?" Tom asked. Pete Hallwell, the CFO at Maximo Health Center Complex, responded, "Yes, pretty much so." Tom continued, "The foundational assumptions behind these rules and measures are primarily based in Cost Accounting and commonly referred to as cost-world thinking. In order to save money and minimize your expenditures for supply parts or inventory or supplies, you must reduce the amount of money you spend for these items. In order to reduce the amount of money you spend on these items, you must never buy more than the maximum amount. In addition, in order to reduce the money spent on these items, you must not spend money until absolutely necessary, which means you only order parts or supplies when they reach or go below the minimum level," Tom explained to a very captive audience.

Tom continued, "These assumptions seem valid, and if implemented correctly and monitored closely, they should deliver a supply system that controls dollars and maintains inventory within the minimum and maximum

- Rule 1: Determine the maximum and minimum levels for each item.

- Rule 2: Don't exceed the maximum level.

- Rule 3: Don't reorder until you reach or go below the minimum level.

FIGURE 9.1
The rules of the Min/Max system.

levels. However, most systems of this type, even in a perfect world, don't seem to generate the desired results that are required," and again, Tom could see most in attendance shaking their heads in agreement. "For some reason, there always seem to be situations of excess inventory for some items and of stock-out situations for others. There always seem to be constant gyrations between too much inventory and too little inventory. The whole operational concept behind the Minimum/Maximum systems was supposed to prevent these kinds of occurrences from happening, and yet they still do," Tom explained.

"Perhaps the best way to make this point, is with a couple of examples," Tom said. "The first example deals with a company that measured and rewarded their procurement staff based on the amount of money they saved with parts purchases. For the procurement staff, their primary way to accomplish this objective was to buy in bulk, and for the most part this was usually quite easy to accomplish. Their suppliers preferred, and sometimes demanded, that their customers buy in bulk to receive the benefit of 'quantity discounts.' The more you bought, the less it cost per unit. The assumption being that the purchase price per part could be driven to the lowest possible level by buying in large quantities, and the company would save the maximum amount of money on their purchase. It seemed like a great idea, and certainly a way to meet the objective of saving money. Sometimes these supply items were procured in amounts well in excess of the maximum, but the company got them at a great price!" Tom explained.

Tom continued, "The bottom line was that by using this cost-saving strategy, the company had a warehouse full of low-cost inventory that had used a large portion of their cash. The problem was, they didn't have the right mix of inventory to build even a single product. They had too many of some items and not enough of others. The bigger problem was they ran out of money to purchase any more parts, especially the parts and materials they desperately needed!" Tom explained. "Do you suppose they wished they had at least some of the money back so they could buy the right parts, in the right quantity, at the right time, so they could produce products or deliver their service?" Tom asked the group. Without exception, everyone agreed with this question.

Tom continued, "The other cost saving example is one a friend of mine was involved in that was with a company who was a contractor to the Federal Government. In their contract with the Government, the Government had offered a very lucrative clause to save money. This company was given a budgeted amount to buy parts on a yearly basis, and based on this budgeted amount, the Government offered to split fifty-fifty any amount the company could underrun their parts budget. The company took the total budgeted dollars and divided it by twelve to establish the monthly parts budget. They also held back a percentage of the budgeted amount each month, so they could claim cost savings and split the difference. Any parts purchase that would have exceeded the targeted monthly budget was postponed until the next month, even if it was urgently needed. The ability of this company to make money slowed dramatically. They were literally jumping over dollars to pick up pennies. There were many jobs waiting for parts that couldn't finish until they had the parts to finish, but they had to wait, sometimes for several days or weeks, to get the parts, because of the cost-saving mentality."

Then, Tom said, "In both of these examples, it's an issue of bad cost metrics driving the bad behavior. In both of these cases, cost savings were employed as the primary strategy. In the first example, the company ultimately went bankrupt and went out of business. They couldn't pay back the loans on the money they had borrowed to buy all of the low-cost parts because they couldn't make enough finished products. In the second example the company avoided bankruptcy because they provided a needed service for the Government, so they were ultimately spared by seeing the error of their ways, and they decided to spend the budgeted dollars to buy the needed parts."

Pete spoke up and commented on what he heard so far, "This is all so very interesting Tom!" Tom responded by saying, "I'm just getting started." Tom continued, "If the system as a whole isn't producing the desired results, then what segment of the system needs to be changed to produce the desired results? Perhaps the minimum and maximum levels are the wrong rules to engage, and saving money is the wrong financial measure to consider. In order to solve today's problems, we must think at an order of magnitude higher than we were thinking when we developed yesterday's solutions. In other words, yesterday's solutions are causing most of today's problems."

"One of the most important aspects of any service, manufacturing, production, or assembly operation system, is to have and maintain the ability to supply raw materials or parts or supplies at a very predictable level. If the parts availability goes to zero, then your production or service activities will stop. The continual availability of parts, monitored accurately, implies a supply-chain system that contains all of the necessary and robust features to support the customer demand requirements," Tom explained. "Does everyone understand this basic comment?" Tom asked the group, and again, everyone in the audience shook their heads in agreement.

Once again, Tom continued, "The Minimum/Maximum supply-chain system was developed years ago, and at the time it brought forward some favorable improvements. Then and now, the functional theory behind the supply-chain Minimum/Maximum concept is that, supplies and materials should be distributed and stored at the lowest possible level of the user chain. In essence, this is a push system, one that pushes parts through the system to the lowest possible level. It seems to make some sense because parts must be available at the lowest level in order to be used. In this type of system, the parts are consumed until the minimum quantity is met or exceeded, and then an order is placed for more parts. The parts order goes up the chain from the point-of-use location back to some kind of central supply center. Or the necessary orders are placed directly back to the vendor, depending on the situation."

Tom continued, "When the orders are received at the central supply center, they are pushed back down the chain to the lowest point of use locations," Tom explained and then flashed a figure (Figure 9.2) on the screen.

"This drawing defines a simplified version of this parts Flow activity. This flow might not be applicable to all situations, but I believe it applies to Maximo's Hospitals. Some companies, and smaller businesses, will have fewer steps, in that they order directly from a vendor and receive parts back into their business without the need for large, more complex, distribution systems. However, the thinking behind the Minimum/Maximum system will still apply, even to those smaller businesses," Tom explained.

"Larger companies, or those with numerous geographical locations, like Maximo, will most likely have developed some type of a central supply and/or distribution locations that feed the next level of the supply distribution system. Maybe a regional warehouse versus local distribution points. The distribution points in turn feed the companies or business segments that use the raw material and parts at the final point of use location to build products or deliver their service. Some distribution systems may even be more complex than what is displayed here. But even with increased complexity, the results they are trying to achieve remain the same, which is to get the parts to where they need to be when they need to be there," he explained.

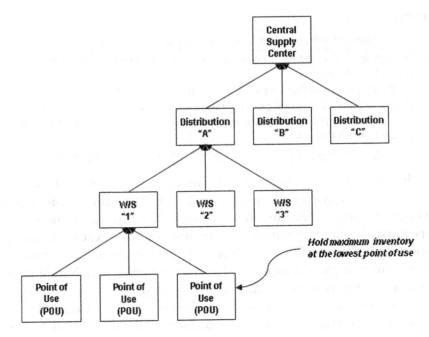

FIGURE 9.2
Supply chain parts Flow activity.

"The model of a central supply system versus a decentralized system has moved back and forth for many years. Some will say that the supply system should be centralized at the user location to make supply activities easier and more responsive. Others argue that the supply chain activities should be decentralized to save money and reduce operating expense. Even with these different and opposing views, it seems that the current method is for the decentralized model of supply systems," Tom explained. Tom then suggested that they take a short break in order to digest what he had explained so far.

After the break, Tom continued his detailed explanation. "For all of its intent to save money and reduce operating expenses, this decentralized system can and usually does cause enormous hardships on the very systems it is designed to support. With all of the intended good this type of system is supposed to provide, there are some top-level rules that drive the system into chaos. Let's look at some of these rules and understand the negative aspects that derive from them," as he flashed a Table 9.1 on the screen.

TABLE 9.1

Top-Level Rules for Minimum/Maximum Supply System

1. The system reorder amount is the maximum amount no matter how many parts are currently in the bin box.
2. Most supply systems only allow for one order at a time to be present
3. Orders for parts are triggered *only* after the minimum amount has been exceeded.
4. Total part inventory is held at the lowest possible level of the distribution chain—the point-of-use (POU) location.
5. Parts are inventoried once or twice a month and orders placed, as required.

"This table provides a summary listing of the top-level rules for the min/max supply system," Tom explained. "Even though the Minimum/ Maximum system appears to control the supply needs and cover the inventory demands, there are some significant negative effects caused by using this system. First and foremost, there is the problem of being reactive to an inventory or parts situation, rather than proactive. When minimum stock levels are used as the trigger to reorder parts or supplies, some supply-chain systems, as they are currently organized and used, will have a difficult time keeping up with the demands being placed upon them. And there is an increased probability that stock-outs will occur, possibly for long periods of time," Tom explained.

"Stock-outs occur most often when the lead time to replenish the part exceeds the minimum stock available. In other words, availability of the part between the minimum amount and zero is totally depleted before the part can be replenished from the vendor," Tom explained and flashed a new figure on the screen. Tom then said, "This figure (Figure 9.3) displays a graphical representation of this stock-out effect. The curved line shows the item usage through time and the possibility of a stock-out situation," he explained.

Tom added, "Of course, when parts are reordered, they are ordered at a level equal to the maximum amount, and the problem appears to quickly correct itself. However, there can be a significantly large segment of time between stock-out and correction, and if the part is urgently needed, the parts non-availability can cause havoc in the assembly sequence." "Does everyone understand what this figure is actually saying?" Tom asked. When everyone answered in the affirmative, Tom continued. "Some might argue that the solution to the problem is to simply increase the minimum amount to trigger a reorder sooner in the process and avoid the stock-out situation. While it is possible this solution could provide some short-term

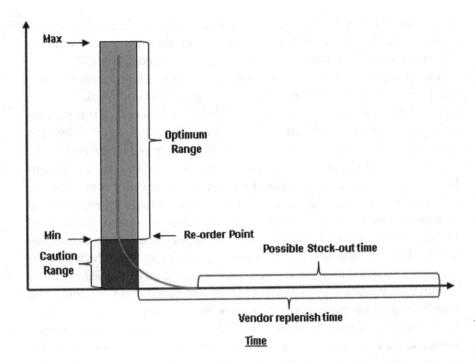

FIGURE 9.3
Graphical impact of the stock-out effect.

relief, in the long run it causes inventory levels to increase, which need-lessly ties up cash and continues at this elevated level. It is also possible that if you raise the minimum level, then the maximum level must be raised also. Many companies use a ratio variable to calculate the spread between minimum and maximum. If that's the case, then total inventory levels will go up, which again costs more money to maintain. This action would be totally counter to the Cost Accounting rules."

Once again Tom continued his presentation, "The Minimum/Maximum supply chain system is based totally on being in a reactive mode. That is you must wait for the part to reach its minimum stock level before a reorder request is activated. In many companies, the most used parts are managed using the Minimum/Maximum concepts and can frequently be out of stock. All of these 'rules' of the Min/Max supply system create the disadvantage of having maybe several thousand dollars, or hundreds of thousands of dollars, tied up in inventory that may or may not get used before it becomes obsolete, modified, or dated because of expiration.

If additional money is spent buying parts that might not be needed, at least in the quantity defined by the maximum limit, then you have effectively diverted money that could have been used to buy needed parts."

Just to reinforce the point he just made, Tom said, "As an example for purposes of discussion, suppose we pick a random part with a Minimum/Maximum level already established, and we track this part for a twenty-six-week period using the current system rules and follow the flow and cyclical events that take place. What happens at the end of the twenty-six weeks? For this example, we will assume that the maximum level is ninety items; the minimum reorder point is twenty items; and the lead time to replenish this part from the vendor averages four weeks. The average is based on the fact that there are times when this part can be delivered faster, say three weeks, and other times it is delivered slower, say five weeks. Let's also assume that usage of these parts varies by week, but on average is equal to about ten items per week," Tom explained.

Tom then flashed Table 9.2 on the screen and said, "This table shows the reorder trigger happening when current inventory drops below the minimum amount of twenty items. The first reorder would trigger between weeks six and seven, and again between weeks seventeen and eighteen, and again between weeks twenty-five and twenty-six."

"During this twenty-six-week period there would be a total of about eight weeks of stock-out time. Remember, there is an average of four weeks of vendor lead time to replenish this part. This repeating cycle of maximum inventory and stock-outs becomes the norm, and the scenario is repeated time and time again." Tom explained. Tom followed Table 9.3 with a new figure (Figure 9.4) which uses the data from this table.

"As I said, in this figure (Figure 9.4) we have used the data from our table to graphically display the results of the Minimum/Maximum system, and it demonstrates the potential negative consequences that can occur when using this system. If the vendor lead time is not considered as an important reorder variable, then stock-outs will continue to occur. Stock-outs can become a very predictable negative effect in this system," he explained.

In addition, Tom added that the graph shows the negative consequences of the supply system and demonstrates why supply-chain systems using the Minimum/Maximum concepts will periodically create excessive inventory and stock-out situations. The primary reason this happens is because part lead times are not properly taken into account. "This is amazing material Tom!" Pete said.

TABLE 9.2

Simulated Data for Minimum/Maximum Supply System

Week	Current Inventory	Actual Items Used	End of Week Inventory	Items Added (Replenish)
1	90	10	80	
2	80	15	65	
3	65	15	50	
4	50	15	35	
5	35	5	30	
6	30	15	15	
7	15	15	0	
8	0	0	0	
9	0	0	0	
10	0	0	0	90
11	90	15	75	
12	75	15	60	
13	60	8	52	
14	52	12	40	
15	40	10	30	
16	30	10	20	
17	20	15	5	
18	5	5	0	
19	0	0	0	
20	0	0	0	
21	90	15	75	90
22	75	18	57	
23	57	15	42	
24	42	12	30	
25	30	15	15	
26	15	15	0	

Tom continued, "In most cases, the most prominent measures for the Minimum/Maximum systems are focused in cost world thinking, rather than what the system needs. If the lead times from the vendors are not considered, then there remains a high probability that stock-outs will continue. The stock-out situation exacerbates itself even further when at the point-of-use a user has experienced a stock-out situation in the past. In that situation the users will often try to protect themselves against stock-outs by taking more than is needed." "Do we need another break?" Tom asked. Virtually everyone in the room indicated that they would rather continue.

TABLE 9.3

Theory of Constraints Distribution and Replenishment Model

Week	Current Inventory	Actual Items Used	Weekend Inventory	Items Added (Replenish)
1	90	10	80	
2	80	15	65	
3	65	15	50	
4	50	15	35	10
5	45	5	40	15
6	55	15	40	15
7	55	15	40	15
8	55	10	45	5
9	50	10	40	15
10	55	15	40	15
11	55	15	40	10
12	50	15	35	10
13	45	8	37	15
14	52	12	40	15
15	55	10	45	15
16	60	10	50	8
17	58	5	53	12
18	65	10	55	10
19	65	10	55	10
20	65	10	55	5
21	60	15	45	10
22	55	18	37	10
23	47	15	32	10
24	42	12	30	15
25	45	10	35	18
26	53	15	38	15

Tom continued, "It is also possible that some companies will preorder inventory based on some type of forecast for the coming year, and this strategy only exacerbates the problem even more. At best, it is extremely difficult to forecast what a consumer may or may not buy. I've always said that forecasts are always wrong and the further into the future you make the forecast, the 'wronger' it will be. This problem is encountered at the manufacturing level and the retail level. Manufacturers will produce excess finished good inventory that must be stored at a great cost or sold to retailers at a discounted price. Because of the flaws in their forecasting methods, some stores are left with large amounts of inventory when new

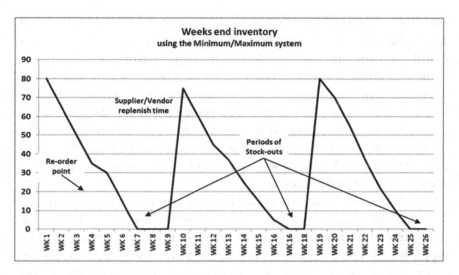

FIGURE 9.4
Consequences of Min/Max supply system.

models or products are released. This becomes most visible when stores offer 'year-end clearance sales' or 'inventory liquidation' events. They guessed wrong with the forecast and have much more inventory than they can sell. In many cases because stores couldn't get enough of the hot-selling product, they missed out on sales. Now they must sell any remaining inventory, sometimes at bargain prices, to generate enough cash to go buy more inventories for the coming year. This cycle of too much and too little repeats itself year after year." Tom then said, "So, what's the answer to this logistics dilemma?"

Tom began to answer his own question by saying, "One of the primary operating functions of the supply-chain system is to build and hold inventory at the lowest possible distribution level. This assumption is both correct and incorrect. The correct inventory should be held at the point-of-use location, but not based on minimum or maximum amounts. Instead, the necessary inventory should be based on the vendor lead times to replenish and maintain sufficient inventory to buffer the variations that exist in lead time. The Theory of Constraints Distribution and Replenishment Model is a robust parts replenishment system that allows the user to be proactive in managing the supply-chain system. It's also a system based on usage, either daily or weekly, but not some minimum amount. Some parts/inventory will require much more vigilance in day-to-day management." And with this comment,

Tom flashed a new table on his screen and explained, "This table (Table 9.4) defines the suggested criteria required to implement a Theory of Constraints Distribution and Replenishment Model in a supply-chain system."

Tom continued, "The Theory of Constraints Distribution and Replenishment Model argues that the majority of the inventory should be held at a higher level in the distribution system and not at the lowest level. It is still important to keep what is needed at the lowest levels, but don't try to hold the total inventory at that location." Again, Tom checked for understanding, and when he was comfortable that everyone was following what he had just said, he continued.

"The Theory of Constraints model is based on the characteristics of a 'V' plant distribution model. The 'V' plant model assumes that distribution is fractal from a single location, which in this case is either a central supply location or a supplier/vendor location (the base of the 'V') and distribution is made to different locations which are the arms of the 'V.' The 'V' plant concept is not unlike any supply-chain distribution methodology. However, using a 'V' plant method has some negative consequences, especially when working under the Minimum/Maximum rules that I presented earlier. If one is not careful to understand these consequences, the system can suffer dramatically," Tom explained. He continued, "One of the major negative consequences of 'V' distribution is distributing items too early and sending them down the wrong path to the wrong location. In other words, inventory is released too early and possibly to the wrong destination. This is especially likely to happen when the same type of inventory or part is used in several locations."

TABLE 9.4

Criteria for the Theory of Constraints Distribution and Replenishment Model

1. The system reorder amount needs to be based on daily or weekly usage and part lead time to replenish.
2. The system needs to allow for multiple replenish orders, if required.
3. Orders are triggered based on buffer requirements, with possible daily actions, as required.
4. All parts/inventory must be available when needed.
5. Parts inventory is held at a higher level, preferably at central supply locations or comes directly from the supplier/vendor.
6. Part buffer determined by usage rate and replenish supplier/vendor lead time. Baseline buffer should be equal to 1.5. If lead time is 1 week, buffer is set at 1.5 weeks. Adjust as required, based on historical data.

Tom then asked the group a question, "Has it ever happened that at one location you have a stock-out situation, and one of the rapid response criteria for finding the part is to check another hospital within Maximo's complex?" Pete answered his question by saying, "Yes, it happens often!" Tom responded, "If this is the case, then parts/inventory distribution has taken place too early in the system. Sometimes, it's not that the system does not have the right parts/inventory, but it's just that they are in the wrong location. Distribution from a higher level in the chain has been completed too quickly."

Tom continued his presentation, "The Theory of Constraints Distribution and Replenishment Model also argues that the use of Minimum/Maximum amounts should be abolished. Instead the inventory should be monitored based on daily or weekly usage, with replenishment occurring, at a minimum weekly, and possibly daily for highly used items. The end result of these actions will be sufficient inventory in the right location at the right time, with zero or minimal stock-outs to support the activities that take place within your hospitals. Instead of using the minimum amount to trigger the reorder process, it should be triggered by daily usage and vendor lead time to replenish," and with that, Tom flashed another table onto the screen.

Tom then said, "As an example, suppose we apply the Theory of Constraints Distribution and Replenishment Model rules to exactly the same criteria that we used for the Minimum/Maximum system we discussed earlier. We will use the same part simulation and the same period of time, with the same usage numbers. The difference will be in this simulation, we will change the rules to fit the Theory of Constraints Distribution and Replenishment Model, based on usage amount and vendor lead time rather than minimum and maximum amount."

Tom explained, "This table (Table 9.3) represents the simulated data for a random reorder scenario using the Theory of Constraints Distribution and Replenishment Model. In this example we will assume that the maximum level is ninety items, which is the starting point for the current inventory. We will also assume that there is no minimum reorder point, but rather reorder is based on usage and vendor lead time. We will also assume that the lead time to replenish is still four weeks and that the average usage of the part is about ten per week. Does everyone understand?" Tom asked, and again, it appeared that everyone did, so Tom continued with his example.

Tom began again, "The data in this table also assumes that no parts inventory is held at the next higher level and that the parts replenishment has to come from the vendor and consumes the allotted vendor lead time. However, if the parts/inventory were held at a higher level in the distribution chain, such as a central supply or a distribution point, and replenishment happened daily and/or weekly, then the total inventory required could go even lower than the data suggests. This could happen because distribution is completed weekly, rather than waiting the full four weeks for delivery. Is everyone still with me?" has asked and again, everyone was.

Tom continued, "The part usage rates are exactly the same as the previous run and the starting inventory is equal to ninety parts. This also assumes we have a weekly parts/inventory replenish after the initial four weeks of lead time has expired. In other words, every week we have delivered what was ordered four weeks ago. In the Theory of Constraints scenario, the reorder point is at the end of each week based on usage. The total number of parts used is the same number of parts that should be reordered." Tom then flashed a new image on the screen (Figure 9.5).

Tom continued, "The figure on the screen demonstrates the effects of using the Theory of Constraints Distribution and Replenishment Model. One of the most notable things you see in this graph is that total inventory required through time has decreased from ninety items to approximately forty-two items or roughly a forty-seven percent reduction. In essence, the required inventory has been cut in half. The other notable feature is that even though the inventory level has been cut in half, the number of

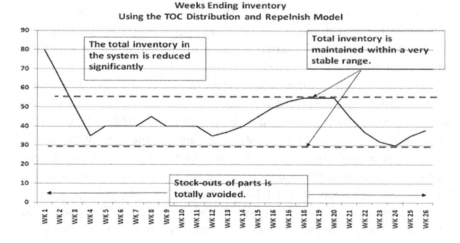

FIGURE 9.5
The overall effect of Theory of Constraints Replenishment method.

stock-out situations has been reduced to zero!" Tom said with vigor. The group was somewhat flabbergasted in that by reducing the inventory by half, there were no stock-outs!

Tom continued, "When the Theory of Constraints Distribution and Replenishment Model is used to manage the supply chain, there is always sufficient parts inventory to continue your work in your various hospitals. The total inventory is also much more stable through time, without the large gaps and gyrations from zero inventories available to maximum inventory as noted on the Minimum/Maximum system."

With a smile on his face, Tom then said, "Perhaps the best way to explain the Theory of Constraints Distribution and Replenishment Model is with an easy example. Consider a soda vending machine. When the supplier, the soda vendor, opens the door on a vending machine, it is very easy to calculate the distribution of products sold. The soda person knows immediately which inventory has to be replaced and to what level to replace it. The soda person is holding the inventory at the next highest level, which in on the soda truck, so it's easy to make the required distribution when needed. He doesn't leave four cases of soda when only twenty cans are needed. If he were to do that, when he got to the next vending machine he might have run out of the necessary soda because he made distribution too early at the last stop." Tom could see by the expressions on everyone's face that they immediately related to this simple example.

"After completing the required daily distribution to the vending machines, the soda person returns to the warehouse or distribution point to replenish the supply on the soda truck and get ready for the next day's distribution. When the warehouse makes distribution to the soda truck, they move up one level in the chain and replenish from their supplier. This type of system does require discipline to gain the most benefits, but it assumes that regular and needed checks are taking place at the inventory locations to determine the replenishment needs. If these points are not checked on a regular basis, it is possible for the system to experience stock-out situations." Tom explained.

"So, let's summarize our conclusions from what you've heard today," Tom said. He continued, "The distinct contrast in results between simulated data runs using the Minimum/Maximum supply system and the Theory of Constraints Distribution and Replenishment Model are undeniable. The true benefits of a Theory of Constraints-based parts replenishment system are many, but the most significant impact is realized in these two areas.

The first benefit is the reduction of total inventory required to manage and maintain the total supply-chain system by nearly fifty percent. This inventory reduction could lead to a significant dollar savings in total inventory required, perhaps thousands of dollars. And think about what would happen to your profit levels," Tom said.

"The second benefit is the elimination of stock-out situations. Without a doubt, not having parts available is an expensive situation because it slows throughput through the systems you have at each hospital. Treatment sites sit idle, waiting for parts or medications to become available. Stock-out situations increase frustration, not only in not being able to complete the work, but also in the time spent waiting for parts to become available. So, think about what might happen to your on-time delivery of services metric," Tom suggested.

Tom completed his presentation by stating, "Looking for parts or medications and experiencing shortages are a continuing problem in most supply-chain systems. These problems are not caused by the hospital staff, but by the negative effects of the supply-chain system and the way it is used. If your current Min/Max supply system is maintained, then the results from that system cannot be expected to change much, if at all. However, if new levels of output are required from the system, now and in the future, then new thinking must be applied to solve the parts and medication supply-system issues. The concepts and methodologies of the Theory of Constraints Distribution and Replenishment Model can positively impact the ability to provide services on time and in the correct quantity."

When Tom finished, he asked, "Are there any questions or comments?" Pete was the first to raise his hand and said, "I followed most of what you were explaining throughout most of your presentation, but I must say, when you finished with the soda vending machine example, it all fell into place." Cynthia, then added, "I absolutely agree with Pete and going forward, I think we can make major improvements to our profit margins and on-time delivery of treatments!" Bruce Johnson, the Accounting Manager then commented, "While I had never heard of the Theory of Constraints before you arrived, in the future I will be finding and reading everything I can. Do you have other elements of Theory of Constraints that you'll be teaching us?" Tom just smiled and said, "As they say, you ain't seen nothin' yet!" "In fact, I know we had planned to discuss something referred to as the Goal Tree, but I'd like to schedule another session to speak about that." They scheduled the meeting for the next week and with that, the meeting came to a close.

10

Drum Buffer Rope at Simpson Water Heaters

The next week, Tom flew back to Detroit to meet with the leadership team that Matt had assembled to hear Tom's presentation on Drum Buffer Rope. Tom drove his rental car to Simpson Water Heater's facility and signed in. Matt came to meet him and they both walked to the conference room. When everyone was seated, Tom began, "Unlike the last presentation on the *Ultimate Improvement Cycle*, I want to keep today's discussion much simpler. In a Theory of Constraints environment, production planning and scheduling is done so with a tool known as the Drum-Buffer-Rope. Drum Buffer Rope is designed to regulate the flow of work-in-process through a production line based upon the pace of the slowest resource, the constraint operation, also known as the capacity constrained resource."

Tom continued, "In order to optimize the flow of product through your factory, material is released according to the capacity of your capacity constrained resource. The production rate of the capacity constrained resource is equated to the rhythm of a drum. The rope is the communication mechanism that connects the constraint to the material release to the first operation, in order to make certain that raw material is released in time to guarantee that the constraint always has material to work on. So, the first purpose of the rope is to assure that the constraint is never starved for work and not inundated with excess work-in-process inventory, sort of like you have here at Simpson Water Heaters," Tom said in a joking manner.

Tom then explained, "Because of the existence of statistical fluctuations and disruptions in the upstream operations, a buffer is established to protect the constraint from ever being starved. By the same token, the rope assures that material is not introduced into the production process faster than the constraint can consume it. So DBR has three purposes, namely, first to protect the constraint from starvation; second, to ensure that excess material is not released into the system; and third, to protect the delivery due dates to the customer." Tom then flashed a Power Point slide on the screen (Figure 10.1).

Tom then flashed a drawing of this system on the screen (Figure 10.2) and said, "Visually these three elements might look like this figure. Here we see the three elements of the Drum-Buffer-Rope system and the interconnectedness of each. The drum sets the pace of the production line and its capacity is hopefully greater than the number of orders in the system. In order to satisfy the shipping schedule, we must first fulfill the constraint schedule. In order to meet the constraint schedule, we

1. A shipping schedule which is based upon the rate that the constraint can produce parts.

   That is, use the throughput of the constraint for promised due dates.

2. A constraint schedule which is tied to the shipping schedule.

3. A material release schedule which is tied to the constraint schedule.

FIGURE 10.1
Three main elements of Drum Buffer Rope.

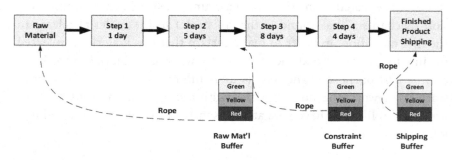

FIGURE 10.2
Visual display of a Drum Buffer Rope system.

must satisfy the material release schedule. Failure to release materials per the schedule will jeopardize the constraint schedule which will in turn jeopardize our shipping schedule. Because of this linkage of schedules, managing the buffers becomes critical!" Tom then asked the group if they had any questions.

Greg Thompson, the Production Manager raised his hand and asked, "If we implement Drum Buffer Rope, what happens to our current scheduling system?" Tom responded, "That's a great question Greg, and if you can hold on for a bit, I will answer it."

Tom continued, "In this visual representation of a Drum Buffer Rope system, I have displayed three buffers, the raw material buffer, the constraint buffer and the shipping buffer. And if you have an assembly operation that feeds parts into your process, you can place a buffer there as well. These buffers are comprised of two different dimensions which are both space and time. Now what do I mean by that?" he asked the group. "Since we don't want to have excess inventory in our process, the buffers contain some physical inventory and a liberal estimate of lead time from various points within our total process."

Tom continued, "In the case of the raw material buffer, we place an amount of needed raw materials at the beginning of the process, as well as a time buffer to prevent material shortages at the beginning of the process. In the case of the constraint buffer, we place an amount of physical inventory in front of the constraint and a time buffer based upon the lead time from raw material release until the products arrive at the constraint operation. Likewise, if you have an assembly operation, the buffer would contain some amount of material and a time buffer based upon the lead time from the constraint operation to the assembly operation. The shipping buffer contains some amount of work-in-process inventory and a time buffer based upon the lead time from either the constraint operation (or assembly operation) to completion into finished product. So how much is 'some amount of material?'" Tom asked rhetorically.

Tom continued, "In order to size the buffer correctly, the arrival of parts to the buffer must be monitored and compared to the scheduled arrival time. By monitoring the buffer, we are essentially sending a signal to the plant as to when we need to expedite parts. You'll notice a section of the drawing of our Drum Buffer Rope system labeled as 'buffers.' When parts do not arrive into the buffer on schedule, it in essence creates what is referred to as a 'hole' in the buffer. If we divide the buffer into three zones, we will be able to successfully manage the buffer. So, what are these zones?" he asked.

Tom continued his explanation, "The first zone, which is the green zone in our drawing, means that everything is going according to the scheduled arrival date or time, so holes in the green zone are no cause for concern. The second zone, the yellow zone in our drawing, tells us that the parts are not arriving on schedule and that it is time to locate the missing parts and create an expediting plan, in the event the parts need to be expedited. The third zone, the red zone in our drawing, means that the parts will definitely not be arriving into the buffer on schedule and that the jobs need to be expedited. Managing the constraint buffer focuses attention on late arrivals to the constraint and tells us when we need to expedite and when not to expedite. Any questions so far?" Tom asked and when there were none, he continued.

"How much physical inventory we need is a function of how stable or consistent our process is at producing product. That is, if we are never creating holes in our green zone, then our buffer is probably too high. By contrast, if we are constantly penetrating our red zone, then the buffer is clearly too low. If we have over-sized our buffer, then we are needlessly increasing operating expenses and cycle time, while at the same time decreasing inventory turns and cash flow. If we have undersized our buffer, then we run the risk of starving our constraint and losing valuable throughput. My advice to you is to err on the side of conservatism, because losing valuable throughput is much more damaging to your plant than increasing operating expenses or reducing cash flow. Remember, according to the Theory of Constraints, Throughput is revenue minus Operating Expense, which is the key driver of your profitability," Tom explained.

Tom continued, "You may be wondering just how much of the buffer should be physical parts and how much should be time? Believe it or not, it depends upon the variability of our process. If we have a highly variable operation feeding the constraint, or one that has many disruptions, then most of our buffer will be in the form of physical materials. If, on the other hand, our feeder operation contains very little variability, then most of the buffer will be in the form of time. As you improve your process by reducing waste and variation using Lean and Six Sigma, rendering it more consistent and stable, then the ratio of physical inventory to time will change accordingly. Remember the purpose of these buffers is to protect our constraint from starvation and our delivery of product to customers."

Tom looked directly at Greg and said, "The Drum Buffer Rope system is a finite scheduling method that attempts to balance and control the optimum flow of materials through a plant in accordance with the demands of the market, while minimizing lead time, inventory and operating expenses." Again, Tom looked at Greg and said, "Greg, I'll get more into your question about what happens to your current scheduling system shortly."

Tom continued his Drum Buffer Rope explanation, "In addition to protecting the constraint from starvation and/or inundating the process with excess inventory, buffer management accomplishes another critical aspect. Buffer management provides you with a vehicle to systematically identify and quantify potential improvement opportunities in key non-constraint operations. By focusing improvements on the sources or causes of buffer holes, it provides you with the opportunity to improve throughput and reduce both cycle times and inventory. If you are continuously finding holes in your red zone, then you know that there are problems in one or more of the upstream processes. If you know this, then your improvement actions need to be focused on the operation creating the holes. As you continue to improve your process, these holes in your buffer will eventually disappear and provide you with the opportunity to safely reduce the size of your buffers and consistently improve throughput, reduce cycle times and reduce inventory."

"As you analyze and prioritize the causes of the holes in your buffer, another important nuance occurs. You will be able to form a picture of protective capacity throughout your process. This is important for several very important reasons," and Tom posted another overhead on the screen (Figure 10.3).

1. The non-constraint that has the least protective capacity will have the highest probability of becoming the next constraint when we break the current constraint.

2. It provides you with a way of estimating how much of the non-constraint capacity can be sold in a targeted market of the non-constraint products, if they are in a form that can be sold. However, you will only be able to exploit this market if it will not jeopardize the constraint buffer and the constraint throughput.

3. You are able to focus in on and prioritize improvement efforts in the right non-constraints.

FIGURE 10.3
The importance of protective capacity.

"Okay, so let's now answer Greg's question about how we use Drum Buffer Rope with your current scheduling system," Tom said. "The real question is, can Enterprise Resource Planning or ERP and Theory of Constraints exist together in the same manufacturing facility? The short answer is a resounding yes! The Theory of Constraints is very often seen as an alternative to ERP, but it doesn't have to be. Scheduling in your ERP system begins by identifying a due date for an order and then attempts to start the order as late as possible, but still meet the date. Scheduling through a plant uses production rates and time to schedule each resource," Tom explained.

"The Theory of Constraints uses a much simpler approach. It begins by identifying the constraining operation and other resources are scheduled around the constraint. Remember, the rate of production that can pass through the constraint is the definitive rate that can pass through the entire plant and as I explained, that rate is the drum-beat. So, with this in mind, you use ERP to schedule production in your plant around the beat of the drum. The next step is to set up buffers ahead of the constrained resource to ensure that it is never starved due to any unforeseen irregularity upstream. You then set up a buffer downstream of the constraint so that a downstream problem can never interfere with the constraints output." "Are you with me so far Greg?" he asked, and Greg indicated that he was.

Tom continued, "The buffer can be inventory or what ERP refers to as a safety stock. It can also be spare resources or whatever works in a particular environment, to never allow the constraint to move away from its drumbeat. Finally, a rope is tied to all the other resources so that they never fall behind or get too far ahead of the constraint. While falling slightly behind is not usually a problem, getting too far ahead is simply a waste which should be avoided. Together using the drum, the buffer, and the rope makes Theory of Constraints a very simple system to implement and you use the ERP system to effectively manage the constraint. Simply schedule your upstream resources to keep the buffer full, and schedule downstream resources based on the output of the constraint. The bottom line is that ERP works on rules and the Theory of Constraints can easily be combined with it to give you a superior scheduling system." Tom then turned to Greg and asked, "Did that answer your question?" Greg responded and said, "I think so, but I may have questions for you in the future."

"Let me say a couple more things comparing Drum Buffer Rope and ERP," Tom said. "In their pure forms, ERP assumes infinite capacity and works to schedule all steps in the process. Drum Buffer Rope, on the other hand, assumes finite capacity and only schedules the constraint. Typically, ERP prohibits late release of materials, while Drum Buffer Rope prohibits early release, simply because early release only serves to drive up work-in-process inventory. Also, ERP drives material requirements all the way through the bill of materials, no matter how much stock is on hand, while Drum Buffer Rope takes existing stock and buffers into consideration. The bottom line is that ERP and Drum Buffer Rope are different solutions to scheduling, but they can co-exist. Simply use ERP to manage the constraint and schedule upstream resources to keep the buffer full and schedule downstream resources always forward from the output of the constraint. As I said earlier, ERP works on rules and those rules can be taken from Theory of Constraints easily," Tom explained.

"Are there any questions or comments?" Tom asked. Matt raised his hand and said, "What you've given us today is a new way forward for us and I'm very excited to get moving on everything. I mean I can see clearly how our new replenishment solution and now, our new scheduling system will move us into new levels of profitability. My question is more one on technique." "And what question are you referring to?" Tom asked. Matt responded with another question, "How do we go about developing our company-wide improvement effort?" Matt asked. "That's a great question Matt, so let's schedule another meeting and I would be happy to present the details of how we do that," Tom said. "Who would you like to be invited to this session Tom?" Matt asked. Tom replied, "Let's have the same team that's here today," Tom replied. And with that, the meeting ended.

11

Maximo's Goal Tree

As in previous sessions, the same group filed into Maximo's conference room, and Tom welcomed everyone and began. "In today's session, I want to present a simple strategic tool that I have used in many companies to create improvement plans and that tool is something known as the Goal Tree. In the spirit of learning a tool and making it your own, I have changed the way the Goal Tree was originally presented, but I'll get to that change later. So, before we get into how to create a Goal Tree, let's review the basics of the Goal Tree," Tom explained.

"The Goal Tree is a logic diagram that is actually simple to construct, and one that I think you will feel confident using." Tom then explained, "[1] Bill Dettmer, who is generally credited as being the man who developed the Goal Tree, tells us of his first exposure to the Goal Tree back in 1995. Bill had attended a management skills workshop conducted by Oded Cohen at the Goldratt Institute. Back then, the Goal Tree was referred to as an Intermediate Objectives Map (IO Map), but in recent years, Dettmer has recommended that the IO Map should now be referred to as a Goal Tree. Bill now believes that it should be the first step in the Theory of Constraints full Logical Thinking Process analysis. He believes this because it defines the standard for goal attainment and its prerequisites, in a much more efficient manner." "Just so you know, Theory of Constraints' Logical Thinking Process represents a series of logic trees used to analyze an organization to locate its weak points. We won't be covering these logic trees today, but I wanted to make you aware of their existence" Tom explained.

"It is my belief that the Goal Tree is a great focusing tool that will help everyone understand why an organization is not meeting its goal. The thing I like most about the Goal Tree is that it can be used as a stand-alone tool, which results in a much faster analysis of the organization's weak points. In this session we will discuss the Goal Tree as a stand-alone tool," Tom explained.

"There are two distinctly different types of logic at play which are sufficiency-type logic and necessity-type logic. Sufficiency-type logic is quite simply a series of 'if-then' statements. If I have 'this,' then I have 'that.' On the other hand, necessity-based logic trees use the syntax, In order to have 'this' I must have 'that.' The Goal Tree falls into the necessity-based category. For example, in order to have a fire, I must have a fuel source, a spark, and air. If the goal is to have a fire, it must have all three components. The fuel source, spark, and air are referred to as Critical Success Factors (CSFs)." "Take away even one of the CSFs and you won't have a fire," Tom explained.

Tom continued, "Our first deliverable today is that we must first define our *span of control* and our *sphere of influence*. Our span of control includes all of those things in our system over which we have unilateral change authority. In other words, we can decide to change those things on our own, because they are within our control and don't require approval from someone outside our system. On the other hand, our sphere of influence are those things we may want to change, but we must get approval to do so." Pete then said, "I would think our span of control covers everything within our four walls, from the time we receive materials, medicines or parts, until we deliver our services to our customers." He then added, "Our sphere of influence, simply put, would be everything before receiving materials, medicines or parts, as well as the delivery of our services to our customers. Do I have that right Tom?" he asked, and Tom indicated that was right.

Tom continued, "The distinction between what our span of control and sphere of influence is very important, simply because our sphere of influence is not a fixed entity. In your systems here at Maximo, you can influence way more than you can control and it's probably much more than you realize. Generally speaking, as Pete just said, many things within the walls of your hospital facilities represent you span of control. But having said that, not everything fits into this category. For example, things like governmental regulations under which your hospitals are regulated, are not considered within your span of control. You might be able to influence them, but you certainly don't have control over them. So, for now, let's go with your definitions Pete, but we must exercise caution." With Maximo's span of control and sphere of influence defined in limited terms, the creation of their Goal Tree began.

Tom continued and inserted a new slide onto the screen, "This figure (Figure 11.1) demonstrates the hierarchical structure of the Goal Tree. The Goal Tree consists of a single Goal, several Critical Success Factors (CSFs), which must be in place to achieve the goal, and a series of Necessary Conditions (NCs) which must be in place to achieve each of the CSFs. The Goal and CSFs are written as terminal outcomes, as though they are already in place. The NC's are, more or less, written as activities that must be completed in order to achieve each of the CSFs. We'll be completing our own Goal Tree, but a completed Goal Tree's basic structure looks like this," Tom explained.

Tom continued, "Suppose that your organization is profitable, but you want to become a highly profitable one. You assemble the key members of your staff to develop an effective plan to achieve this goal. In the Goal Tree drawing on the screen (Figure 11.2), after much discussion, you agree on your Goal as 'Maximum Profitability,' and place it inside the Goal box. This goal statement, which is the desired end state, is written as a terminal outcome as though it's already been achieved." You think to yourself, "What must I have in place for our goal to be realized?" You think, "I know that we must have Maximum Throughput of patients, Minimum

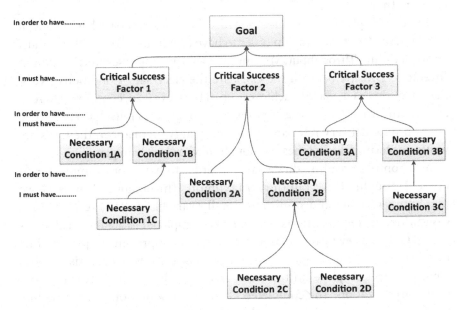

FIGURE 11.1
Basic structure of a Goal Tree.

FIGURE 11.2
The Goal Tree with goal and Critical Success Factors.

Operating Expenses and Minimum Inventory, so you place each of these in separate CSF boxes. One-by-one you continue listing those things that must be in place to achieve your goal and place them into separate CSF boxes like the figure below (Figure 11.2). In a Goal Tree you should have no more than 3 to 5 CSFs."

Tom then explained, "Because the Goal Tree uses necessity-based logic, it is read in the following way: In order to have Maximum Profitability, I must have Maximum Throughput, Minimum Operating Expenses, and Minimum Inventory. Directly beneath the CSFs are the Necessary Conditions (NC's) that must also be in place to achieve each of the CSFs." So, continuing to read downward, "In order to have Maximum Throughput, I must have two NC's, high on-time delivery rates and excellent quality. Remember, the CSFs are written as terminal outcomes, as though they're already in place."

"You continue reading downward, in order to have, for example, based upon Throughput Accounting, Maximum Throughput, I must have maximum revenue and minimum totally variable costs. The Necessary Conditions represent actions that must be completed to achieve each individual CSF, so they form the basis for Maximo's improvement plan. In like manner, your team completes all of the NCs, until you are satisfied that what you have in place on the Goal Tree will ultimately deliver the goal of the organization. The completed Goal Tree might look something like this figure (Figure 11.3)," and he flashed it on the screen. Tom pointed out the existence and direction of the connecting arrows for each entity which

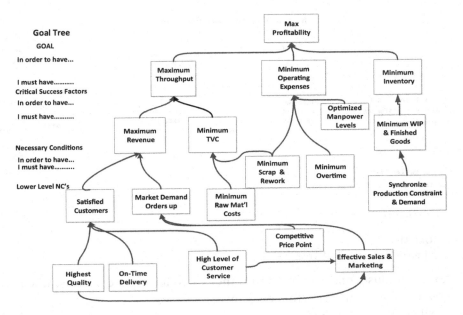

FIGURE 11.3
Completed Goal Tree.

are used to tie each entity together. He also explained that this Goal Tree was actually one for a manufacturing company and when Maximo creates their own Goal Tree, the entities will probably be completely different.

Tom asked if there were any questions or comments so far and Pete said, "I can see how this tool can be used by Maximo to create our improvement plan. But my question is, how detailed should you make the wording in each of the boxes?" "Good question Pete," Tom replied. "Typically, the wording is intended to be a sort of shorthand note so that your team can look at it and know the details of what you are saying. If you look at the wording in this figure, you'll see that in each box they are, in effect, short statements of your intended results and actions you plan to take to achieve each one," Tom explained and continued on with his presentation.

"So, let's work on creating your Goal Tree," Tom said. "The Goal that we start with is the responsibility of the owner or owners, so since all of the leaders in each of the hospitals within Maximo, it is your responsibility to state the Goal." Tom explained. "My suggestion is that you discuss the potential Goal as a group and when you all agree, we will continue constructing your Goal Tree. One thing to keep in mind is that for each hospital within Maximo, you will be creating your own Goal Tree. But for

Maximo's Corporate Goal Tree

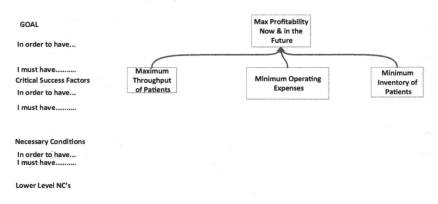

FIGURE 11.4
Maximo's Corporate Goal Tree.

now, you must consider what you want as a conglomerate of sorts, when creating this Goal Tree," Tom explained.

All six leaders of the hospital complex met to develop Maximo's Goal statement. After about an hour, the group of executives notified Tom that they had agreement on what they now referred to as their Corporate Goal. The group of executives agreed that Pete would be the one to present their final Corporate Goal. Pete began his explanation, "Tom, after much discussion, we have concluded that our Corporate Goal will be to have maximum profitability across all six hospitals. We also discussed what our Critical Success Factors should be, and we came up with the following (Figure 11.4)" Pete explained. "As you can see, our Goal is to achieve Maximum Profitability both Now, and in the Future," Pete added. Tom replied, "I like the way you added a reference to the future."

"Okay, since you have the leaders of each hospital here today, I think you should take a shot at completing your Corporate Goal Tree. Remember, for each individual hospital within Maximo's Complex, when you return to your individual hospitals, you need to get a group together to create your own, individual Goal Tree," Tom explained. "But for now, I want everyone to work on your Corporate Goal Tree," Tom added. And with these basic instructions, the corporate group began to work on their Goal Tree. "If you have any questions, I'll be right here to answer them," Tom said. The group formed to create the Corporate Goal Tree consisted of the following leaders from each of the hospitals (Figure 11.5), along with Pete Hallwell.

- Maximo Children's Hospital, specializing in children's ailments, Tom Jones.

- Maximo Women's Hospital, specializing in pregnancies, Philip Zagst.

- Maximo Veteran's Hospital, specializing in military veterans, Marie Thomas.

- Maximo Oncology Hospital, specializing in cancer treatments, Terry Sample.

- Maximo Surgical Hospital, specializing in surgical operations, Patricia Smith.

- Maximo Emergency Hospital, specializing in emergency patients, Ted Simpson.

- Corporate CFO Pete Hallwell.

FIGURE 11.5
Maximo's corporate leaders.

Tom Jones was the first to speak and said, "It's my suggestion that Pete Hallwell lead us through the creation of our Corporate Goal Tree." Everyone in the room agreed with Tom and so the effort began. Pete stepped to the front of the room and said, "I think one of the most important things we must keep in mind as we're creating our Goal Tree is to consider all we have learned about Throughput Accounting." Again, everyone agreed with Pete. "We have already agreed with what we have for our Goal and Critical Success Factors, so let's start with our first Critical Success Factor, Maximum Throughput of Patients," Pete suggested and loaded the partial Goal Tree on his computer screen (Figure 11.6).

Maximo's Corporate Goal Tree

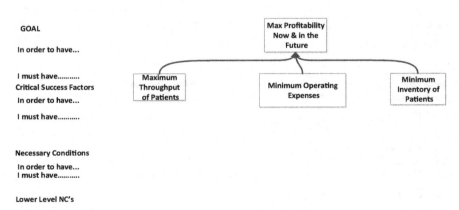

FIGURE 11.6
Original partial Goal Tree.

Pete began again, "So what must we do to obtain Maximum Throughput of Patients?" he asked. Terry Sample was the first to respond and said, "Clearly, in all of our hospitals, in order to achieve Maximum Throughput, we must first identify our system constraint, if we are to follow the guidelines of Throughput Accounting."

Everyone agreed with Terry, except Patricia Smith. She recommended that they also include Goldratt's second step, meaning they should not only identify the system constraint, but they should also exploit it. Everyone agreed with Patricia, and they were about to insert this comment into the partial Goal Tree, when Ted Simpson said, "Wait, why should we only apply the first two steps in Goldratt's 5 focusing steps?" "What do you mean Ted?" Pete asked. "Shouldn't we apply all five steps?" Ted replied. Heads were bobbing up and down until Pete said, "Great point Ted," and he added it to their Goal Tree (Figure 11.7). "Ted, that was a great point to bring to our attention," Pete said.

"I was just thinking that if we want to get the full potential, then we have to first identify the constraint, then exploit it, then subordinate everything else to the system constraint," Ted said. "And if the first three steps don't cut it, then we would need to elevate the constraint until it's broken. And when it is broken, we have to react to the new system constraint," Ted added. "That's a great point Ted!" Pete exclaimed. "So, let's see how that reads," Pete said. "In order to have Maximum Profitability Now and in the

Maximo's Corporate Goal Tree

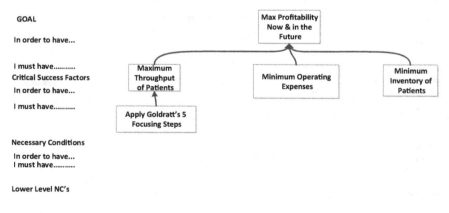

FIGURE 11.7
Applying Goldratt's Five Focusing Steps.

Maximo's Corporate Goal Tree

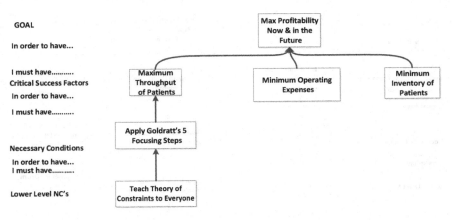

FIGURE 11.8
Goal Tree with lower level NC.

Future, we must have Maximum Throughput of Patients. And in order to have Maximum Throughput of Patients, we must Apply Goldratt's 5 Focusing Steps," Pete read.

Continuing on Pete said, "So, in order to Apply Goldratt's 5 Focusing Steps, what must we have?" he asked the group. Philip responded and said, "I think we must educate our employees on the Theory of Constraints?" "I like that Philip, how about everyone else?" Tom asked. Everyone in the room agreed on that being the next Necessary Condition, so he added that one to their Goal Tree (Figure 11.8).

The corporate group continued working on their Corporate Goal Tree until they were satisfied with their end product and decided it was time to review their finished tree with Tom (Figure 11.9). Tom was on the phone in the hallway, so Pete went looking for him. Tom saw Pete and hung up his phone. "What's up Pete?" Tom asked. "We think we have a finished product for you to review," Pete replied. "Wow, that's one of the fastest Goal Tree exercises I've ever seen, so let's go check out your finished product," Tom said, and they both walked into the conference room. Pete had used Visio to construct their Corporate Goal Tree, so he loaded it onto his screen for easy review.

Tom took several minutes to review what the corporate group had prepared and began speaking. "I don't think I have ever seen a simpler Goal Tree than this one," Tom said. "And because it's a corporate level Goal

Maximo's Corporate Goal Tree

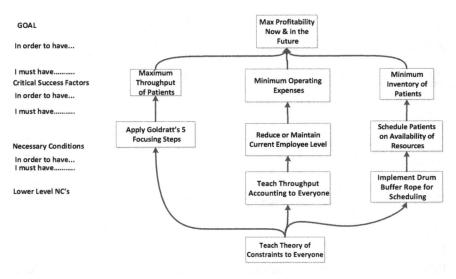

FIGURE 11.9
Completed Corporate Goal Tree.

Tree, I believe that it will serve its purpose for the Maximo Complex," Tom explained. "I say this, because you will be preparing a much more detailed one for each individual hospital," he said. "If you look at this Goal Tree, you have indicated that the key to maximizing profitability, lies at the base of it where it says, 'Teach Theory of Constraints to Everyone' and that says it all," Tom explained. "So, my assignment to all of you is to get a group together at each hospital and create a lower level Goal Tree," he stated. "But having said this, we are not finished yet," Tom said. "In the spirit of learning a new tool and making it your own, I want to show you how I have changed the original usage of the Goal Tree," Tom said. "But for now, let's take a short break," Tom said.

When everyone had returned from their break, Tom continued and inserted a new figure on the screen (Figure 11.10), "Earlier I said that I have changed the way the Goal Tree was first introduced. This change has to do with how the Goal and Critical Success Factors are worded (and some of the NC's). The Goal Tree you see on the screen is from a manufacturing company I consulted for and we will use it as an example." Tom also said, "You'll also notice that each block has a locator number inserted. I did this so that if there is a question, you can locate the specific CSF or NC much easier."

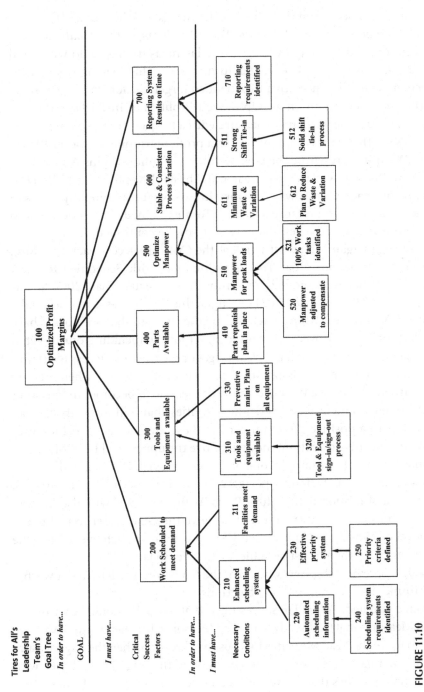

FIGURE 11.10

Manufacturing Goal Tree example.

Tom continued, "One of the key learnings in the book, [1] *The 4 Disciplines of Execution: Achieving Your Wildly Important Goals*, was the concept of Lead and Lag Measures. The lag measure has to do with Goal achievement and should be written in such a way that there is a clear measurement of Goal units with a well-defined target. So, for example, instead of the Goal being written as 'Optimized Profit Margins,' let's word it as though it was a performance measure with a target," Tom explained.

"Let's say that your company's current profit margins are around 19 percent. What if we re-wrote the Goal as follows: Profit Margins Above 25%? Written this way, we can measure it and it has a clear target, just like a finish line in a race. In this way everyone knows what the company wants to achieve and how to measure success," Tom explained. "Any questions so far?" Tom asked, and when there weren't any, he continued.

Tom began again, "Now let's look at the Critical Success Factors (CSFs). The first CSF in our Goal Tree is written as Work Scheduled to Meet Demand. What if we added something like 'Greater Than 20%' to our original CSF? Can you now see how vague this CSF was as it was originally written? Written in this manner, it is neither measurable nor does it have a target for the improvement team to shoot for. By including our target, it becomes measurable and has a clear target or measure of success to attain."

Tom continued his explanation, "I chose to do so because, when they are measurable and have a target, as many of them do, it becomes much easier for the improvement team to define activities that will move these Lead Measures in a positive direction. And if these lower level Lead Measures move in a positive direction, they will move the upper level Lead Measures in like manner. For example, one of the lower level NC's is stated as '410- Parts replenishment plan in place > 99% on time %.' If this is achieved, then the assumption is that '400- Parts Available > 99%' will also be met. And if this CSF is met, then it should move the Goal closer to its hoped-for level of 25%. As we know, each CSF contributes to achievement of the Goal, but all of them must be achieved to meet the final Goal target." Tom added, "So, review this new version of the Goal Tree and let me know what you think of it." There were no objections, so they moved on.

Tom continued, "What I'm suggesting is that the CSFs should be written as Lead Measures that tie directly to the Lag Measures. In other words, if we were able to move the Lead Measures in a positive direction, then the Lag Measure would eventually improve as well. Let's look at the original Goal Tree with the remaining CSFs that I have changed using these simple guidelines." Tom loaded a new slide onto the screen for everyone to see (Figure 11.11).

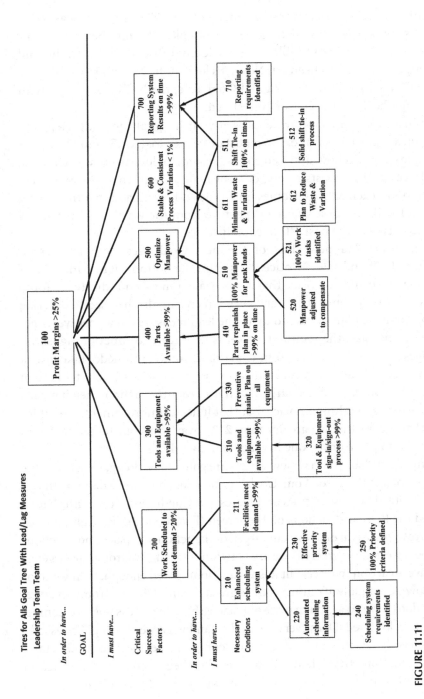

FIGURE 11.11

Goal Tree with new guidelines implemented.

Tom continued, "As you can see, many of the CSFs are now measurable and display a clear success target. For example, CSF number 400 is now written as '400 Parts Available > 99%.' Clearly, this CSF is measurable and the target to reach has been set. Now let's look at the Necessary Conditions (NC's)." "As written in the original Goal Tree, the NC's are written with the same clarity as the CSFs," Tom stated.

"When time is a factor, which it is at your hospitals, my next step is to develop a real-time status or current state of the Goal, CSFs and NCs. I use a simple Green, Yellow, and Red coding system to describe how each of the Goal Tree entities exists in our current reality. With this new approach, the status of each entity becomes much easier. I might add that the coding system I will now describe is a departure from the way I had been using the Goal Tree in the past," Tom explained.

Tom inserted a new slide of the new Goal Tree onto the screen (Figure 11.12) and said, "Notice the key on the bottom right hand side of the Goal Tree and you'll see that a box shaded in green indicates that the measure is at or above the target level. Green can also be used to describe actions that we plan to take to drive the lead measures in a positive direction. In this case, the required action is in place and functioning, so no changes need to be made," Tom explained. Tom continued, "Likewise, a yellow box indicates that a lead measure is greater than 5%, but less than 25% away from the defined target. Or if it's a required action, then it means that there is something in place, but that it needs improvement. And if it's red, that means that it's greater than 25% away from our target or there's no action in place or the one in place is not working."

Tom began, "So, just to review what we're going to be doing, we will use the instructions at the base of our Goal Tree to assess how we're doing with our Goal, Critical Success Factors and Necessary Conditions," and with that he posted the three instructions on the screen (Figure 11.13). "Basically, if what we have in place is at or above our target, or the action is in place and functioning well, we color it green. If we are between 5% and 25% from our target or we have an action in place, but it isn't functioning well enough, then we color it yellow. And finally, if our measure is greater than 25% away from our target or we don't have an action in place or what we have in place is not functioning, then we color it red. Does everyone understand what we're doing?" he asked.

"Everyone at this manufacturing company seemed to understand the instructions that I had laid out, so they began color-coding each of the entities in their Goal Tree," Tom explained. "One-by-one the team

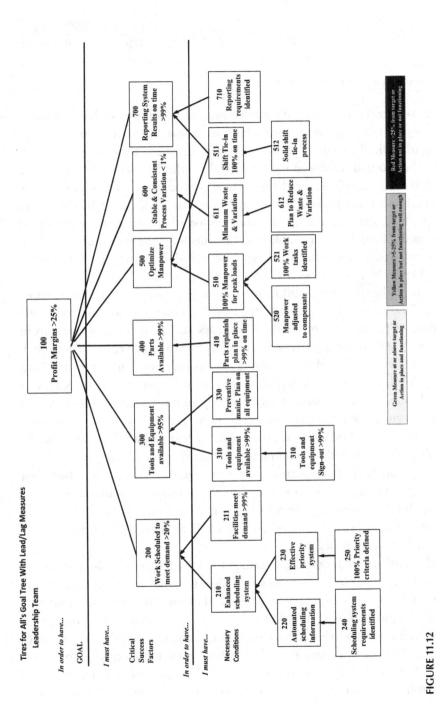

FIGURE 11.12
Goal Tree with coding system for status.

Green Measure at or above target or Action in place and functioning	Yellow Measure >5-25% from target or Action in place but not functioning well enough	Red Measure >25% from target or Action not in place or not functioning

FIGURE 11.13
Instructions for assessing Goal Tree entities.

discussed each of the individual entities, and although they had disagreements at times, they were able to work their way through them and come up with a final product. When they were finished, they called me back into the room and showed me their final results," Tom explained, and he loaded their completed Goal Tree assessment on the screen (Figure 11.14).

Maximo's team looked at the final Goal Tree with each of the colors highlighted. Pete was the first to comment on what Tom had just presented and said, "Tom, I have a couple of comments for you about this assessment method." "Sure Pete, what are they?" Tom asked. "First, I want you to know that I really like this assessment method using the Goal Tree. I've never seen anything like this before and I can't wait to get started on each of our hospitals," Pete said. "Having said this, I do have one question for you," Pete added. "What question is that Pete?" Tom asked. "The percentages away from target for the yellow and red boxes, are they hard and fast rules?" Pete asked. "Remember when I told you to learn a new tool and make it your own?" Tom said. "Well, it applies to these percentages as well," Tom added. "You guys can decide on what the assessment rules are for your hospitals," Tom said. "So, I'd like you guys to spend some time assessing your own Corporate Goal Tree," Tom instructed. And with that, the corporate team began their assessment.

With the instructions complete, the Maximo corporate team began working on their new version of their Corporate Goal Tree. Their first action item was to make sure they had the appropriate lead and lag measures, and then where appropriate, they needed to add target values. Once again, the corporate team elected to have Pete Hallwell lead their effort, and with that, they began.

All members of the corporate team participated actively in the assessment of the Corporate Goal Tree, and while there were numerous disagreements during their assessment session, at the end of the day, they had completed their Corporate Goal Tree. When they were finished, they called Tom back into the conference room to get his opinion on their finished product (Figure 11.15). Tom spent several minutes reviewing Maximo's Corporate Goal Tree, and when he was finished with his initial review, he moved to the front of the room to make his initial comments to the corporate team.

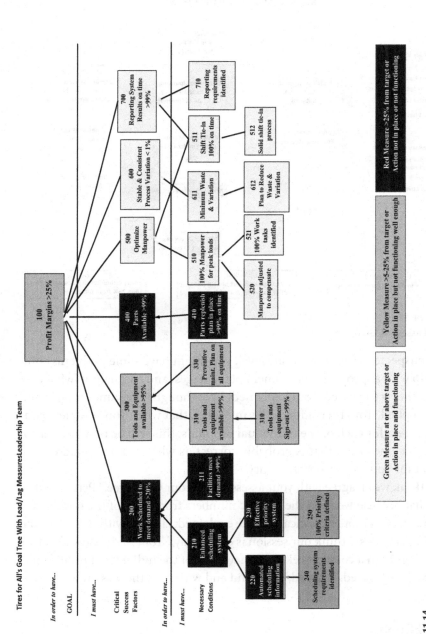

FIGURE 11.14

Final assessed Goal Tree.

Maximo's Corporate Goal Tree

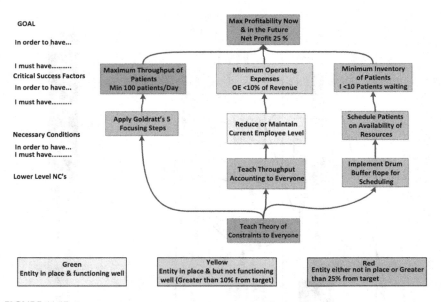

FIGURE 11.15

Final assessed Goal Tree.

"I suspected at the Corporate level, you might have some problems coming up with appropriate assessment percentages, and based upon what I see here, this is the case," Tom explained. "We thought the same thing Tom," Pete replied. Tom then added, "It's my belief, that when you complete your Goal Trees for each of the individual hospitals, this will be much easier for you. The one entity that is probably correct, is what you have entered as a target for your overall profitability.

"I think we all agree with your assessment of our Goal Tree," Pete added. "I say that because we need the specific numbers from each of the hospitals to set our targets more realistically," Pete explained. "I agree with you, Pete, and having said this, I think our session is over today," Tom said. "How about we get together in a couple weeks to review each of the individual hospital Goal Trees?" Tom asked. "Agreed," Pete said and with that, the session was over.

REFERENCE

1. Jim Huling, Chris McChesney and Sean Covey, *The 4 Disciplines of Execution: Achieving Your Wildly Important Goals*, 2012, New York: Free Press.

12

Developing an Improvement Plan at Simpson

When Tom finished his last session at Simpson Water Heaters, he had been asked by Matt Maloney how to create an improvement plan. Tom explained that when he returned, he would teach Simpson Water Heaters how to do just that. Tom and Matt had talked and set up a new session for the next day in Detroit. Tom prepared his materials for this session and flew into Detroit. Tom had rented a hotel room fairly close to Simpson Water Heaters, so it would be a short drive there in the morning.

As usual, Tom woke up early, showered, got dressed, and ate breakfast. When he returned to his hotel room, he called Matt to chat about today's session. Tom explained that he would be presenting a tool known as the Goal Tree and Matt seemed very anxious to learn more about it. Tom explained that he would first teach how to create a Goal Tree and then use it to create an improvement plan for Simpson Water Heaters. Tom was scheduled to begin in 45 minutes, so he got into his rental car and drove to the site. Tom entered the manufacturing complex, parked, and walked to the lobby. The security guard called Matt to let him know of Tom's arrival. Matt came to the lobby and the two of them walked to the conference room.

Matt reintroduced Tom to the group and Tom began today's session. "Good morning everyone," Tom began. "Today's session is all about an improvement tool known as the Goal Tree and I think at the end of today, you will see how valuable this tool is and what it can do for you here at Simpson Water Heaters," Tom said. "There's another side of the Theory of Constraints that we haven't talked about yet and that is something referred to as the Logical Thinking Tools. These Logical Thinking Tools are a series of Logic Diagrams that can be used to both assess your company and locate those things that stand in the way of improving your overall company. The one problem that many people feel after they have been through a training session on these tools is that they don't have a good idea of how to begin using them. We're not going to discuss these tools, but rather we will discuss another logical thinking tool known as the Goal Tree," Tom explained.

"The Goal Tree is a sort of 'short cut' to assessing your company's weak points and it's much simpler to use than the Logical Thinking Tools," Tom explained. "The man generally credited with developing the Goal Tree is Bill Dettmer, of whom I have the greatest respect. When he originally created the Goal Tree, he referred to it as the Intermediate Objectives Map, but he has since then changed the name to the Goal Tree," Tom stated. "I want to make one thing perfectly clear, before we begin," Tom said. "As I said, we won't be discussing the Logical Thinking Tools, but I want everyone to understand that I am a huge fan of these logic trees. In the future, we might have a session on these tools, but for now, we will only be discussing the Goal Tree," Tom explained.

When everyone arrives, Tom began his explanation, "When using any of Theory of Constraints' Thinking Process tools, there are two distinctly different types of logic at play, sufficiency and necessity based logic. Sufficiency-based logic tools use a series of if-then statements, that connect cause and effect relationships between most of the system's undesirable effects. Necessity-based logic uses the syntax, in order to have x, I must have y or multiple y's. The Goal Tree falls into the category of necessity-based logic and can be used to develop and lay out your company's strategic and tactical actions that result in successful improvement efforts."

"As mentioned earlier, the Goal Tree dates back to at least 1995 when it was casually mentioned during a Management Skills Workshop conducted by Oded Cohen at the A.Y. Goldratt Institute, but it was not part of that workshop, nor did it ever find its way into common usage as part of the Logical Thinking Process (LTP). It was described as a kind of Prerequisite Tree without any obstacles." Tom explained.

"Bill Dettmer," he continued, "the originator of the Goal Tree, tells us that one of the first things we need to do is, define the system boundaries that we are trying to improve, as well as our span of control and sphere of influence. Our span of control means that we have unilateral change authority, while our sphere of influence means that at best, we can only influence change decisions. Dettmer explains that if we don't define our boundaries of the system, we risk 'wandering in the wilderness for forty years.'" Tom continued.

Tom began again, "The hierarchical structure of the Goal Tree consists of a single Goal and several entities referred to as Critical Success Factors (CSFs). The CSFs must be in place and functioning if we are ever going to achieve our stated goal. The final piece of the Goal Tree are entities referred to as Necessary Conditions (NCs), which must be completed to realize each of the CSFs. The Goal and CSFs are worded as terminal outcomes, as though they were already in place, while the NC's are stated more as activities that must be completed."

Tom loaded a Power Point slide into his computer (Figure 12.1) and explained, "This is a graphic representation of the structure of the Goal Tree, with each structural level identified accordingly. The Goal, which is defined by the owners of the organization, sits at the top of the Goal Tree, with three to five Critical Success Factors directly beneath it. The CSFs are those critical entities that must be in place, if the Goal is to be achieved. For example, if your Goal was to create a fire, then the three CSFs which must be in place are (1) a combustible fuel source, (2) a spark to ignite the

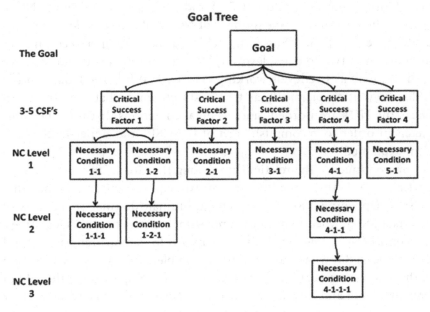

FIGURE 12.1
Basic structure of a Goal Tree.

combustible fuel source and (3) air with a sufficient level of oxygen. If you were to remove any of these CSFs, there simply would not be a fire. So, let's look at each of these components in a bit more detail."

Tom continued, "Steven Covey suggests that to identify our goal we should, 'Begin with the end in mind,' or where we want to be when we've completed our improvement efforts, which is the ultimate purpose of the Goal. A Goal is an end to which a system's collective efforts are directed. It's actually a sort of destination, which implies a journey from where we are, to where we want to be. Bill Dettmer also makes it very clear that the system's owner or owners determine what the goal of the system should be. If your company is privately owned, maybe the owner is a single individual. If there's a board of directors, they have a chairman of the board who is ultimately responsible for establishing the goal, based on input from the other board members. Regardless of whether the owner is a single person or a collective group, the system's owner(s) ultimately establishes the goal of the system."

"In the Goal Tree, there are certain high-level requirements which must be solidly in place, and if these requirements aren't achieved, then we simply will never realize our goal. These requirements are referred to as Critical Success Factors (CSFs) and Necessary Conditions (NCs). Each of the CSFs have some number of NCs that are considered prerequisites to each of the CSFs being achieved. Bill Dettmer recommends no more than two to three levels of NC's, but in my experience, I have seen as many as five levels working very well. While the Goal and the CSFs are written primarily as terminal outcomes, that are already in place, the NC's are worded more as detailed actions that must be completed in order to accomplish each of the CSFs and upper-level NCs," Tom explained.

Tom continued, "The relationship among the Goal, CSFs and the supporting NC's, in this cascading structure of requirements, represents what must be happening if we are to reach our ultimate destination. For ease of understanding, when I am in the process of constructing my Goal Trees, the connecting arrows are facing downward to demonstrate the natural flow of ideas. But when our structure is completed, I reverse the direction of the arrows to reveal the flow of results. In keeping with the thought of learning a tool and making it your own, I have found this works well for training purposes even though this is the complete opposite of Dettmer's recommendations for construction of a Goal Tree."

"As we proceed, it's important to understand that the real value of a Goal Tree is its capability to keep the analysis focused on what's really important to the success of the system. Dettmer tells us that a 'Goal Tree will be unique to that system and the environment in which it operates.' This is an extremely important concept because 'one size does not fit all.' Dettmer explains that even two manufacturing companies, producing the same kind of part, will probably have very dissimilar Goal Trees," Tom explained.

"A Goal Tree could very quickly and easily be constructed by a single person, but if the system it represents is larger than the span of control of the individual person, then using a group setting is always better. So, with this in mind, the first step in constructing a Goal Tree is to clearly define the system in which it operates and its associated boundaries. The second consideration is whether or not it falls within your span of control or your sphere-of-influence. Defining your span of control and sphere of influence, lets you know the level of assistance you might need from others, if you are to successfully change and improve your current reality," Tom continued.

"Once you have defined the boundaries of the system, your span of control, and sphere of influence you are attempting to improve, your next step is to define the ultimate goal of the system. Remember, we said that the true owner(s) of the system is/are responsible for defining the goal. If the true owner or owners aren't available, it is possible to articulate it by way of a 'straw man,' but even then, you need to get concurrence on the goal from the owner(s) before beginning to construct your Goal Tree. Don't lose sight of the fact that the purpose of the Goal Tree is to identify the ultimate destination you are trying to reach," Tom stated.

He continued, "Dettmer tells us that the Goal Tree's most important function, from a problem-solving perspective, is that it constitutes a standard of system performance that allows problem-solvers to decide how far off-course their system truly is. With this in mind, your goal statement must reflect the final outcome and not the activities to get you there. In other words, the Goal is specified as an outcome of activities and not the activity itself."

"Once the Goal has been defined and fully agreed upon, your next order of business is to develop three to five Critical Success Factors (CSFs) that must be firmly in place before your Goal can be achieved. As we explained earlier, the CSFs are high-level milestones that result from specific, detailed actions. The important point to remember is that if you don't achieve every one of the CSFs, you simply will not achieve your goal," Tom explained.

Tom continued, "Finally, once your CSFs have been clearly defined, your next step is to develop your Necessary Conditions (NCs), which are the simple building blocks for your Goal Tree. The NC's are specific to the CSF they support, but because they are hierarchical in nature, there are typically multiple layers of them below each of the CSFs. As already stated, Dettmer recommends no more than three layers for the NC's, but on numerous occasions I have observed as many as five layers working quite well. With the three components in view, you are now ready to construct your Goal Tree. Let's demonstrate this through a case study where a company constructed their own Goal Tree."

Tom then said, "The company in question here, is one that manufactures a variety of different products for diverse industry segments. Some orders are build-to-order, while others would be considered orders for mass production parts. This company had plenty of orders to fill, but unfortunately, they were having trouble not only filling them, but filling them on time. As a result, this company's profitability was fluctuating between making money one month, to losing money the next month, sort of like you here at Simpson Water Heaters. Because of this, the board of directors decided to make a leadership change and hired a new CEO to effectively 'right the ship.'"

Tom continued laying out this case study, "The new CEO had a diverse manufacturing background, meaning that in his career he had split his time between job shop environments and high-volume manufacturing companies. When the new CEO arrived, he called a meeting of his direct reports to not only meet them, but to assess their proficiencies and capabilities. He soon realized that most of the existing management team had been working for this company for many years, and that their skills appeared to be somewhat limited. Before arriving, the new CEO had concluded that the best approach to turning this company's profitability around and stabilizing it, would be to use the Theory of Constraints Thinking Processes. But after meeting his new team, and evaluating their capabilities, and since time was of the essence, he decided instead to use the Goal Tree to assess his new company and lay out an improvement strategy."

He continued, "The CEO's first order of business was to provide a brief training session on how to construct a Goal Tree for his new staff. The first step was to define the boundaries of their system, which included receipt of raw materials from suppliers to shipping of their products to their customers. Within these boundaries, the team concluded that they clearly had defined their span of control, because they had unilateral change authority. They also decided that they could influence their suppliers, and somewhat the same with their customers, so their sphere of influence was also defined."

"In advance of this first meeting with his staff, the CEO had met with the board of directors, to determine what the goal of this company actually was. After all, he concluded, it's the owner or owner's responsibility to define the goal of the system which was 'Maximum Profitability.' After discussing his meeting with the board of directors to his team, and the goal they had decided upon, the CEO posted the goal on the top of a flip chart as seen in this figure (Figure 12.2)." Tom explained.

Tom continued, "The CEO knew that the board of directors wanted maximum profitability both now, and in the future, so he added the future reference to the Goal box. But before moving on to the Critical Success Factors (CSFs), the CEO decided that it would be helpful if he explained the basic principles of both the concept of the system constraint, and how to use Throughput Accounting (TA). His staff needed to understand why focusing on the constraint, would result in Maximum Throughput, but equally important, his staff needed to understand how the three components of profitability, Throughput (T), Operating Expense (OE), and Investment/Inventory (I) worked together to maximize profitability. With this in mind, the CEO explained Throughput Accounting to his new team, along with the basics of the Theory of Constraints."

Tom continued with his case study, "The CEO first explained the basics of the Theory of Constraints and then explained that Throughput (T) was equal to Revenue (R) minus Totally Variable Costs (TVC) and that Net Profit was equal to Throughput minus Operating Expense (OE), or T – OE. Finally, he explained that Return on Investment (ROI) was equal to NP/I, where I is the Inventory value. With this brief training behind them, he then

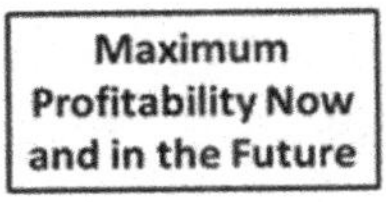

> Maximum
> Profitability Now
> and in the Future

FIGURE 12.2
Goal statement.

challenged his staff to tell him what they needed to have in place to satisfy this profitability goal, both today and tomorrow. That is, what must be in place to maximize Net Profit now and in the future?" After these explanations were completed, the CEO returned to their Goal Tree creation.

After much discussion, his staff offered three Critical Success Factors which the CEO inserted beneath the Goal in the Goal Tree (Figure 12.3). After learning the basics of Theory of Constraints' concept of the constraint, and basic Throughput Accounting (TA), his staff knew that because they needed to increase Net Profit (T − OE), then maximizing Throughput had to be one of the CSFs. They also concluded that, in order to maximize Net Profit, minimizing OE had to be another CSF. And finally, because return on investment (ROI) was equal to Net Profit divided by their investment (i.e. NP = (T ÷ I), they needed to include minimum investment (i.e. inventory) as one of the CSFs.

The CEO felt very good about the progress they had made with their first Goal Tree, but it was time for lunch, so they decided to break and come back later to complete the Goal Tree. When his staff returned from lunch, they reviewed what the CEO had presented on TA, just so it was fresh in

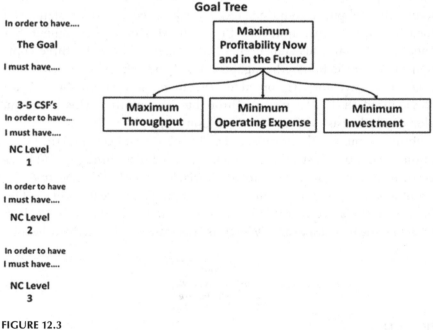

FIGURE 12.3
Goal Tree with goal and three CSFs.

their minds, as they began again to review and construct the rest of their Goal Tree. The CEO started, "In order to maximize profitability now and in the future, we must have Maximum Throughput, minimum Operating Expense and minimum Investment, which is mostly inventory. Are there any others?" he asked. His staff looked at each other and agreed that these are the three main CSFs.

Knowing that what was needed next were the corresponding Necessary Conditions (NCs), the CEO started with Maximum Throughput. "In order to have Maximum Throughput, what do we need?" he queried. His CFO put his hand up and said, "We need to maximize our revenue stream." Everyone agreed, but the Junior Accountant immediately raised her hand and said, "That's only half of it!" The CEO and CFO looked at her and said, "Tell us more." She explained, "Well you explained that Throughput was revenue minus Totally Variable Costs, so minimal Totally Variable Costs has to be a Necessary Condition too." The CEO smiled and said, "So, let me recap that what we have so far is that 'In order to have Maximum Throughput, we must have maximum Revenue and minimal TVC's.'" "And everyone agreed," Tom reported.

Tom continued explaining his case study, "The CEO continued, 'In order to maximize Revenue, what must we do?' The Operation's Manager said, 'We must have satisfied customers,' and before he could say another word, the Marketing Director added, 'We must also have sufficient market demand.' The CEO smiled, scanned the room for acceptance again, and added these two NC's to the Goal Tree (Figure 12.4). The CEO thought to himself, I am so happy that I chose to use the Goal Tree rather than the full Thinking Process analysis."

Continuing on Tom said, "The CEO then said, 'Let's stay with the satisfied customer's NC. In order to have satisfied customers, we must have what?' The Quality Director raised his hand and said, 'We must have the highest quality product.' The Logistics Manager added, 'We must also have high, on-time delivery rates.' And before the CEO could add them to the tree, the Customer Service Manager added, 'We must also have a high level of customer service.' The CEO smiled again and said, 'Slow down, so I don't miss any of these everyone.' Everyone laughed. The CEO looked at the lower level NC's for satisfied customers and asked if they needed anything else. Everyone agreed that if they had the highest quality product, with high on-time delivery rates and a high level of customer service, then the customers should be highly satisfied."

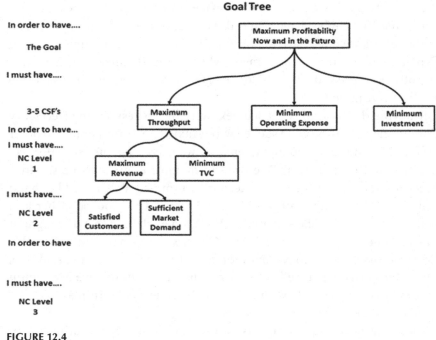

FIGURE 12.4
Partial Goal Tree.

Continuing Tom said, "The CEO continued on beneath the CSF for Maximum Throughput and asked, 'So, what do we need to supplement or support sufficient market demand?' The CFO said, 'We need a competitive price point and by the way, I think that would also help satisfy our customers.' The CEO added both NC's and connected both of them to the upper level NC of sufficient market demand. The CEO stepped back and admired the work they had done so far, but before he could say anything, the Sales Manager said, 'If we're going to have sufficient market demand, don't you think we also need effective sales and marketing?' Again, everyone nodded their heads in agreement, so the CEO added that NC as well."

"Before the CEO could say anything more, the Junior Accountant raised her hand and added, 'I was thinking that three of the ways we could have effective sales and marketing would be related to the three lower level NC's assigned to satisfied customers. I mean, can we do that in a Goal Tree?' The CFO was the first person to speak and he added, 'I think that's a fantastic idea!' The CEO thanked her and added the connecting arrows," Tom explained.

Tom continued, "The CEO then said, 'Great job so far, but what's a good way for us to minimize TVC?' Without hesitation, the Quality Manager said, 'That's easy, we need to minimize our scrap and rework.' The Quality Manager then said, 'I think that would also be an NC for one of our other CSFs, minimum operating expense.' Everyone agreed, so the CEO added both the NC and the second connecting arrow. Once again, the Junior Accountant raised her hand and added, 'I think that we should add another NC to the CSF, minimum operating expense, and that we should say something like optimum manpower levels and maybe also minimized overtime.' The CEO smiled and added both of the NC's to the tree."

"So, what about our CSF, Minimum Investment?" asked the CEO. The Plant Manager raised his hand and said, "How about minimized WIP and Finished Goods inventory?" The C EO l ooked f or o bjections, b ut w hen nobody objected, he added it to the tree. He then asked, "What about an NC underneath that one?" The Plant Manager looked at him and said, "We need to synchronize our production around the constraint and demand." "What do you mean?" asked the CEO. "I mean," the plant manager replied, "we need to stop producing parts on speculation and start building based on actual orders. I've been reading about Theory of Constraints' version of scheduling referred to as Drum Buffer Rope and I think we need to move in that direction," he added. "And with that, the CEO added his comments to the Goal Tree," Tom stated.

Tom continued, "When he was finished a dding t he n ew i tems t o t he Goal Tree (Figure 12.5), he turned to the group and began clapping his hands in appreciation for their effort." He explained, "I've been doing this for quite some time now, but I have never seen a group come together more than you have today." He added, "I was a bit apprehensive when we began today, that maybe some of you would push back and not contribute, but I was totally wrong."

Tom, nearing completion of the first part of his case study, then said, "The CFO raised his hand and said, 'For me, I have never seen this tool before, but going forward, I will be using it a lot. In fact, I was thinking that this tool can be used to develop individual department improvement plans.' 'Tell us more,' said the CEO. 'Well,' the CFO replied, 'if an NC, for example, applies mostly to a specific g roup l ike P roduction o r S ales & M arketing, then that could be seen as the Goal for that group. I'm very happy to have been here today to complete this exercise.' Everyone else agreed with him. The C EO t hen s aid, 'Ladies a nd g entlemen, t his e xercise i s n ot o ver y et.'

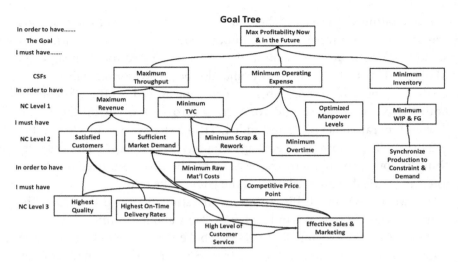

FIGURE 12.5
Completed Goal Tree.

'What else is there to do?' came a question from the CFO. 'We'll get back together tomorrow morning and I'll explain the next steps,' he explained.

Tom continued with his case study, "Bright and early the next morning, the executive team began filing into their conference room, full of anticipation on just what they would do with their completed Goal Tree. The CEO hadn't given them any instructions on how to prepare for today's work, so they were all eager to have the events of the day unfold. When everyone was seated, the CEO welcomed them and offered his congratulations again on the great job they had done the day before." "Good morning everyone," he said as everyone responded with a "good morning" back to him. As he scanned the room, he noticed that there was one person missing, the Junior Accountant. When he asked the CFO where she was, he explained that she was working on the monthly report and wouldn't be joining them today. The CEO looked the CFO square in his eyes and told him that nothing was more important than what they were going to do today. "Go get her!" he stated emphatically. The CFO left and returned minutes later with the Junior Accountant, and the CEO welcomed her. He then said, "We created this as a complete team and we're going to finish it as a complete team."

"The CEO explained, 'When the Goal Tree was originally created by Bill Dettmer [1], it was to be used as a precursor to the creation of a Current Reality Tree (CRT). That is, he used it as the first logic tree in Theory of

Constraints' Thinking Processes to help create the CRT.' He continued, 'And although I fully support this approach, I have found a way to use the Goal Tree to accelerate the development of an improvement plan.' The CEO passed out copies of the completed Goal Tree and began." Tom explained and continued on.

"I want everyone to study our logic tree, focusing on the lower level NC's first," he explained. "As we look at these NC's, I want everyone to think about how we are doing with each of these," he continued. "By that I mean, is what we said is needed to satisfy a CSF or upper level NC, in place and functioning as it should be. We're going to use a color-code scheme to actually evaluate where we stand on each one," he said. "If you believe that what we have in place is good and that it doesn't need to be improved, I want you to color it green. Likewise, if we have something in place, but it needs to be improved, color it yellow. And finally, if an NC is either not in place or is not 'working' in its current configuration, color it red," he explained. "Does everyone understand?" he asked, and everyone nodded in agreement. "It's important that we do this honestly, so be truthful or this exercise will all be for not." Tom explained.

Continuing Tom said, "The CFO raised his hand and asked, 'How will we use our color-coded tree?'" "Good question," said the CEO. "Once we have reviewed our Goal, CSFs, and NCs, we will start with the red entities first and develop plans to turn them into either yellows or greens. Likewise, we'll then look at the yellows and develop plans to turn them into green ones," he explained. As he was explaining his method, the CEO could see heads nodding in the affirmative, meaning that everyone understood his instructions. With that, the CEO passed out green, yellow, and red pencils. "I want everyone to do this individually first and then we'll discuss each one openly, until we arrive at a consensus," he explained. "While you're considering the state of each entity, I also want everyone to also think about a way we can measure the status of many of these in the future," he said. "I'll be back in a couple of hours, so please feel free to discuss your color selections as a group," he added. "With the instructions complete, the team began reviewing their Goal Tree and applying the appropriate colors to each entity."

"Right on schedule, the CEO returned and asked how the session was coming. The Plant Manager spoke first, 'I was amazed at how much disagreement we had initially, but after we discussed each item, we eventually came to an agreement on how we believe we're doing.' The CFO jumped into the conversation and added, 'I was amazed at how we came together as a team, just by creating our Goal Tree.' 'I have to admit that when you told me to go get our Junior Accountant, I was a bit taken back. But at the end of the day, she was a very important addition to this team,' he added. And with that, the Junior Accountant was somewhat embarrassed, but thanked the CFO for recognizing her contribution to the effort," Tom explained.

"So, where is it?" asked the CEO. "Where is your finished product, your Goal Tree?" The CFO went to the flip chart and there it was (Figure 12.6). The CEO then asked, "Did you also discuss what kind of metrics we might use to measure how we're doing?" "Yes, we did," said the CFO. "And?" the CEO asked. "We need to do more work on that," he answered. "So, what's next?" asked the CFO. "After studying the finished product," Tom reported, "the CEO thanked everyone for their effort and then said, 'Let's take a break and come back later and I'll explain how we can use this tree to develop our final improvement plan.'"

Tom continued, "The team reassembled later that day to discuss their next steps. Everyone seemed enthusiastic about what they would be doing going forward. When everyone was seated, the CEO turned to the group

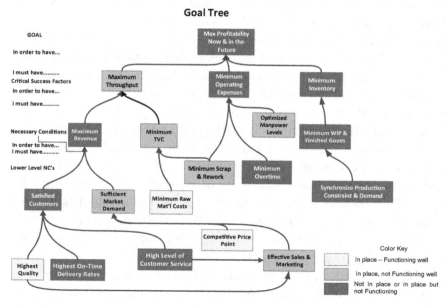

FIGURE 12.6
Color-coded Goal Tree.

and asked, 'So, how does everyone feel about this process so far?' The Plant Manager was the first to respond, 'I can't speak for anyone else, but the development of the Goal Tree was a real eye-opener for me. I never imagined that we could have analyzed our organization so thoroughly in such a short amount of time. I mean think about it, when you add up the total amount of time we've spent so far, it's not even been a full day's work!' As he spoke, everyone was nodding their heads in agreement."

"The CFO was next to speak and said, 'I can absolutely see the benefit from using this tool and one of the things that impressed me the most, is that everyone contributed. But what really captivated me is, that for the first time since I started working here, we actually are looking at the system rather than isolated parts of it. One of the things that I will take away from this is that the total sum of the localized improvements does not necessarily result in an improvement to the system. The Goal Tree forces us to look at and analyze all of the components of our organization as one entity.' Tom explained.

Tom continued with the case study, indicating this last part would answer Matt's original question of how to create an improvement plan, 'OK, let's get started,' said the CEO. 'Today we're going to plan on how turn our problem areas, those we defined in red, into hopefully strengths,' he said. 'Does anyone have any ideas on how we can turn our bottom three reds into either yellows or greens?' 'In other words, what can we do that might positively impact delivery rates, customer service and synchronize production to the constraint and demand?' he asked."

"The Plant Manager was the first to speak and said, 'If we can come up with a way to schedule our production, based upon the needs of the constraint, it seems to me that we could really have a positive result for on-time delivery rates and at the same time it would reduce our WIP and FG levels?' he said more in the form of a question. The CFO then said, 'Since you mentioned Drum Buffer Rope (DBR) yesterday, I've been reading more about it and it seems that this scheduling method is supposed to do exactly what you just described,' he said directly to the Plant Manager."

Continuing on Tom said, "The CEO responded by saying, 'He's right, DBR limits the rate of new product starts, because nothing enters the process until something exits the constraint.' 'So, let's look at what happens to the reds and yellows, if we were to implement DBR,' he added and pointed at the Goal Tree up on the screen. "The way I see it is, if we implement DBR, we will minimize WIP. If we minimize WIP, we automatically

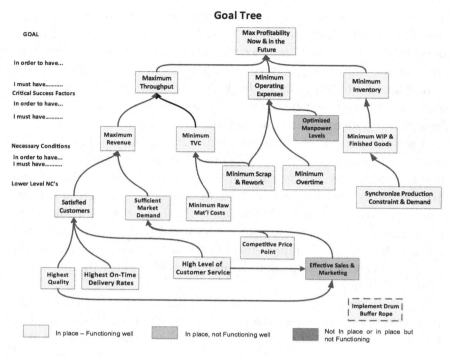

FIGURE 12.7
Goal Tree with Drum Buffer Rope inserted.

minimize FG's, which minimizes our investment dollars, which positively impacts our profitability,' he explained enthusiastically. 'We should also see that on-time delivery rates jump up, which should result in much higher levels of customer satisfaction,' he added. 'This should also allow us to be more competitive in our pricing and stimulate more demand and with our ability to increase throughput, we will positively impact profitability,' he explained. The Junior Accountant then said, 'Last night I read more about the Theory of Constraints and it seems to me that one thing we could do is stop tracking efficiency in our non-constraints and if we do that, we should also reduce our WIP.'"

"The Quality Director spoke up and said, 'I'm thinking that if we effectively slowdown in our non-constraints, we should see our scrap and rework levels improve significantly, because our operators will have more time to make their products. And I also believe that we should implement TLS.' 'What is TLS?' asked the CFO. 'It's an improvement method which combines the Theory of Constraints, Lean, and Six Sigma,' the

Quality Director explained. 'This improvement will reduce our scrap and rework levels and in conjunction with DBR, will reduce both our operating expenses and TVC. The combination of these improvements will both contribute to our profitability,' he added," Tom explained.

"'One other thing is that we should see our overtime levels drop, which will also improve profitability,' said the CFO. 'I am just amazed that by making these three basic changes, we could see a dramatic financial improvement,' he added. The team continued working on their Goal Tree until it was complete (Figure 12.7)," Tom added.

Tom then said, "The stage was set for major financial gains by first, developing their cause and effect relationships, and by looking at their organization as a system rather than making improvements to parts of it. That's a very important message for everyone to glean from all of this. Not all improvement efforts will happen rapidly like it did in this case study, but it is possible to make rapid and significant improvements to your organization by looking at it from a holistic point of view. The fact is, isolated and localized improvements will not typically result in improvement to the system. So, let's take a break for now and when we get back, we'll complete our case study."

13

The Expanded Case Study at Simpson Water Heaters

When everyone was back from their break, Tom began again with his case study. "The CEO began to explain, 'Before we develop our performance metrics, let's first discuss the purposes of an organization's performance metrics. In general, we need some type of feedback mechanism that tells us how we're doing. A way to be able to know that the direction we're traveling is on course. That is, in the event that we need to make any midcourse corrections. These performance metrics should be system related, in that they tell us how the system is performing, rather than how individual processes are working. Remember, our focus is on system performance, and not individual performance. So, think about what our performance metrics should be? But before we answer that question, let's talk about their purpose,' he added and loaded a Power Point slide (Figure 13.1)." The CEO continued, "Performance measures are intended to serve at least six important functions or roles."

Tom continued, "The CEO then explained, 'So with these functions in mind, let's now look at how we can use our Goal Tree to create our series of performance metrics. If we use the Goal Tree as our guide, we should start with our goal, Maximize Profitability Now and In the Future, and create our first tracking metric,' he explained. 'Earlier in our discussion, I introduced you to Throughput Accounting which defined Net Profit as Throughput minus Operating Expense or NP = T – OE. The metric of choice for this Goal Tree then, should be NP which we insert into our 'Goal box.' In addition, I prefer to give most of the metrics a target to shoot for. With this metric, I believe that our Net Profit should be greater than twenty-five percent (NP > 25%),' he stated. 'We must then look at each

1. First, and foremost, the measures should stimulate the right behaviors.

2. The performance measures should reinforce and support the overall goals and objectives of the company.

3. The measures should be able to assess, evaluate, and provide feedback as to the status of the people, departments, products, and the total company.

4. The performance measure must be translatable to everyone within the organization. That is, each operator, manager, engineer, etc., must understand how their actions impact the metric. Performance metrics are intended to inform everyone, not just the managers!

5. The performance metrics chosen should also lend themselves to trend and statistical analysis and, as such, they shouldn't be "yes or no" in terms of compliance.

6. The metric should also be challenging, but at the same time be attainable. There should be a stretch involved. If it's too easy to reach the target, then you probably won't gain nearly as much in the way of profitability. If it's too difficult, then people will be frustrated and disenchanted.

FIGURE 13.1
Six purposes of performance metrics.

CSF and NC and select appropriate performance metrics and targets for as many as might be appropriate. Keep in mind that not every box will have a defined metric, but let's get as many as we can.' "The CEO," Tom said, "then told the executive team that he wanted them to work on the rest of the metrics as a team and that he would return later."

Tom explained, "Because the operational status of companies varies from company to company, there is no standard set of metrics and targets to recommend. But for the company in this case study, the team stayed focused and was able to identify appropriate metrics and targets. They started with the Goal, then worked through the CSFs, and then onto the NCs. Let's get back to the case study and see what they were able to do."

The CFO was the first to speak and said, "It's clear to me that having performance metrics for the three CSFs is imperative, since they are the three components of profitability." Tom interjected, "The team decided to first, determine which entities could actually have metrics tied to them. After they had determined all of the metrics, they would then develop targets for each specific performance metric. The figure on the screen (Figure 13.2)

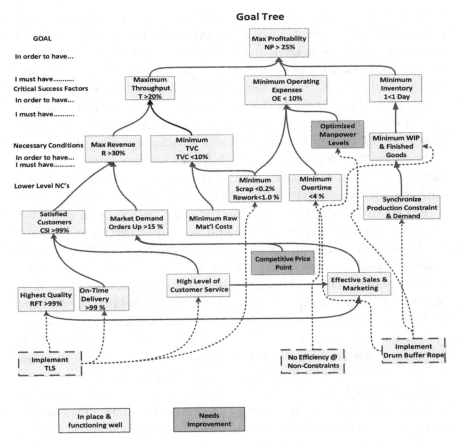

FIGURE 13.2
Color-coded Goal Tree with targets.

is the Goal Tree with appropriate metrics defined by this executive team, along with their targets." Tom explained.

Tom then explained, "All of the team members contributed to this effort and were all amazed at the finished product they had developed. As they were admiring their Goal Tree with the performance metrics they intended to track, the CEO entered the room. He studied the completed Goal Tree and then moved to the front of the room. He thanked everyone for their effort and told them that they could return to their offices. The CFO stood and said, 'With all due respect sir, we haven't finished yet.'"

Tom continued with the case study explanation, "The CFO stood, faced the group and asked, 'Where do you think we should start? I mean should we start at the top with the Goal or should we start at the bottom and work our way up?' The Junior Accountant raised her hand and said, 'I think we should start at the lower levels and work our way to the top.' 'Why do you feel that way?' asked the CFO. 'If we follow the direction of the arrows, and then set, and reach our target, then the level directly above will be the net result of our efforts,' she replied. 'Could you give us an example?' asked the CFO. 'OK, for example, if we set our target for Highest Quality, Right the First Time (RFT) at greater than 99% and we achieve it, plus, our on-time delivery rate to 99% and we achieve that, then we have a great chance of having our Customer Satisfaction Index (CSI) be greater than 99%. So, it's kind of like sufficiency type logic using if-then statements,' she explained."

The Quality Director then spoke up and said, "I can see your point, but I can also make the argument based on necessity-based logic. By that I mean, we could start with the Goal and give it a target of 25%. So, with necessity-based logic, we could say that in order to have a profitability of 25%, we must have a Throughput improvement of at least 20%, while holding our operating expenses to less than 10% and holding our on-hand inventory to less than one day." The CFO re-entered the conversation and said, "I see both points of view, but I must tell you I like following the direction of the arrows on our Goal Tree. I say this because, when we implement Drum Buffer Rope and the combined Theory of Constraints, Lean, and Six Sigma methodology, we drive improvement upward and our metrics respond to what we're doing." The Junior Accountant then said, "I don't think it matters which direction we go, because at the end of the day, the metrics will tell us how we're doing," she said.

Tom continued, "A short while later the CEO returned to the conference room to find the completed Goal Tree, with metrics and targets posted on the screen at the front of the conference room (Figure 13.3). He studied it, turned to the group and asked someone to explain it to him. The CFO turned to the Junior Accountant and said, 'I think since you contributed most to our success, that you should be the one to do that.' The Junior Accountant just smiled and said she would be happy to, and did so with confidence, agility and a seemingly true understanding of this new tool. She finished her presentation by telling the executive team that this tool will serve her well in her new position as CFO with her new company and everyone gasped in disbelief."

Tom concluded his meeting and said, "The Goal Tree is an amazingly simple tool to not only learn, but in my experiences, it's a tool that most

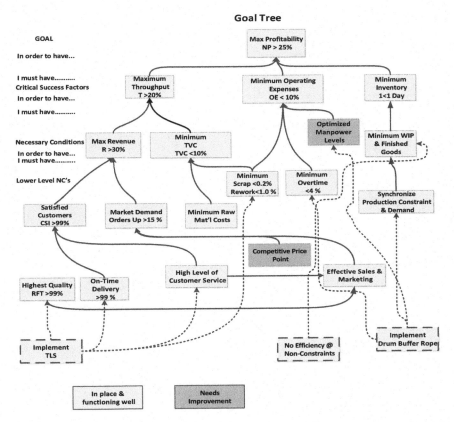

FIGURE 13.3
Completed Goal Tree.

people feel comfortable using. As you learned, in a very short amount of time, this team not only learned how to create their Goal Tree, they were able to use it to develop their strategic and tactical improvement plan. I am forever grateful to [1] Bill Dettmer for providing us with this amazing tool and I encourage everyone to read Bill's book, *The Logical Thinking Process – A Systems Approach to Complex Problem Solving.*" "Now, what I want you to do before I return the next time, is create your very own Goal Tree." And with that, Tom left to drive to the airport for his flight home.

REFERENCE

1. H. William Dettmer, *The Logical Thinking Process – A Systems Approach to Complex Problem Solving*, 2007, American Society for Quality Control Press, Milwaukee, WI.

14

Maximo's Improvement Plan

When Tom Mahanan left Maximo Health Center Complex the last time, he had just completed a session on the construction of a Goal Tree. He had also instructed the corporate members in attendance to return to their respective hospitals and create a Goal Tree for each one. He had told them he would be back in two weeks to review their completed Goal Trees. Tom looked at his schedule and decided to contact Pete Hallwell to set a date for his next trip. He dialed Pete's number, and after several rings, the phone was answered. "Hello, Pete Hallwell here," the voice said on the other end. "Hi Pete, it's Tom Mahanan," Tom said. "Oh, hi Tom, what's up?" he asked. "I want to schedule another visit to review your individual hospital Goal Trees," Tom said. "When would you like to come Tom?" Pete asked. "You tell me Pete, what's the best day and time?" Tom asked. Pete looked at his schedule and said, "How about Tuesday at 8:00 am?" he asked. Tom looked at his schedule and said, "That works for me Pete, I'll see you then."

Tuesday morning Tom drove to Maximo's Corporate offices, signed in, and the guard called Pete to let him know that Tom was in the lobby. Shortly thereafter, Pete arrived in the lobby, and the two of them went to the conference room. Pete reintroduced Tom to the group, which consisted of the same members that were there during his training session on the Goal Tree. And with that introduction, Tom began. "Good morning everyone, happy to be back with everyone," he said. "So, how did everyone do with the individual Goal Trees?" he asked. Everyone seemed to indicate that they had been able to create their Goal Trees without any problems. Pete then said, "What we did is to hold a general training session for all of the hospitals in our complex and that seemed to work very well. In fact, we created a Goal Tree for our Oncology Hospital as part of our overall training." "I like that approach Pete, so can I see what you came up with?"

Maximo Oncology Hospital Goal Tree

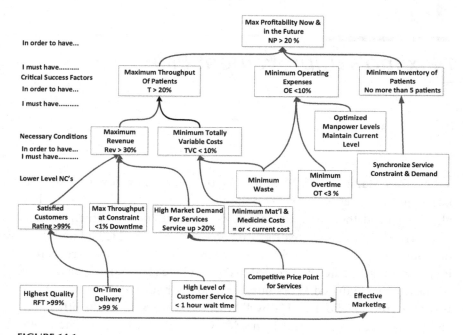

FIGURE 14.1

Maximo Oncology Hospital Goal Tree.

Tom asked. "Of course," Pete responded and loaded a completed Goal Tree on the screen (Figure 14.1).

What Tom saw on the screen was a well-designed Goal Tree that contained target values for many of the Goal Tree entities. After reviewing the Goal Tree, Tom said, "I am very impressed with what you have put together on this Goal Tree." He continued, "The flow of information looks very good, but what impresses me the most is your use of 'lead and lag measure' just like we discussed in our training. I also like how you have set target values for each of your key entity statements. Now all that's left to do, is your assessment exercise." And with that comment, Pete flashed another overhead on the screen (Figure 14.2) and said, "You mean like this?"

Tom looked at their assessed Goal Tree and said, "Wow! You guys really hit a home run! I have to be honest with everyone, I truly didn't expect such a completed Goal Tree to be ready for this visit! Congratulations everyone for a job well done!" he exclaimed.

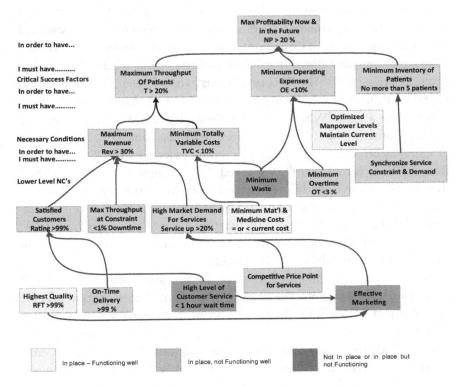

FIGURE 14.2
Assessed Maximo Oncology Hospital Goal Tree.

And with that, Pete spoke up and said, "What we decided is that this Goal Tree can be used by all six of our hospitals!" "Yes, there will be slight modifications for each hospital, but at the end of the day, this Goal Tree will fit each of our hospitals." "What a great idea Pete!" Tom exclaimed. "So, what is your next exercise Pete?" Tom asked. Pete responded immediately and said, "Tom, this is where we will need your help." "In what way Pete?" Tom asked. Pete responded and said, "For example, for the Necessary Condition, Maximum Throughput at Constraint, what improvement would you recommend that we implement to achieve our target of less than 1% downtime?" "It depends upon what the cause or causes of your downtime are Pete?" Tom replied. He added, "Do you have an analysis of your downtime?"

Pete responded and said, "I think I can speak for Terry Sample, when I say that one of the reasons we have downtime here is that we frequently run out of meds for our treatments." Terry nodded in agreement. Tom responded and said, "The Theory of Constraints has the perfect solution, if this is truly what's causing your downtime." Pete replied, "Tom, what's the solution you're referring to?" "The Theory of Constraints Replenishment Solution would be ideal and I can teach your teams how to set that up," Tom replied.

Pete then asked, "What about the Necessary Condition, Synchronize Service Constraint and Demand?" Tom responded and said, "The Theory of Constraints offers a scheduling method referred to as Drum Buffer Rope." "What is that Tom?" Pete asked. "It's a simple scheduling method that focuses on the rate of the system constraint," Tom replied. "I would assume you have waiting rooms full of patients waiting to receive treatments?" He added. "That's exactly what we have at all of our hospitals!" Pete exclaimed. He added, "Is that something simple for our employees to learn?" "Yes, absolutely, Pete," Tom replied.

Tom then said, "I will schedule all of the necessary training and I will assist your hospitals with the implementation of your key strategies for improvement." Then Tom added, "One thing that I don't see on your Goal Tree is any reference to 'Emergency Services?' Pete?" Pete responded and said, "We all discussed that, and those hospitals that have Emergency Departments, have it in their Goal Trees." "Okay, I just wanted to make sure that was included," Tom replied. "At some point I want to present a case study on a hospital Emergency Department for STEMI type heart attacks, but we'll address this later on." Tom said.

"So now, let's look in more detail at your Goal Tree, so I can demonstrate how you can add your improvement efforts to develop your final improvement plan," Tom said. "For example, we just discussed two improvement initiatives, namely Drum Buffer Rope and Theory of Constraints' Replenishment Solution," He explained. Tom then updated their Goal Tree to reflect these additions, plus a couple others and loaded it onto the screen (Figure 14.3). "By adding these improvement tools to your Goal Tree, you will be able to see how many of the Goal Tree entities will be impacted," he explained. "Just follow the hashed arrows and you'll see what I mean," he added.

"It's important to remember that these connecting arrows can impact multiple NC's and CSFs," Tom added. "Does this make sense to you?" he asked. Pete responded and said, "It makes perfect sense!" "So, your new assignment is to focus on each of the individual Goal Trees and

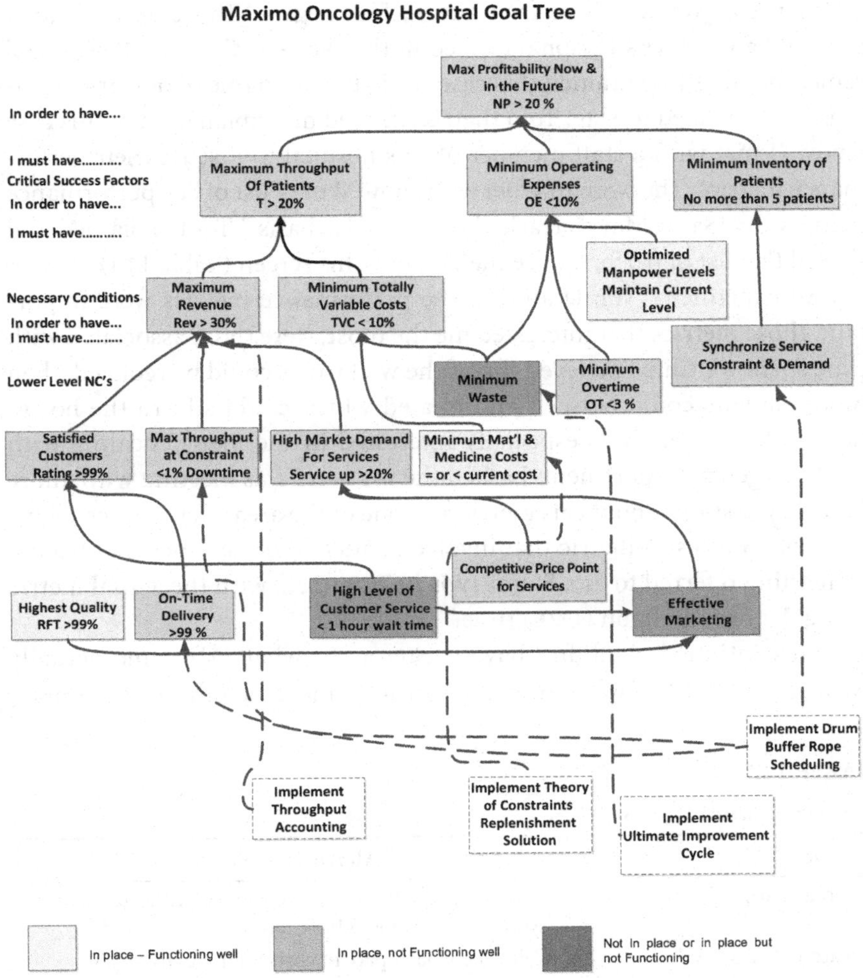

Maximo Oncology Hospital Goal Tree

FIGURE 14.3
Goal Tree with improvements added.

record what you believe will be the best improvement strategy for each hospital," Tom explained. "So, when can we hear about the Emergency Department Case Study?" Pete asked. "Let me check my computer to make sure I have it with me and if I do, would you like to hear it now?" Tom asked. Pete scanned the conference room, and everyone indicated that they'd like to hear about it now. "So, everyone, take a break and I'll get it loaded," Tom said.

When everyone was back from break, Tom began, "This case study took place at Saint Mary's Hospital located in the Western Chicago. Pete, you'll remember that I mentioned this case study to you in one of our first meetings." Tom related to Pete. Tom then continued his explanation of this case study. "I met with a staff member of this hospital to discuss their performance metrics. The woman I met with showed me a list of key performance metrics that Saint Mary's tracked on a regular basis." Tom explained and loaded this list of performance metrics onto his screen (Table 14.1).

Tom explained, "While all of these performance metrics were important, those metrics that interested me the most, were those associated with time spent waiting. I believed that if the wait times could be reduced, then more patients could be seen and treated which could add to the hospital's bottom line. I was especially interested in the metric dealing with the Emergency Department. I asked the woman I was meeting with, more specific questions about this metric and one of the areas that interested me the most was a sub-metric that involved patients in the process of having something referred to as a Stemi-type heart attack, with the actual metric being, Door to Balloon (D2B) time."

Tom continued, "I didn't have a clue as to what D2B time actually was, so I asked the woman to explain it in more detail, but in simpler

TABLE 14.1

Key Performance Metrics

Metric	Metric Description
Average Hospital Stay	Appraise the amount of time your patients are staying in your hospital after admission.
Treatment Costs	Calculate what a patient costs your facility.
Hospital Readmission Rate	Calculate how many patients are coming back after they are discharged.
Patient Wait Time	Calculate your patient satisfaction score by assessing their average wait time.
Patient Satisfaction	How patients felt while being taken care of in your hospital?
Patient Safety	Identify any incidents happening in your hospital and reduce the patients' exposure to further risk.
ER Wait Time to See a Doctor	Evaluate the time patients spend from checking in to the ER until they see a doctor.
Costs by Payer	Evaluate which type of health insurance they have and what it costs.

terms." She responded and said, "Door to Balloon is a time measurement in Emergency Room/Cardiac Care Unit, specifically in the treatment of ST Segment Elevation Myocardial Infarction, or simply, a STEMI heart attack." I responded by saying, "What did you just say?" She chuckled and said, "The time interval starts with the patient's arrival in the Emergency Department and ends when a catheter guide-wire crosses the culprit lesion in the Cardiac Cath lab. In everyday language, this just means that a balloon is inflated inside one of the heart's primary blood vessels to allow unimpeded blood flow through the heart."

She continued her explanation, "The clock starts ticking either as a walk-in to the Emergency Department, or in the field where a patient is being attended to by medical personnel. This metric is enormously important to patients simply because the longer this procedure is delayed, the more damage occurs to the heart muscle due to a lack of oxygen to the heart muscle. It's damaged because the cause of this problem is typically due to a blockage within the heart that prevents oxygen from being supplied to the heart, and without proper amounts of oxygen, muscle damage results. The inflated balloon 'unclogs' the blood vessel. Graphically, door to balloon might look like this (Figure 14.4)," and he loaded a picture on his laptop's screen. "For those of you who have no experience with this, this is a graphic summary of the D2B Time," Tom added.

Tom explained, "Seeing this graphic image of what this procedure involved, made it much easier for me to understand. My conclusion was that this might be a good place to start the improvement effort within

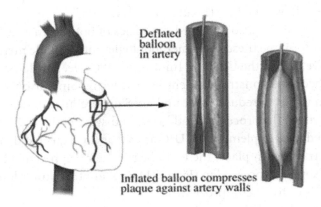

FIGURE 14.4
D2B time graphic.

Saint Mary's. I then asked this same woman if there was a specific metric value or standard that Saint Mary's had to achieve." She replied and said, "Yes, the current median standard for Door to Balloon (D2B) time is 90 minutes, and Saint Mary's was actually doing quite well against this standard." She continued, "We have a median score of 66 minutes, but we are anticipating that the standard would be changing to 60 minutes in the future." I then asked, "When you say median, do you actually mean that it's the average or mean time?" She responded and said, "No, for some reason this standard is tracked based on the median."

"We continued discussing this standard and finally decided that this would be a good place to start the improvement effort at Saint Mary's. On further discussion with this woman, she explained that in addition to this new time benefitting the patient by experiencing much less heart muscle damage, there was also a financial incentive for the hospital. Apparently, reimbursement rates for Medicare and Medicaid patients were tied to completing the D2B time below the standard median time. We decided to put together a team of hospital subject matter experts to study this metric and look for ways to achieve this future target, before it was mandated to do so," Tom explained.

Tom continued, "The team was formed, and I conducted a training session for the team members focusing on how to use my integrated Theory of Constraints, Lean, and Six Sigma improvement methodology. I explained to the team that the Theory of Constraints and its Five Focusing Steps offers a much quicker solution to this type of project. When I described Theory of Constraints' Five Focusing Steps, I used the hospital's jargon such as the following figure (Figure 14.5) describes."

Tom continued, "I also reviewed the basics of both Lean and Six sigma and how to combine these three methodologies into a single methodology which I have named the Ultimate Improvement Cycle. I explained to them that the Theory of Constraints identifies the focal point for improvement, while Lean works to reduce waste and Six Sigma reduces and controls the variation within the process." In addition, "I displayed the UIC's tools and actions needed to implement the UIC as well as the expected deliverables. With this training in place, the team began their improvement effort by creating a simple Process Map (Figure 14.6) of another, lower level metric known as Door to Doctor process."

"After completing the simple process map of Door to Doc time, I instructed the team to 'Walk the Gemba' by going to both the Emergency

1. Identify the system constraint—In a physical process with numerous processing steps, like D2B Time, the constraint is the step with the smallest amount of capacity. Or another way of stating this is the step with the longest processing time.

2. Decide how to exploit the system constraint—Once the constraint has been identified, this step instructs you to focus your efforts on it and use the improvement tools of Lean and Six Sigma to reduce waste and variation but focus your efforts mostly on the constraint. This does not mean that you can ignore non-constraints, but your primary focus should be on the constraint.

3. Subordinate everything else to the constraint—In layman's terms, this simply means don't over-produce on non-constraints, and never let the constraint be starved. In a process like the Door to Balloon Time, it would make no sense to push patients into this process, since they would be forced to wait excessively. But of course, the hospital cannot predict when patients with heart attacks will show up needing medical attention. But by constantly trying to reduce the constraint's time, the wait time should be continuously reduced.

4. If necessary, elevate the constraint—This simply means that if you have done everything you can to increase the capacity of the constraint in Step 2, and it's still not enough to satisfy the demand placed on it, then you might have to spend money by hiring additional people, purchasing additional equipment, etc. That is, anything that would reduce the time in the constraint. With a standard as important as D2B Time, this step would not be out of the question.

5. Return to Step 1, but don't let inertia create a new constraint—Once the constraint's required capacity has been achieved, the system constraint could move to a new location within the process. When this happens, it is necessary to move your improvement efforts to the new constraint if further improvement is needed. What is thing about inertia? What this means is to make sure things you have put in place to break the original constraint (e.g. procedures, policies, etc.) are not limiting the throughput of the process. If necessary, you may need to remove them.

FIGURE 14.5
Theory of Constraints' Five Focusing Steps in medical terms.

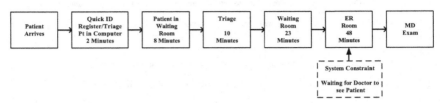

FIGURE 14.6
Current State Door to Doctor Time.

Department and Cardiology Department to observe what happens during this process and to have conversations with employees from both departments about problems they might have encountered. This was a fact-finding mission aimed at understanding how patients are managed through this treatment process. The team collected many observations during this walk, most of which would be used to construct their Current State Process Map, for D2B Time," Tom explained.

Tom continued, "The team then developed the following problem statement: *Hospital's current state cycle time is 66 minutes (median) for Door to Balloon Time when patients arrive at the Emergency Department and are classified as a STEMI candidate. The Hospital's goal is less than 60 minutes (median) 100% of the time.* In addition, the team set two primary performance goals as follow:

1. Hospital's median Door to Balloon Time at 60 minutes or below.
2. Decreased Door to Balloon Time will improve patient outcomes as measured by quality metrics. Additionally, these quality metrics are tied to the hospital's reimbursement based on the result of those outcomes."

"The team then developed a business case for their efforts: In addition to the quality and reimbursement benefits, this project will help in the marketing of the hospital's Cardiology services. Improved performance in quality metrics will lead to awards and preferred provider status. Examples include: Chest Pain Accreditation, Top 100 Heart Hospital, Blue Cross Distinction for Cardiac Care." Tom explained.

"As a final step before their improvement work began, the team developed their performance metrics to be used to judge the final impact of

TABLE 14.2

Performance Metrics for D2B Time

Metric/Unit: Complete cycle time in Median Minutes	Baseline: Median = 66 minutes	Goal: Future median = <60 minutes	Future estimated median = 53 minutes

their improvement efforts on D2B Time which are include in the following table (Table 14.2)," Tom explained.

Tom continued, "The team had access to D2B time data that had been collected on previous patients passing through this process. The team then analyzed the data to better understand what was happening on previous D2B events, and to determine the location of the constraint within this process. The team met with me and showed me what they had discovered (Figure 14.7) as a summary of this analysis before any improvements were initiated. They broke their analysis into three separate phases which were, Door to EKG, EKG to Table, and Table to Balloon."

"I reviewed what they had done and then told the team that 'I really liked the analysis they put together and how they had identified the system constraint in this system. Based upon their analysis, the first stage, Door to EKG, only took an average of 4.75 minutes, while the second stage, EKG to Table, took, on average, 36.7 minutes, while the third stage, Table to Balloon, took 21.2 minutes. This clearly demonstrates where they had to focus their improvement efforts and that is EKG to Table.'" Tom continued. "I explained that I realize that you're measured on the median time to

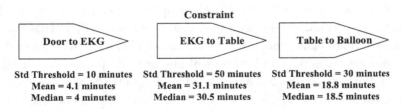

**Door to Balloon Time After Improvements
Standard Threshold 90 minutes
Mean 52 minutes
Median 53 minutes**

Constraint

Door to EKG   EKG to Table   Table to Balloon

Std Threshold = 10 minutes   Std Threshold = 50 minutes   Std Threshold = 30 minutes
Mean = 4.1 minutes   Mean = 31.1 minutes   Mean = 18.8 minutes
Median = 4 minutes   Median = 30.5 minutes   Median = 18.5 minutes

FIGURE 14.7
Door to Balloon Time process.

complete the full Door to Balloon Time, but my belief is that you should measure your progress using mean values, rather than median times. The reason I said this is because as you work to reduce variation in this system, the values for mean and median will come closer together and statistical tools and tests are all based on mean values. At any rate, this was a great first step," I concluded.

Tom continued, "One of the tools I taught the team was an Interference Diagram, which I presented to everyone on a previous visit here." I suggested that this would be a good tool for this team to use to dissect the process to develop improvement opportunities. I also explained, that the purpose of the Interference Diagram, or ID for short, was to identify any barriers or obstacles or interferences that stand in the way of achieving a goal or objective. I then explained that the Interference Diagram can then be used to develop an improvement plan on how to reduce the EKG to Table phase time. In the case for Phase 2, EKG to Table, the goal developed by the team was identified simply as "EKG to ED Exam Room Table Faster."

Continuing on, "The team then reassembled and developed a list of 'interferences' that stood in the way of achieving the goal they had set of reducing the EKG to ED exam room table time. One-by-one, the team recorded the interferences or obstacles that stand in the way of reaching their goal and created a slide to show me (Figure 14.8). They then called me and asked me to come to their meeting room so that they could have me see their completed Interference Diagram."

"I reviewed the work they had done, looked at the group and simply said, 'Awesome work everyone!' The team leader walked me through the entire diagram, and I was very impressed to say the least. I had many questions about the writings within each box of the Interference Diagram, and without exception every question was answered to my satisfaction," Tom explained.

"I then told the team that I will be leaving Saint Mary's shortly, but the next thing I would recommend that you create is a SIPOC Diagram. I explained that in any process improvement activity, a SIPOC is a tool that summarizes the inputs and outputs of one or more processes in a table format. For anyone who has never seen this diagram, the acronym SIPOC stands for Suppliers, Inputs, Process, Outputs, and Customers which form the columns of the table. Over the next week, the team worked hard to create the SIPOC Diagram (Figure 14.9), Tom explained. The team then

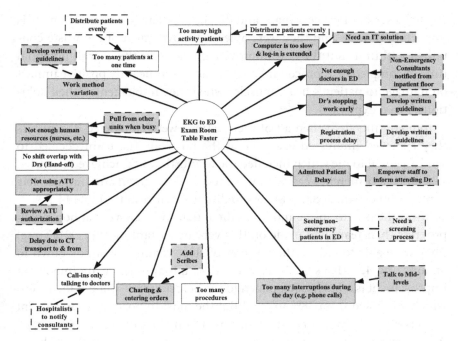

FIGURE 14.8
Completed Interference Diagram.

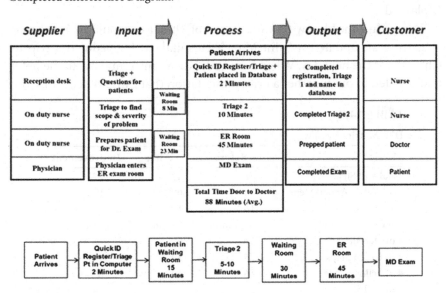

FIGURE 14.9
Completed SIPOC diagram.

created a series of process maps and did an excellent job of analyzing this important process and they were able to remove much of the waste contained within it. But the real improvement came in the overall potential time to complete this procedure, which had a significantly positive impact on damage to patient's heart muscles when they implemented their solutions," Tom explained.

Tom continued, "When all of their actions were completed, the results they achieved impressed everyone at the hospital. The team decided to send an email to me which included the results they had achieved and then scheduled a conference call with me. I received the email and immediately contacted the team at Saint Mary's to discuss their results (Table 14.3)."

"I was the first to speak and I told them that I was amazed at how much progress their team had made on this very important metric, D2B Time! They were able to reduce the number of steps required from 69 down to an amazing 42! That's a 27-step reduction, but another really important improvement is what has happened to the percentage of value-added steps which increased from 38% to 69%! But the most important improvement of all is the D2B cycle time which dropped from 66 minutes to 53 minutes! And after learning about how important this time is to a patient's heart muscle, this 13-minute reduction is a fantastic accomplishment!" Tom explained.

"In conclusion, I knew that my Board of Directors would be interested in getting an update on Saint Mary's Hospital, so I scheduled a trip to Chicago for the next day. When I arrived, I drove my rental car to the hotel and decided to put together a brief presentation that I would deliver to The

TABLE 14.3

D2B Metrics Review

Metric	Before	After	Improvement
Total # of Steps	69	42	−27
% of Value-Added Steps	38%	60%	31%
# of Swim Lanes	16	15	−1
Total Cycle Time	66 minutes	53 minutes	13 minutes
# of Decisions	13	6	−7
# of Green Steps	26	29	3
# of Yellow Steps	16	10	−6
# of Red Steps	27	3	−24

TABLE 14.4

Metrics Review

Metric	Metric Description	Before	After
Average Hospital Stay	Time patients spend in hospital	4 days	2 days
Patient Wait Time	Average wait time for services	2 hours	1 hour
Patient Satisfaction	How patients feel about services	77%	95%
ER Wait Time	Time patients wait to see doctor	1.5 hours	45 minutes
Readmission Rates	Patient return after discharge	22%	8%

Board. In addition to the amazing work the team had done on D2B Time, there had also been other teams working on improving the other metrics, so I included some of them in my presentation to the Board. I put together a before and after review of some of the more important metrics that were part of the D2B improvement effort (Table 14.3)," Tom explained.

Tom completed his explanation by explaining that he had also put together a before and after review of some of the more important metrics that the hospital tracks (Table 14.4).

The Maximo Group reviewed these metrics and were amazed at the improvement results that Saint Mary's had achieved. Pete then asked, "Tom, can we expect to see the same level of improvement that Saint Mary's achieved?" Tom replied, "Yes, and one metric not listed in this table was Profit Margins, which sky-rocketed just like these metrics did!" "I know I can speak for everyone here when I say, I am excited to get going on our improvement effort!" Pete added. And with that comment, the session ended.

"Tom, I have a question for you," Pete said. "When will you be able to come back and train our employees on Drum Buffer Rope?" he asked. "If you can, we can arrange that training for later this week. Look at your schedule and let me know," Tom replied. "Will do Tom," Pete replied and with that Tom left.

15

More Training at Maximo

The next day, Tom received a voice mail from Pete Hallwell indicating that his team would be available for training on Drum Buffer Rope on Thursday morning. Tom called Pete back and confirmed that he was available for this training session on Thursday, so they set it up to begin at 8:00 Thursday morning. Tom spent the rest of the day putting together the training materials for this session. On Thursday morning Tom arrived at Maximo Health Center Complex was met by Pete Hallwell and the two of them took the elevator to the seventh floor. As the two of them entered the conference room, Tom could see the same familiar faces that had been involved in most of his presentations in the past. Pete reintroduced Tom and he began.

"Good morning everyone," Tom said and everyone in unison said good morning back to him. "As all of you know, I am here today to discuss the Theory of Constraints scheduling system known as Drum Buffer Rope, or DBR for short," Tom explained. Tom continued, "In their book, *The Goal*, Goldratt and Cox effectively use a story written in a novel format to walk the reader through the steps necessary to move a manufacturing organization from the traditional manufacturing concepts to a facility managed using the concepts of Drum-Buffer-Rope (DBR). And while Maximo is not a manufacturing complex, the same principles and actions apply to service industries, just like Maximo," Tom explained.

"The thinking behind Drum Buffer Rope is really quite simple, but mostly just logical. Thinking logically is nothing new, but it is not the way most people think. The fundamental view of Drum Buffer Rope is to focus on the system as a whole rather than only a single segment of the system, at least until you have clearly identified the constraint. This idea of looking at the global system is a major shift in the way systems have previously been viewed and managed. Prior to global, systems thinking, the pervasive point of view was, and still is in many companies, that any systems improvement, at any location, would improve the overall system. The idea being that the sum total of several isolated improvements would somehow equal an improvement to the overall system. But such is not the case. The effects of employing the 'shotgun' approach to systems management can cause a series of devastating systemic effects," Tom explained.

"Just to review, a system can be defined as a sequence of steps or processes that are linked together to produce something as an end result. With that definition in mind, it's easy to understand how virtually everything can be linked to some kind of a system," Tom explained. Tom continued, "Engineering organizations have systems, banks have systems and hospitals have systems. Almost anything you can think of is the product of a system. By design, a system can be as small and unique as two processes linked together, where the output of one process becomes the input for the next process. On the other hand, systems can be very complex, with many processes linked together, maybe even hundreds or more. Just because a system is complex does not mean it can't be improved, it just means it's complex, and that's okay. Even in a system as simple as two linked processes, one of those two processes could very well constrain the other one. It's just the nature of how things work," Tom explained.

"If a systems constraint did not exist, then the system should, at least theoretically, be able to produce at infinite capacity. But infinite capacity is not a level that is ever achieved from any system, simply because all systems are restricted, at some point in time, by some type of output limitation. This limitation is usually determined by the presence of some kind of system, capacity limit. No matter how good the system is, there is still only so much it can do. Sooner or later whatever kind of system is being analyzed, it will reach its maximum system capacity and be unable to deliver more. If higher system outputs are required beyond the current capacity, then it should be clear that the system must be changed," Tom explained.

"For years, organizations have dedicated considerable time and effort to remove variation from their systems. The overall goal is to remove as much variation as possible from the system. But, no matter how much effort is extended, variation will still exist! If you were asked; how long it takes you to get to work every day, your response might be something like, 'about thirty minutes.' The instant you answer with the word 'about,' you have introduced variation into the system. You know that historically speaking, some days you get to work in twenty-five minutes and yet other days it can take thirty-five or forty minutes. In your 'get to work' system, things can happen that will either speed up the process or slow it down," Tom continued.

"Variation exists in everything, but especially within any system. You understand that some processes will produce at a faster or slower rate than others, and this is the premise behind variation. Because of variation, the output from a system will not always be predictable, but rather it will operate within a range that constantly changes. This variable range is known as statistical fluctuation, and it exists in every system. It's important to understand that you cannot make variation go away. The theory and practice of Six Sigma has pioneered the race to variation reduction," Tom stated.

Tom continued, "But even with the most valiant efforts of time and money, not all variation can be removed. You can reduce the amount and the severity of variation, but it will still exist in some form. Once you understand that variation is a constant variable in any system, it's easier to understand that at some point, you will reach the minimum variation that is controllable in the system, and any efforts to reduce variation beyond that point are generally fruitless. Perhaps, instead of spending so much time and effort on techniques to remove variation, the focus should really be on techniques to manage variation."

"When viewing a system through the eyes of Drum Buffer Rope, it becomes quickly apparent that improving every step in the process is not what is required, nor will the sum total of all of those discrete system improvements equal an improved overall system. When conducting a full systems analysis, with the intent of implementing Drum Buffer Rope, an important consideration to know and understand is the location of the system constraint, or the slowest operation," Tom explained. "In Goldratt's Five Focusing Steps, this is Step 1, identify the system constraint. Once you know where the slowest operation resides, you now have the information necessary to know where to focus your attention within the system. Why is it important to understand where the slowest operation is? Because this is the location that controls and determines the output for your entire system. In essence, the entire system will produce no faster than the slowest operation can produce," Tom continued.

"With the constraining operation identified, you have collectively quarantined the *drumbeat* for your entire system. Knowing the drumbeat is of strategic importance to implement and gain any system improvements. The drum provides you with the necessary information of knowing where to focus your improvement efforts. Historically, many organizations conduct many improvement projects, because there is a belief that every organization and every process should strive for improvement. However, the sum of many efforts does not always equal what is good for the system as a whole," Tom explained.

He continued, "The problem with this type of thinking is it is a totally unfocused shotgun approach to solving the problem. In effect, it presents an improvement policy that states: if I select a wide enough range, then I should hit the target, or at least come close to the target. When you take the shotgun approach you might hit everything a little bit, but miss the full impact required to make real change and improvements. If your shotgun approach includes trying to improve non-constraints, as most do, then the system as a whole gains nothing!"

"The improvement of non-constraints in isolation of the entire system, without a comprehensive analysis, is just a way of treating the symptoms and not the real issue, which is the system constraint. Without the ability and the accurate information necessary to focus on the real issues, the disease goes merrily on. Improvement of non-constraints is a noble gesture, but one that yields little, if any, real improvements. Every process within a system does not need to be improved at the same time, because some system processes are more important than others. Without knowing where your constraint resides, your efforts to improve will be unfocused and consequently worthless, serving only to consume large amounts of money, resources, and time," Tom explained.

"Once you have identified the systems constraint, it must be subjected to the red-carpet treatment. Nothing in your system is more important than the constraint! Once you have this information, you must decide how to best manage the constraint. If the output from your entire system depends solely on the output of the constraint, then wouldn't you think it merits special attention? One of those considerations is to exploit the constraint, which is Step 2 of the Five Focusing Steps. Exploitation simply means that you evaluate the process to get the most out the constraint activity," Tom stated.

He continued his explanation,

"Rarely is a constraint being utilized at, or near, the maximum that it can do. The exploitation effort simply means looking for things that the constraints can stop doing. This could be an excellent opportunity to employ the Interference Diagram (ID) to define the interferences that stop you from getting more from your constraint. You may want to implement Lean concepts to reduce waste or Six Sigma to better control variation and quality. It might also mean taking actions as simple as keeping your process busy during breaks and lunch time, or perhaps implementing a second shift or a third shift, or even off-loading work to non-constrained processes or resources."

"Exploitation does not mean buying a new machine or adding more resources, at least not yet. It simply means that you need to find ways to get more out of the current process than you are currently getting. There is a very high probability that during the exploitation exercise, the constraint capacity could be improved above and beyond the capacity of the next constraint in the system. If such is the case, then you simply go back to Step 1 and redefine the constraint. In a normal improvement effort, this repeating cycle between Steps 1 and 2 might be completed several times before the system has stabilized. When the system becomes stable, then go to Step 3 of the Five Focusing Steps and implement the subordination rule to synchronize your patient flow. The end result is to stabilize and synchronize the system, and then focus on the constraint. Let the non-constraints work as required to serve sufficient quantities of patients to keep the constraint busy," Tom explained. He then added, "I know I'm giving a very detailed explanation, but it's important for you to have a complete explanation, if you are to successfully implement Drum Buffer Rope."

And with that comment, Tom continued, "The second consideration is to make sure the constraints are busy all the time. In other words, never let your constraint run out of work to do. If the constraint stops or slows down, then the entire system will stop or slow down. The best way to accomplish this objective is to make sure there are always patients in the queue in front of your system constraint. In other words, create a *buffer of patients* in front of the constraint. The entire system output has total dependency on the constraint output, and constraint output is directly proportional to system output. Think in terms of the right amount of work, in the right location and at the right time."

"The system constraint not only determines the number of patients you can treat, but it also determines the correct amount of patient inventory that should be maintained in the system. The correct inventory level of patients will be reached almost by default when system subordination is actively pursued and implemented," Tom explained.

"The *rope* is actually a mechanism that controls two different functions. First, it is the mechanism that determines how much and when to release new patients into your system. The most common practice is to tie an artificial 'rope' from the constraint operation back to the front of the line. When the constraint produces and completes one patient treatment, and passes it to the next operation, then the rope is pulled to signal the front end of the line to release one more patient into the system. The rope signal is equal to the output of the constraint operation, no more and no less. This release mechanism, tied to the drumbeat of the constraint, will allow for a synchronized patient flow and a smooth transition of patients through the system," Tom explained.

Tom continued, "The second function of the rope is to initiate and maintain subordination for all other processes in the line. By default, following the cadence of the rope release signal causes subordination to the remaining non-constraint process steps to be executed. The non-constraint process steps can only work on what has been released to work on. By releasing work only to the drumbeat of the constraint, all other operations will be held in check to the rule of subordination. Even if the non-constraints can do more work, they are restricted by subordination and only allowed to work on patient work required by the constraint."

"The systems inventory not only includes the patients located at the buffer, but also the cumulative total of patients at other process locations as well. Bad things can and do happen after processing patients at the constraint. There is also a buffer referred to as a shipping buffer, which in a hospital environment would be completing treatment and release of patients. The constraint buffer provides the necessary protection in front of the constraint, and the shipping buffer provides protection after the constraint. The shipping buffer is just a mechanism to absorb and manage the inevitable variation that will occur. Buffer sizing at these two locations is a variable, but you do need to start with something. Consider, as a starting point for the buffer at the drum (the constraint) location to be about one and a half patients or whatever units of time you are measuring," Tom explained.

"For example, if your constraints can treat ten patients in one day, then the buffer should be set at fifteen units (or $10 \times 1.5 = 15$). You may decide in time that the buffer is too large or too small, so you can adjust it either up or down depending on the need. The shipping buffer could be three or four hours or less depending on the speed of patients through your system. It doesn't need to be necessarily large in quantity or long in time. It just needs to be sufficient to protect against variation after the constraint. It's also important to consider your shipping buffer time in your scheduling calculation, in order to determine the correct release time into the system for on-time completion of patient treatment. If you watch your buffer locations carefully, you can make good decisions to increase or decrease them based on some supportive historical data. If your buffer is constantly on the high end, then reduce it. If it is constantly on the low end, then increase it. Apply the rule of common sense to determine the correct buffer," Tom stated.

Tom continued, "When you know and understand the constraint location, and you buffer the work activity, and you send the correct release signal to the front of the line to release more patients, then you have in essence implemented a system of synchronized flow," Tom said and loaded the following figures (Figure 15.1) onto the screen, which defines the DBR steps and integration.

"But wait!" Tom exclaimed. "With a synchronized flow, and actively implementing system subordination, there is a very high probability that the performance metric of efficiency will deteriorate quickly, at

DBR = Synchronized Patient Flow

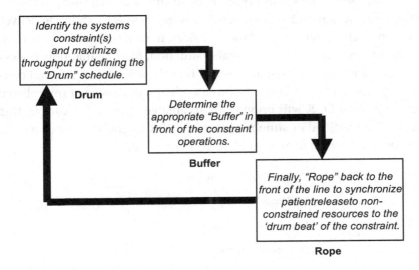

FIGURE 15.1
DBR's steps and flow.

least for some period of time. It will manifest an unacceptable efficiency performance metric that is considered undesirable by many companies. The new mantra will be to 'stop the synchronization nonsense and improve the efficiency.' Be careful what you consider to be nonsense. In this case, the real nonsense is the efficiency metric. When the synchronized flow is implemented, then excess capacity at non-constraints will be quickly exposed, at least for some period of time. Based on the efficiency metrics it will appear that everything is falling apart, and you are headed in the wrong direction. But through time, the new system reality and thinking will expose new evidence about what is actually happening in the system. The new reality is this," Tom explained and loaded a new overhead on the screen (Figure 15.2).

Tom then said, "It's important to remember that constraints can exist in one of two types. The first type is the *internal constraint*, which simply means that the market demand for your services is higher than the capacity of your system to deliver it. Future patients want much more of what you offer then what you can deliver. It's a good situation for your hospitals to be in, but only up to a certain point. If you can't figure out a way to meet patient demand, then your competitors will usually figure out a way to do it for you. This situation is ideal for implementing traditional Drum Buffer Rope to meet the demand and capture more patients."

He continued, "The second type of constraint is an *external constraint*. In this case the demand for your services is less than your ability to deliver it. The market is buying less of your services, in some case much less than you can deliver. This is a less desirable situation, but one that nonetheless can exist. This situation usually means that there is not an internal constraint to contend with. If this is the case, then it is somewhat improbable that traditional DBR will provide an acceptable answer. Instead, in this situation, a modified or simplified form of DBR might be more practical. This form is referred to as Simplified DBR, or S-DBR."

- Throughput rates will increase.

- Lead times through the system will be reduced.

- Work-in-process inventory will go down.

- On-time delivery will improve.

FIGURE 15.2
The new reality from DBR.

"The concept of S-DBR was developed by Bill Dettmer and Eli Schragenheim, and is defined in their book [1] *Manufacturing at Warp Speed*. The S-DBR concept assumes that the constraint is external to your system and resides in the market segment. Customers aren't buying as much of your service that you can deliver, or there is significant variation in market demand, which can cause the constraint to float back and forth between internal to external locations. In this situation, the constraint becomes interactive by moving between the market constraint (external) and the production constraint (internal). This oscillating cycle between internal and external constraints can cause its own brand of chaos in deciding which market segments should be pursued and which ones might be better left alone. Either way it is a decision that must be dealt with," Tom explained.

"In the scenario of an external constraint, the drum is determined and activated only when the system has firm service requests in place. The rope is now determined by the service requests that actually exist, which are released based on service due dates. If the service requests exceed the capacity of the system, then the constraint has become internal and different actions must be taken. This also assumes that the internal constraint will exist only for short periods of time and can be overcome by actions like implementing additional shifts or short-term overtime. Dettmer and Schragenheim have argued, quite successfully, that the market is the true constraint of any system," Tom explained.

"There is another unique situation that can require the implementation of a third type of DBR, known as Multiple-Drum-Buffer-Rope (M-DBR). The situation for M-DBR is created when a single buffer location is required to supply services to more than one treatment center, and each treatment center has its own drum that is keeping pace at a different rhythm," Tom explained as he loaded a new overhead onto his screen (Figure 15.3) which demonstrates an example of an M-DBR configuration.

Tom then said, "Even with all the respectable improvements that can be achieved with a synchronized flow using traditional DBR, S-DBR or even M-DBR, there can also be some problems associated with achievement, especially with traditional DBR. It's not a bad problem, just one you need to be aware of. When you follow Goldratt's Five Focusing Steps, it is possible during Step 2 (the exploitation step) that a constraint can be improved to the point that it is no longer the constraint, and at times this can happen very quickly. When it does happen, you have effectively

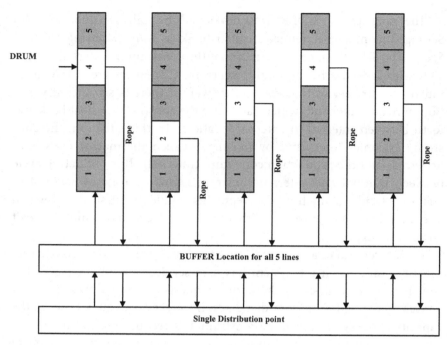

FIGURE 15.3
M-DBR model.

'rolled' the constraint to a new location, which means you only finished Step 2 before it is now time to go back to Step 1 again. The original system process that was considered to be the constraint today is no longer the constraint tomorrow. These types of rapid system improvements can obviously cause some problems."

"When a new constraint is identified in the system, then the system effectively has a new drumbeat. When that happens, you also have to move the buffer location to reside in front of the new constraint, and you have to move the rope signal from this new location back to the release point of patients at the front of the line. In some systems it might be possible to roll the constraint several times to several different locations before an acceptable level of system stability is achieved. This fast action of fixing and rolling the constraint can and will cause a certain amount of chaos in a system. Hospital employees will quickly become confused about 'Where is the constraint today?' Improvements can happen so fast that the negative effects of change will outweigh the positive effects of improvement," Tom explained.

Traditional Drum Buffer Rope

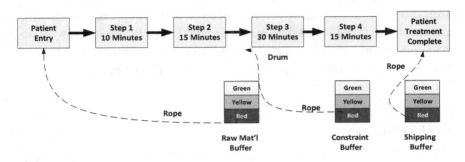

FIGURE 15.4
Traditional Drum Buffer Rope.

"So, in conclusion, I want to show you a simple graphic of traditional Drum Buffer Rope," he said as he loaded a new Power Point slide on his screen (Figure 15.4). "As we progress through our improvement efforts at Maximo Health Center Complex, the use of DBR will have many applications," Tom explained. "I hope today's session has provided you with numerous ideas for the application of DBR," Tom explained and then asked if there were any questions of comments.

Pete Hallwell was the first to respond and said, "Tom, for me I can see numerous potential applications for Drum Buffer Rope within our complex of hospitals. For example, at Maximo Oncology Hospital, where we specialize in cancer treatments, I can see DBR as a way to treat patients at a much faster rate, thus allowing us to serve the public much better. Patricia Smith, from Maximo Surgical Hospital, specializing in surgical operations, was next to speak and said, "I agree with Pete, and I can see us increasing the number of surgical operations, which will have a pronounced impact on revenue and profitability." Tom Jones, from Maximo Children's Hospital, specializing in children's ailments, then said, "At our hospital, using Drum Buffer Rope, I can see us treating many more children using the same resources!" When nobody else had comments, Tom declared this session to be over.

Pete stayed in the conference room, and when everyone had departed, he said to Tom, "Tom, that was an excellent session and I can't wait to get started with our improvement efforts. I realize we have already begun with the development of our Goal Tree, but I'm talking about the actual implementation of the tools and methods you've given us. So, how soon can you come back and get us started?" "I think we should be able to begin serious improvement efforts next week, say Tuesday, if that works for you Pete?" Tom asked. "Sounds great to me Tom, see you then!" Pete exclaimed. "Oh, and one other thing Pete, when we implement Drum Buffer Rope, we'll do it in conjunction with Theory of Constraints' Replenishment Solution to maximize your results," Tom said. "Can't wait," Pete replied.

REFERENCE

1. Bill Dettmer and Eli Schragenheim. 2001. *Manufactruing at Warp Speed*. Boca Raton, FL: St. Lucie Press.

16

Simpson Water Heaters' Goal Tree

Before leaving from Simpson Water Heaters the last time, Tom had instructed Matt to lead an effort for Simpson to create their own Goal Tree. Simpson's team had done that very thing, so Matt decided to call Tom and schedule his next visit. He called Tom, and they set up a meeting for the day after tomorrow.

Tom arrived at Simpson Water Heaters, met Matt in the lobby, and the two of them walked to the conference room. The conference room was full, and Tom could tell by the look on people's faces that they were anxious to begin this session. Tom looked at the projection on the screen, and he could see a completed Goal Tree. Tom noticed that it was very similar to the one he had presented to them when he taught them how to create a Goal Tree, but he decided not to say anything. Matt reintroduced Tom to the group and began explaining the Goal Tree to Tom. "What you see on the screen is our final Goal Tree," Matt said. "The first thing we did was to review our performance metrics," he explained as he loaded an overhead onto the screen (Table 16.1) with Simpson's metrics highlighted.

"As you know Tom, our results have been pathetic and we have been given an ultimatum to 'fix' them rapidly," Matt said. If you look at each metric individually, they are clearly the worst in the entire portfolio of companies. Our % On-Time Delivery is only 68.1%, while our % Scrap and Rework are 8.8% and 15.6%, respectively. Our Stock-Out % is a miserable 19.1%, and our Efficiency % is at 94.7%, which we all know now that this is not a good place to be. And finally, our % Profit Margins are horrific at negative 1.2%. With all of these metrics in mind, we created the Goal Tree that was on the screen when you walked in (Figure 16.1).

"As you can see with most of entities in our Goal Tree, we have addressed our performance metrics in some way. For example, we have set our

TABLE 16.1

Metrics Review

Company Name	% On-Time Delivery	% Scrap	% Rework	Stock-Out %	Efficiency %	% Profit Margins
Tamsen Auto Parts	68.9	4.8	10.1	11.2	95.4	5.7
Simpson Water Heaters	68.1	8.8	15.6	19.1	94.7	−1.2
Watson Rubber Articles	70.9	6.8	8.8	9.9	88.7	7.8
Jackson Electronics	75.4	4.9	14.2	13.4	89.9	9.1

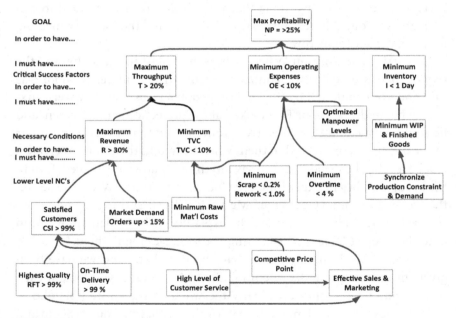

FIGURE 16.1

Simpson Water Heaters, Goal Tree.

targets for scrap at less than 0.2% and our rework at less than 1.0%. We also address our on-time delivery by setting our target at greater than 99%. Our critical success factors are all tied to what we learned about Throughput Accounting, with some of the necessary conditions tied to what you taught us about Theory of Constraints replenishment method and Drum Buffer Rope," Matt explained.

"From my perspective, it looks like you did a very good job, but my concern is that you might have to reduce some of your targets, simply because some of them may be very difficult to achieve," Tom said. "It is our belief that, if we are going to improve our performance metric values, then we had to set targets that were way off from where they are now," Matt replied. "Okay, so your next activity would be to assess how you stand with each of your entities," Tom said. "We have already done that Tom," and Matt loaded another overhead on the screen (Figure 16.2).

"At the base of the Goal Tree, you will see three different shades with each one having a different meaning, in that they are either in place and functioning well, in place, but not functioning well, or either they are not in place or they are but they're not functioning," Matt explained. Tom replied, "Very well done everyone, but if I'm seeing correctly, you only have one that is in place and functioning well?" "Yes, that is correct," Matt replied. "And to make matters worse, we only have three entities that are in place, but not functioning well. The bulk of our entities are

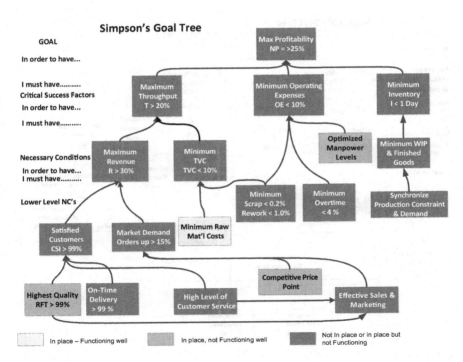

FIGURE 16.2
Assessed Goal Tree.

mostly either not in place or are in place, but are not functioning," Matt added. "It's very clear to me that if your assessment is correct, Simpson has an unbelievable amount of work ahead," Tom replied. "We agree, and here's what we think we need to do," Matt said as he loaded another overhead (Figure 16.3) onto the screen.

Matt began again, "As you can see on this version of our Goal Tree, we have added four different initiatives. One of the first things we intend to do is to use Throughput Accounting to make all of our real time financial decisions, which included eliminating the metric efficiency in our nonconstraint process steps." "That's a good move Matt," Tom said. "We've also decided, based upon your training, that we should implement both Drum Buffer Rope and Theory of Constraints' Replenishment Solution in order to synchronize our production constraint with the customer demand for our products," Matt explained. "That's another really good idea Matt," Tom responded.

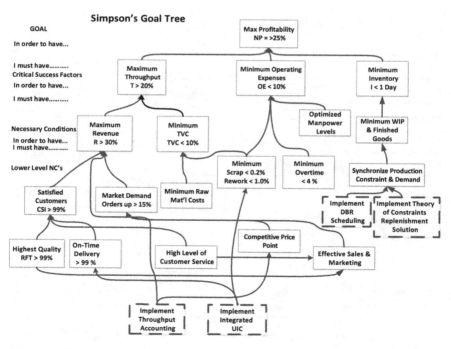

FIGURE 16.3
Goal Tree with improvement initiatives.

"And finally, which I believe is the key to our success is that we intend to implement your Ultimate Improvement Cycle, and it will be one of the first initiatives that we will undertake," Matt added. "Another very good effort Matt," Tom responded. "Have you given any thought to what these initiatives will do to change the status of your Goal Tree?" Tom asked. Matt responded and loaded another figure onto his screen (Figure 16.4).

Matt continued, "We firmly believe that with these four improvement initiatives implemented correctly, we will have an amazing impact on all of our Goat Tree entities. In fact, we believe with just these four improvement initiatives, all of our Goal Tree entities will have the results that you see here on the screen. I know what you're probably thinking, maybe something like, these guys are crazy, but in our hearts, based upon how you explained all of these improvement ideas, we will drive our performance metrics to a level that we had never dreamed were possible." Tom looked in disbelief and simply said, "I do hope you are right, but I must admit, I have never seen improvement predictions that have ever come close to yours!"

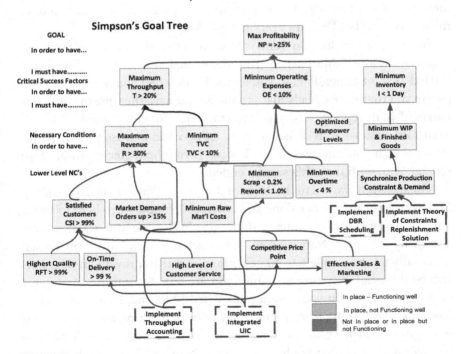

FIGURE 16.4
Future Goal Tree assessment.

TABLE 16.2

Future Performance Metric Predictions

Company Name	% On-Time Delivery	% Scrap	% Rework	Stock-Out %	Efficiency %	% Profit Margins
Tamsen Auto Parts	68.9	4.8	10.1	11.2	95.4	5.7
Simpson Water Heaters	98.5	0.5	1.4	0.5	63,7	20.7
Watson Rubber Articles	70.9	6.8	8.8	9.9	88.7	7.8
Jackson Electronics	75.4	4.9	14.2	13.4	89.9	9.1

"One other thing I want to show you Tom, is our predictions on what we believe will happen to the levels of our performance metrics," Matt added and loaded a new table on his screen (Table 16.2) with the new metrics highlighted. "As you can see Tom, we believe that our performance metrics will reach new and acceptable levels of performance which should make our Board of Directors very happy," Matt explained.

"So, my question for you Tom, is how soon can we get started on these implementations?" Matt asked. Tom responded and said, "I'd like to get started as soon as possible, so you let me know when you're ready." "I can assure you that we are ready just as soon as you have the time to begin our journey," Matt replied. "Okay, let's start today!" Tom exclaimed. "Today?" Matt said somewhat in disbelief. "Yes, let's go and discuss your first initiative which you said was to implement Throughput Accounting," Tom replied. And with that, this session ended.

Tom and Matt walked to the office of the Nancy Watson, the Accounting Manager, knocked on her door and entered. "Nancy, we're here to begin our company transformation," Matt said. "Why are you starting here Tom, why with me?" Nancy asked. Matt responded and said, "The reason is actually a very simple one Nancy. Many of our improvement decisions will be financial in nature and since you are our Accounting Manager, I decided to start with you." Nancy surprised Matt and Tom, and said, "I haven't said anything to you Tom, but I've been working on our accounting system and have already begun making the necessary changes to it." "What kind of changes have you made Nancy?" Tom asked. "I got to thinking about our current accounting system and decided that what we needed was an effective way to judge the potential impact of our operational decisions on profitability. I decided that would include thing like decisions about purchasing, inventory, pricing, staffing, production methods, and a host of other things. I also decided that we also needed a way to monitor the actual daily effect of those decisions using available operations data," Nancy explained.

She continued, "I went to the library to find information about Throughput Accounting and discovered that Throughput Accounting will help leaders evaluate the impact of operational decisions on profitability before they are made. I also discovered that Throughput Accounting will help managers monitor the actual impact of each decision on profitability, so adjustments can be made. The bottom line is that it is simply a way to help managers make the best daily operational decisions in order to achieve improved business performance."

"After our training session, I sat down at my computer and created a simple Throughput Accounting file in Excel in order to analyze the effect of possible decisions on Throughput, ROI and Net Profit, using our existing data. I identified and evaluated several possible operational decisions for return to our positive profitability which included several different ideas. A couple of my ideas were to raise our prices selectively on some items with low Throughput values and also to aggressively resolve delinquent accounts, to quickly generate Throughput," Nancy explained.

Nancy then said, "Perhaps the greatest change was a shift in thinking that affected virtually every aspect of our business. In essence, I shifted away from my normal focus on revenue and cost-cutting and began focusing on the Throughput 'margin' contributed by revenue generation. Needless to say, I am excited about shifting away from Cost Accounting and instead, gaining more insight into all that Throughput Accounting has to offer."

The three of them met for several hours discussing what needed to happen to convert their real-time decision-making to a Throughput Accounting methodology. When they were finished, Tom spoke up and said, "I want to thank you Nancy for the effort you have put forth so far by embracing the concepts of Throughput Accounting. All three of us understand that we must generate reports based on the requirements of GAAP, but for real time decision making, Throughput Accounting is the method of choice." Tom then said, "Nancy, I'd like you to put together a performance metric report, based upon what Simpson has done so far." "I'll get to work on that right away Tom," she replied.

Tom and Matt left Nancy's office and decided to go to the break room to have a cup of coffee and chat about the next steps at Simpson Water Heaters. Tom then asked Matt an important question, "Matt, have you done any training yet on the Theory of Constraints and the Ultimate Improvement Cycle?" Matt replied, "Actually I have held training sessions for my production managers and supervisors on both." "And how was it received Matt?" Tom asked. "Based upon the reaction I received at the end of the training session, I would say it was very well received," Matt replied. "And have you implemented anything yet?" Tom asked. "One of the first things we did was to stop measuring efficiencies in our non-constraints and focused on increasing the efficiency of our constraint operation," Matt replied. "Let me rephrase that Tom. We are still measuring efficiencies in our non-constraints, but the only one we react to is the efficiency of our constraint," Matt added. "What else Matt?" Tom asked.

"I think I told you that prior to me coming to Simpson Water Heaters, the company had tried both Lean and Six Sigma," Matt explained. "Yes, you did tell me that," Tom replied. "Well, we moved our efforts from non-constraints to primarily our constraint operation," Matt explained. "Have you seen any results yet Matt?" Tom asked. "One of the biggest changes we've seen is the drastic reduction in work-in-process inventory along with a major improvement in flow," Matt replied. "We've been doing this for a couple of weeks, and at the end of each week, the flow has improved," he added.

Tom and Matt continued talking and several hours later, Nancy came to Matt's office and said she had the preliminary performance metrics report ready. "Great Nancy! Let's have a look at it," Matt said. Nancy opened her laptop and loaded her Performance Metrics table on her screen (Table 16.3). Nancy began explaining her new table and said, "As you can see, we've had

TABLE 16.3

Simpson's Performance Metrics

Company Name	% On-Time Delivery	% Scrap	% Rework	Stock-Out %	Efficiency %	% Profit Margins
Simpson Water Heaters Before	68.1	8.8	15.6	19.1	94.7	−1.2
Simpson Water Heaters After	75.2	4.8	10.4	13.7	76.3	+4.1

improvements on every metric." The one metric that stood out for Tom was the drop in Efficiency % as it dropped from 94.7% down to 76.3%! For Matt, the most important metric was the change in profit margins which had increased from a negative 1.2% to a positive 4.1%.

Tom then said, "This is a very good start for Simpson Water Heaters, and you've only just begun your improvement effort!" Matt then said, "What I'd like to do next is to implement the Theory of Constraints Replenishment Solution and Drum Buffer Rope. I think that by combining these two together, we'll see a jump in our % On-Time Delivery, a dramatic reduction in our Stock-Out %, and a considerable jump in our % Profit Margins. How soon can we begin these two initiatives Tom?"

Tom responded to Matt's question and said, "Let's try to begin these two initiatives the day after tomorrow?" "Why not tomorrow Tom?" Matt asked. "I have to travel to Chicago to meet with your Board of Directors and give them an update tomorrow," Tom replied. "What do you suggest that I do until then Tom?" Matt asked. "What I would do is assemble your key managers, like Greg Thompson, your Production Manager, Ted Russell, your Purchasing Manager, Cynthia Eberstein, your Quality Manager, plus your production supervisors, and have a review session on the Replenishment Solution," Tom replied. "This will be a big change, especially for Ted, simply because you will no longer be buying parts and materials in bulk anymore," Tom added. "Okay, I'll set that up and I'll see you in a couple of days," Matt replied.

Tom then departed Simpson Water Heaters and drove home. Tom knew he had to put together a summary of the key performance metrics for the Board of Directors to review, so once he arrived home, he began making phone calls to each of the other three portfolio companies. He first called Tamsen Auto Parts and spoke with Bill Johnson, the plant manager. He explained that he needed Bill to put together an update to the six key performance metrics and send it to him. He also called Watson's Rubber Articles and Jackson Electronics, and gave them the same requirement. All three of the plant managers agreed to have the results back to him by the end of the day.

Around 9:00 pm, Tom had received input from all three of the portfolio companies, so Tom decided to create a simple table demonstrating the before and after results for each of the six key performance metrics (Table 16.4).

TABLE 16.4

Before and After Performance Metrics

Company Name	% On-Time Delivery	% Scrap	% Rework	Stock-Out %	Efficiency %	% Profit Margins
Tamsen Auto Parts Before	68.9	4.8	10.1	11.2	95.4	+5.7
Tamsen Auto Parts After	73.1	3.9	8.8	9.0	81.2	+ 9.2
Simpson Water Heaters Before	68.1	8.8	15.6	19.1	94.7	-1.2
Simpson Water Heaters After	75.2	4.8	10.4	13.7	76.3	+4.1
Watson Rubber Articles Before	70.9	6.8	8.8	9.9	88.7	+7.8
Watson Rubber Articles After	82.2	4.1	6.3	5.2	71.1	+10.1
Jackson Electronics Before	75.4	4.9	14.2	13.4	89.9	9.1
Jackson Electronics After	79.9	3.5	9.1	8.2	70.3	+11.6

Tom was happy with the results that he saw with each of the four different companies. Tom was especially happy with the results he saw for Tamsen Auto Parts, Watson Rubber Articles, and Jackson Electronics, simply because most of his efforts with these three companies was via phone and the internet. With the results in place, Tom went to bed.

17

The Board Meeting

Bright and early the next morning, Tom showered, ate breakfast, and drove to the Pittsburgh Airport for his trip to Chicago and his meeting with the Board of Directors. After an uneventful flight to Chicago, Tom picked up his rental car and drove to the Board's headquarters. He checked in with security, and the guard called Jonathan Briggs, the Board Chairman. Jonathan arrived shortly thereafter, and the two of them took the elevator to the conference room. Jonathan introduced Tom to the rest of the Board members, and Jonathan began.

"I want to first thank everyone for inviting me to come to Chicago to give you an update on the four portfolio companies," Tom said. "While I haven't been working with these four companies very long, I think the results you will see shortly are demonstrating improvements to the six key performance metrics we agreed we would track. Much of my time has been spent at Simpson Water Heaters, simply because of their negative profit margins. For the other three companies, most of my efforts have been through telephone calls and internet briefings. As you will see, we have actually seen improvements begins already, even after such a short amount of time," Tom explained, and with that, he loaded his metrics table onto the screen (Table 17.1).

Tom began again, "As I said, much of my time has been spent with Simpson Water Heaters and as you can see, their percent profits have improved from a negative 1.2% to a positive 4.1%. I might add that on my next update, I fully expect that their results will have improved significantly. I say this because the man you hired to run this company, Matt Maloney, was a great hire. He has truly grasped the improvement effort at Simpson Water Heaters, and I am very confident that he will take this company to levels of profitability not seen before."

TABLE 17.1

Before and After Performance Metrics

Company Name	% On-Time Delivery	% Scrap	% Rework	Stock-Out %	Efficiency %	% Profit Margins
Tamsen Auto Parts Before	68.9	4.8	10.1	11.2	95.4	+5.7
Tamsen Auto Parts After	73.1	3.9	8.8	9.0	81.2	+ 9.2
Simpson Water Heaters Before	68.1	8.8	15.6	19.1	94.7	−1.2
Simpson Water Heaters After	75.2	4.8	10.4	13.7	76.3	+4.1
Watson Rubber Articles Before	70.9	6.8	8.8	9.9	88.7	+7.8
Watson Rubber Articles After	82.2	4.1	6.3	5.2	71.1	+10.1
Jackson Electronics Before	75.4	4.9	14.2	13.4	89.9	9.1
Jackson Electronics After	79.9	3.5	9.1	8.2	70.3	+11.6

Jonathan and the other members of the Board of Directors reviewed the results displayed in Tom's table, and Jonathan was the first to comment. "First of all, I am very happy to see that Simpson Water Heaters is no longer losing money," he said. "But I'm equally happy to see that both Watson Rubber Articles and Jackson Electronics are both demonstrating double digit profit margins," he explained. "While I fully expected to see this level of results, I just did not expect to see them so quickly!" He exclaimed. "Well done so far Tom!" He added.

Jonathan then asked Tom what he had already helped these portfolio companies do and Tom responded. "One of the first things I did was to hold a general training session on how to prepare a Goal Tree and then use it to create their own improvement plans," he explained. "As you know, I'm a huge fan of the Goal Tree Tom, so I think that was the right thing to start with," Jonathan said. "Do you happen to have Simpson Water Heater's Goal Tree with you Tom?" Jonathan asked. "I do, would you like to see it?" Tom asked. "Yes, I absolutely would Tom," Jonathan responded. Tom looked through the files on his computer, located the Goal Tree in question, and loaded it (Figure 17.1).

Jonathan and the other Board Members reviewed it, and then, Tom said, "As you can see, they started with the Goal of Maximum Profitability and set their target at greater than twenty-five percent." Jonathan then said, "I see that for their Critical Success Factors they used the three main components of Throughput Accounting, namely, Throughput, Operating Expense, and Inventory." "Yes, they did, and they set their targets for those three at Throughput greater than twenty percent, Operating Expense at less than ten percent, and Inventory at less than a single day," Tom explained. Jonathan then said, "I really like the approach they used and with the lower level Necessary Conditions, it appears as though they have all of the necessary components to achieve their Goal." "Based upon what you know Tom, can you give us an estimate of when you think they will finish implementing whatever it is they're going to implement?" Jonathan asked. Tom responded and said, "Let me show you the next phase of their Goal Tree where they assessed how they were currently doing." And he loaded the assessed Goal Tree (Figure 17.2).

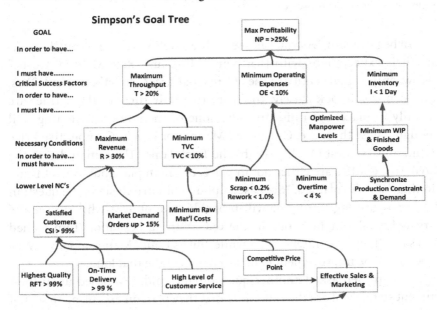

FIGURE 17.1
Simpson Water Heaters' Goal Tree.

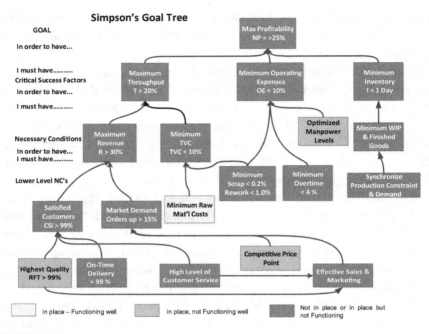

FIGURE 17.2
Simpson Water Heaters' assessed Goal Tree.

Tom began again, "As you can see, only a single Goal Tree entity is meeting their expectations with that being Minimum Raw Material Costs." "Wow, only a single entity in the entire Goal Tree?" Jonathan asked. "Yes, and then if you look closely, you'll see that only three of the entities are actually in place, but unfortunately, none of them are functioning well enough. These three are, Optimized Manpower Levels, Competitive Price Point, and Highest Quality, Right the First Time. The remainder of the Goal Tree entities are either not in place, or are in place but are not functioning," Tom explained. "So, based upon their current state, the question I asked regarding timing, it will probably take quite a while to see the targeted results, right?" Jonathan asked. Without hesitation Tom replied and said, "It will definitely take a while, but as I said, Matt Maloney is very much into the improvement effort, so it won't take that long."

Jonathan then asked another question and said, "So based upon their current state, what are the initiatives that they plan on executing to sort of 'right the ship' as they say?" Tom then loaded another figure (Figure 17.3) on his screen and said, "Here is what they plan on doing going forward.

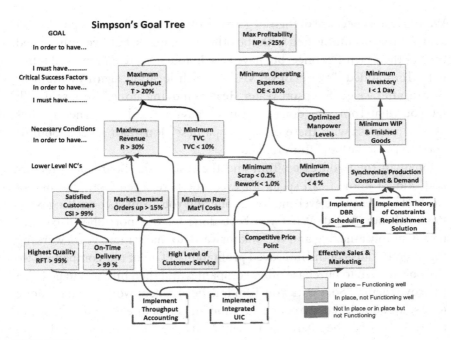

FIGURE 17.3
Simpson's Goal Tree with improvements.

You'll also notice that they have also included an assessment of their future state after implementing their improvement initiatives," Tom added.

Tom began again, "As you can see, there are four major initiatives they want to initiate, which are the implementation of Throughput Accounting, the implementation of my integrated Ultimate Improvement Cycle, and the joint implementation of Drum Buffer Rope and the Theory of Constraints Replenishment Solution. And the amazing part of their assessment is that they firmly believe that after they have implemented these four initiatives, they will meet each and every target value they have set." "Do you believe that's possible Tom?" Jonathan asked. "Normally, I would not, but after having worked with Matt and his team, I do believe that they will," Tom replied. "So again, I ask, how long do you think this effort will take?" Jonathan asked. "With all of the enthusiasm I have seen at Simpson Water Heaters, I believe they will be completed in about three months," Tom explained.

"What about the other three portfolio companies?" Jonathan asked. "I have conducted some training for them, but I wanted to start with Simpson

Water Heaters because of their negative profit margins," Tom replied. "As I said, I have communicated with the other companies, but I've only visited each of their facilities once, but have kept in touch via telephone and internet," Tom added. "We plan on visiting each location again in the near future, after we get Simpson Water Heaters moving along," Tom said. "I'll tell you what Tom, why don't we plan on having regular internet updates as you progress with these other companies?" Jonathan asked. "Sounds good to me Jonathan," Tom replied.

Jonathan then addressed Tom and the rest of the Board of Directors and said, "I know I can speak for everyone here when I say that one of the best moves we've ever made was offering you, Tom, a consulting position with our Board. What you have done for our portfolio of companies is simply amazing and we look forward, to many more years working together. Because of the improved profitability of all of our companies, we the Board, plan to purchase other companies and then hire you to go in an improve them." "So, thank you Tom for the excellent work you have done for us," he added. "I do have one question for you before we end our session today. Would you be interested in helping us select the companies that we plan on purchasing?" Jonathan asked. Tom immediately responded and said, "I absolutely would be honored to help with your selection process."

"The way I'm seeing this consulting offer is that we would have you go into the company first and assess it for possibilities for improvement, and then report back to us with your recommendation on whether or not to purchase it," Jonathan explained. "That's a very interesting scenario Jonathan, but I'd like some time to ponder your offer," Tom replied. "In terms of how you would be paid, we'll leave that up to you," Jonathan added. "Are there any restrictions on how I would be paid Jonathan?" Tom asked. "Well, it must be a reasonable method for payment is all I can say. So, think about it and let me know what you decide," Jonathan replied. "Okay Jonathan, I'll get back to you later on this week," Tom responded.

Tom packed up his computer and headed for the airport for his return flight home to Pittsburgh. As he was driving to the airport, he kept thinking about the offer Jonathan had made to him. He thought to himself, "Should I just bill by the hour or should I consider a completely new way of billing for my work?" He then asked himself, "How would Kevin O'Leary from Shark Tank, go about billing them? I don't think this would fit into a royalty scenario." he said to himself. He arrived at the airport, checked in, and boarded the airplane. He sat in first class again and closed his eyes, still thinking about the best way to bill the Board for this kind of work.

18

Maximo's Improvement Effort

On schedule, Tom arrived at Maximo's Corporate Office where he was scheduled to deliver his sessions on Drum Buffer Rope and the Theory of Constraints Replenishment Solution. He checked in through security, and the guard contacted Pete Hallwell to let him know that Tom was in the lobby. Shortly thereafter Pete arrived and the two of them took the elevator to the seventh-floor conference room. Since Tom had arrived a bit early, nobody was in the conference room yet. Pete then asked Tom, "So Tom, how do you plan on delivering your material today?" Tom responded and said, "My first order of business will be to reacquaint everyone with the concept of a system constraint, then Goldratt's Five Focusing Steps, and then we will discuss Drum Buffer Rope as it applies to a hospital setting. I know we presented DBR before, but I want to key-in on the variety known as Multiple Drum Buffer Rope or M-DBR."

Tom continued, "One thing I want to discuss, somewhat in depth, is the problem of hospital wait times. Every time either myself or someone in my family has been a patient in a hospital, the wait times have been excessive." "That's a fair statement Tom, wait times for most hospitals are clearly excessive," Pete replied. "This is especially a problem in hospital Emergency Departments, so I'd like to begin there, if that's ok with you Pete?" Tom asked. "That's fine with me Tom," Pete replied.

Once everyone was seated, Tom began the session with his water piping diagram so that the team would again see the relevance of why it was so important to identify the constraint and determine the flow of patients. He then walked them through his simple four-step process and presented Goldratt's Five Focusing Steps. He did this just to reacquaint everyone with what they had heard in past sessions. Tom also presented the concept of policy constraints and their potentially devastating effects. When he felt sure that the team understood why it was so important to find both the physical constraint and potential policy constraints, he suggested that they go on their 2-hour Gemba walk at Maximo Emergency Hospital, which specialized in emergency patients. Before they left, Tom instructed them to not get too far into the weeds with their analysis, but rather to identify the most notable steps in the process.

Tom also defined the starting point to be either patient arrival by ambulance or the patient walks in by themselves and the end point to be one of three choices.

- The patient is treated and discharged to go home.
- The patient is admitted to the hospital.
- The patient is transferred to another hospital.

The team left with a new level of enthusiasm and ready to go. They stayed in the Emergency Department (ED) for the entire 2 hours, and when they returned, they had actually created a simple process flow map of what they had observed. One of the team members downloaded the image onto Tom's laptop for viewing on the screen by everyone. The team seemed to be very proud of what they had accomplished. Tom addressed the team and asked, "So, have you identified the system constraint within this process?"

One of the team members said, "We haven't timed every step yet, but we think we all know where the constraint is. We're pretty sure it's the emergency room physicians since we only have three of them," she added. "So, you're telling me that if you can reduce the time waiting for an ED Physician, then you will reduce the wait times?" Tom asked pointing to the slide on the screen (Figure 18.1).

The group indicated that they were sure of it, but Tom kept pushing the subject. "I can tell you this, when my wife and I visited the ED not so long ago, I saw many patients waiting on gurneys and all of the ED patient rooms were full. In fact, we actually were able to see a physician relatively quickly. So, if that's true, then why do you think the constraint is the ED physicians?" Tom asked the group. One of the audience members raised their hand in the back of the room and Tom acknowledged "Mr. Mahanan, the reason so many people in the ED are on gurneys is because sometimes they're waiting for a room to be ready in the hospital," he explained. "We also have to wait for test results so that we can get the right diagnosis for treatment," he added.

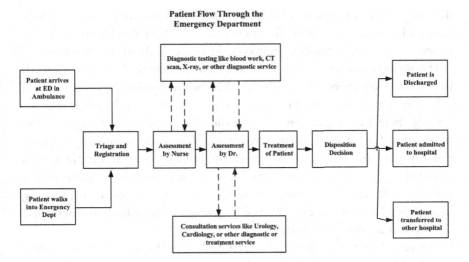

FIGURE 18.1
Patient flow through the ED.

"So, is it possible that the primary reason, or the constraint for the ED, actually lies outside of the ED completely?" Tom asked. "In the ED, you just see the effect, but the cause is someplace else? Can anyone tell me why the patients have to wait so long for a room?" asked Tom. "One reason is that the hospital has a policy that all discharges must be completed before noon or the patient stays until the following day," Pete said. "So, what I'm hearing you say is that we might be up against a policy constraint?" Tom asked. "What would happen to bed availability if this policy didn't exist?" Tom asked.

Tim Bodley, an ED nurse, responded immediately and said, "Holy smokes ... the number of patients waiting for a room would decrease considerably! Are you really saying that it's possible that our ED wait times could be controlled by our hospital's discharge policy?" he asked. Tom responded and said, "I don't want to jump to any conclusions just yet, but yes, it might be entirely possible. I think this team needs to go check out the hospital's discharge process and see what you can find," he said, and the team left the room to find an answer to Tom's point.

The team decided to divide into teams so they could review multiple nursing units and then went to each unit to determine both the steps required to discharge a patient and to determine if there were any policies in place that would have a negative impact on the time it took to discharge patients. The team returned shortly thereafter anxious to talk about what they had found. Tom explained that they needed to invite the supervisory team to the conference room to speak about their findings.

The supervisors were invited for a review of their findings and were all in place shortly, thereafter, anxious to hear what the team had found. Tom asked for someone from the team to speak about what they had learned during their ED inspection. Tim Bodley volunteered and began, "The most important thing I learned today was that if you want to speed up a process, you must first find the constraint, but the constraint is not always something physical. We also learned that the other important thing is that the constraint might not always be in the immediate process you're trying to improve." Tim then reviewed the information the team had discovered during this session with Tom.

The remaining team members each had something to say about what they had learned during their session and told the supervisors that they were sure they will be able to improve the flow through the ED going forward. Tom thanked them for all of their hard work and told them to be back in the morning at 7:00. Everyone packed up their materials and left for the day.

When everyone else was gone, Pete approached Tom and said, "Tom that was the single best session I have ever been associated with in my life!" "I've never seen a team so engaged," he added. "The questions you asked were right on the money and they stimulated thought for the entire team," said Pete. "What I really like is that you don't provide answers to questions … you let the team come up with their own answers. And if the answer isn't quite right, you have a way of asking another question until they do get it right," he said.

"Thanks Pete, but improvement is all about using basic common sense, logic, and discovery. It was clear to me that the wait time problems were not all associated with what's going on in the ED," said Tom. "I think what we'll hear tomorrow will be very enlightening to say the least," he added. "I need to leave now because I've got a conference call with two of my colleagues, so I'll see you in the morning Pete around 7:00," Tom said. "OK Tom, I'll see you in the morning and thanks for a very enjoyable day. I learned so much today about how to effectively lead a team," said Pete.

On the way home, Tom thought about what had happened with this team and what he thought they might present to him in the morning. He thought, "If I can just get them to think holistically, from a system's perspective, they can solve their patient wait times in the ED." When he arrived home, he was met with a kiss from his wife Beverly, eager to hear what he had found at the hospital. Tom explained all that had taken place that day and then they sat down and ate dinner.

"So, how did it go today honey?" asked Tom's wife. "It went very well, once we were able to get the right team in place," said Tom. "It never ceases to amaze me how the leadership of most organizations fails to recognize who the true subject matter experts really are," he continued. "If leadership would only realize that the frontline employees, who live and breathe every day in the system, are the people who know best how to solve the problems, it would be so much easier. If they would only seek input, and truly listen to what they have to say, and then turn them loose to solve the problems, things would be so much better and easier. And Beverly, it doesn't matter what industry it is or how intelligent leadership is, they all miss this important point," Tom said.

The next morning, Tom arrived at Maximo Emergency Hospital around 6:30 and headed to the conference room to prepare for the day. To his surprise, several members of the team were already seated and seemed to be anxious to start the day's activities. By 6:45 am, all of the team members were seated. Tom began the day's session by asking for volunteers to review their findings from yesterday. "So, who wants to tell me what they found yesterday?" asked Tom. Five team members raised their hands, but Tom decided to pick a team member who had been virtually silent the day before. "Why don't we start with you," said Tom pointing to one of the five who had raised their hands.

"Good morning Tom, my name is Jeff Thompson and I'm an ED technician. I want to first say that I don't normally say much when I'm on a team, but today will be different. What I learned yesterday forced me to think differently, and for the first time ever, I am convinced that we can solve the problem of extended wait times in the ED. We all went to the various nursing units around the hospital and we even created a basic process map of the discharge process, which I might add, is full of waste. But the most significant thing we found was the hospital's policy of only completing discharges before noon," he explained.

"And why do you think that is so significant Jeff?" asked Tom. "Because for the afternoon and early evening, no beds can be freed up for new patients!" he said emotionally. "A typical day in our hospital, in terms of when patients actually need an inpatient bed, starts to occur in the early afternoon simply because the morning's surgical cases are finishing up. Plus, the ED is starting to heat up and our various clinics are feeding us patients that might need to be admitted. In all of these cases, everybody needs a bed in an in-house unit," he explained. "So, Jeff, what are you recommending in order to fix this problem?" Tom asked even though he already knew the answer.

Jeff replied, "We need to radically change our discharge policy and then work to remove the waste that exists within it." "So, if you were to implement something, what might this new policy look like?" asked Tom. "To begin with, I would eliminate using a set block of hours that the units have to complete their discharges," he said. "I asked everyone on the various nursing units why they are limited to discharging patients by noon and everyone told me the same thing, 'it's hospital policy,'" he added. "So, Jeff, why do you think the hospital has this policy?" Tom asked. "Because we're stupid!" came a voice from the back of the room and everyone laughed.

With a smile on his face, Tom said, "I don't think it's stupidity. I think it's more the lack of systems thinking. By that I mean, if whoever came up with this policy had been using systems thinking, then they would have realized that it was not a patient-centered policy," he added. "OK, let's assume for a minute that this discharge time policy did not exist, where would the constraint be then?" asked Tom and again several hands went up. "Yes?" said Tom, pointing to one of the women sitting at the end of the table.

"My name is Sally Jones and I'm a nurse in the Emergency Department. I think we don't have enough information to say for sure where the constraint would be," she said. "I think we would need to do extended time studies to determine how long each step in the process takes," she added. "Sally, doing time studies will take a considerable amount of time, so can you think of a different way we might be able to find the constraint?" Tom asked. Sally replied immediately and said, "I'm thinking we could become a patient ourselves and actually walk through the process. I don't mean we would actually be a patient, but we could each attach ourselves to a patient and see where they get hung up," she added.

"Sally, I think that is a great idea," said Tom as everyone else nodded their heads in agreement. "So, why doesn't everyone follow Sally's direction, pick an ED patient, and glue yourself to them," said Tom. "I don't mean that you should be intrusive, just follow their progress," Tom explained. "But before we do that, what did anyone else find yesterday?"

Tom asked. "I too found that the hospital's policy of limiting the time for discharge has a negative effect on bed availability, but I think we have to be careful not to discharge some patients, especially elderly ones, too late in the day," said Jeff. "I say this because some patients might have other problems, such as their nighttime vision being impaired or maybe, if it was in the middle of the night, there may not be buses running and cabs are expensive," he added.

Tom was very impressed with the level of sensitivity that Jeff had expressed, related to patients, and he liked that. Jeff was truly embracing the philosophy of patient-centered care and that was a good thing in Tom's mind. The remaining members of the team presented their findings, and then, Tom dismissed them to go become "a patient" as Sally had suggested. The team left the room and headed for the ED to learn firsthand why the patient wait times were so long. Tom thought more about Sally's recommendation and smiled. "She's a very logical person and seems to have the patient's well-being at the forefront," he thought. The team was gone for approximately 2 hours, and a few members started trickling back into the conference room. When they were all seated, Tom asked them what they had uncovered.

As Tom expected, Sally was the first to respond. "Mr. Mahanan, I followed two patients and both of them were supposed to be admitted to the hospital, but because there were no rooms available, they had to wait on gurneys in the ED," she explained. "I left both of my patients and went to the unit they were expected to be admitted to, to see if I could find the reason there were no beds available," she continued. "In one case, the admittance order had been written, but they were waiting for housekeeping to clean the room before the patient could be officially admitted," she added.

"How long had this patient been waiting and why was it taking so long to get the room cleaned?" asked Tom. "This particular patient was an older woman and she had been waiting for over 3 hours. I was told that the hospital needed to cut costs, so they had recently laid off some of the housekeeping staff. It seems that the remaining housekeeping staff is now supposed to focus on cleaning the surgical areas and the ED first and then patient rooms," she added. "And when housekeeping does come to clean the room, it's only one person doing it. It seems to me that if they had two people doing the cleaning, they could cut the time in half, maybe more. As far as the other patient goes, he was an elderly man who had been waiting for 2 hours," Sally explained. "The other reason the unit gave me was that the discharge paperwork for several patients didn't arrive until after the noon deadline, so the patients had to stay one additional day," she explained.

As Sally explained what she had found, some of the others were nodding their heads in agreement indicating that they had found similar things. Tom was not surprised at what they had found and thought it might be a good time to introduce the team to a different type of constraint. "What Sally found, regarding the layoff of the housekeeping staff, is a classic example of something I refer to as a 'dummy constraint,'" Tom explained. "Think about just how much one of the housekeepers would cost the hospital and compare that to the financial impact of the lost revenue," he explained. "What you're witnessing is the negative impact of Cost Accounting, whereby the key to profitability is thought to be achieved through cost cutting," he continued.

Sally raised her hand and said, "Mr. Mahanan, I think I understand what you are saying. If we hadn't cut the housekeeping staff like we did, and if we didn't have the current discharge policy, then we could process, discharge, and admit more patients at a faster rate. And if we could process more patients, then we could have more cash entering the hospital," she continued. "So, I think that what you're saying is that the cost savings of these so-called dummy constraints pale in comparison to the potential gain in new revenue. Is that right Mr. Mahanan?" she asked. "And, the discharge policy change shouldn't cost anything," she added.

"Yes, Sally, that is exactly what I am saying. In fact, by adding back some of the laid-off housekeeping staff, then setting up the team approach to cleaning the rooms, which you described, and by changing the discharge policy, where do you think the constraint would be located?" asked Tom. At the far end of the conference room table, Jeff raised his hand and said, "I'm pretty certain that, if we were to remove the current constraint, then the next constraint would be the physicians in the ED."

Pete interrupted and said, "I get now why in your training you recommend identifying the current and next constraint … it makes perfect sense!" Sally said, "So how do we go about addressing these two problems so that we can make more beds available?" "Great question Sally," said Tom. "My suggestion is simple. What if we were able to collect some data on how many patients were affected by the extended wait times as a result of the housekeeping and discharge policy? We could then compare the number and frequency of available beds and the financial impact this might have. We can present the analysis at our afternoon report-out?" said Tom.

Jeff was the first to speak and said, "I'm not sure we can do all of that by our afternoon report-out. What if we just presented the concept to them? After all, you did present Throughput Accounting to them and from what I saw, it was received very well," he added. "Maybe Terry's right, let's go collect the data and hold the calculations until tomorrow," Tom replied. "Go see what kind of data are available and be back here by 3:30 so we can put together some talking points," he added. The team split up, with part of them going to the ED to record patient wait times and the other half going to the nursing units to see how many patient discharges were delayed because of the discharge policy.

At 3:30 pm, the entire team returned, and they were obviously anxious to report their findings. Once again, Tom asked who wanted to give their report, and once again, Sally was the first to speak. "My team visited all of the hospital nursing units and found that 15 patients couldn't be discharged because of the discharge policy," said Sally. "In addition, there were 5 patients that were discharged in violation of the policy," she added. "Thank you Sally. How about the team that went to the ED, what did your team find out?" Tom asked.

Jeff spoke up and explained, "We found four patients that had been in the ED for more than 4 hours, three patients that had been there for between 3 and 4 hours, and two patients that had been there between 2 and 3 hours. And, I might add, this was not a super busy day in the ED," he added. Tom listened intently to what the teams had to say and then asked, "But how many people in the ED experienced delayed admittance because they were waiting for a bed?" Jeff replied, "On the basis of the information we gathered, we found that three of the 4-hour patients and two of the 3-hour patients were told by the ED nurses that they would be admitted when an in-house bed became available." Just as they finished their team reports, members of the supervisory team began entering the conference room for the afternoon team report-out.

When they were all seated, Tom asked for a volunteer to summarize what they had learned today. Jeff jumped up and began relating the team's experience saying, "Today was such an eye-opener for us as a team. We collected some very interesting and important data relating to patient wait times and discovered that one of the biggest causes of extended wait times in the ED was actually our discharge policy. It seems as though the policy states that all discharges in the nursing units must be completed before noon, each day. If it's not done by then, the patient must remain for another day and occupy the bed. Not meeting this time requirement is causing extended wait times for ED patients," he added.

One of the ED doctors, Dr. Samuels, was very interested in this comment and wanted to hear more about the data they had collected. The team presented the minimal data they had collected earlier, and after much discussion, Dr. Samuels said, "So, what you are telling us is that, if we change our discharge policy, then our ED patient wait times should decrease?" "That's exactly what we're telling you Dr. Samuels," Jeff replied. "We only have one day's worth of data, but we're confident that by extending, or removing, the discharge time to later in the afternoon, we should be able to reduce the wait time," he added. "I've been thinking about this and I think it will also positively affect our metric, Patient Left without Being Seen," he said.

Sally stood up and said, "There's something else we discovered yesterday and today and that is, on many occasions, one of the reasons why patient rooms are delayed from being ready is that housekeeping takes too long cleaning the rooms. Because of the recent layoffs, there simply are not enough housekeeping employees to clean the necessary rooms, quickly," she added. "Are you suggesting that we rehire these employees?" asked Dr. Samuels. "Remember, Sally, these people cost us money. By being able to decrease the Operating Expense, we hoped to improve our profitability," he added.

"Yes, we know why you took this cost-cutting action, but if you consider the impact on the system, in terms of having rooms available to admit patients, and reduce ED wait times, we think it's a decision that should be reconsidered," said Sally. "As we've learned, there is a better way to improve profitability and that is to increase the amount of new revenue entering the system," she added. "Does anyone else have something they'd like to add?" asked Tom. When nobody else raised their hands, Tom said, "How about the executives … any comments?" he asked.

Dr. Samuels stood up and said, "I think we have a lot of new things to consider and we did promise to consider all recommendations as long as they didn't violate our policies or safety. I do think that at our next executive staff meeting, this Thursday, we need to discuss both of these recommendations and the potential positive impact they could have on revenue.

I feel confident that both of them can be implemented," he added, which brought a smile to the team members' faces.

"Dr. Samuels, did you say you would consider all recommendations from this team?" asked Tom with a piercing look on his face. "My apologies, we'll do more than just consider them; we'll implement them if they don't violate safety or any other healthcare regulations," said Dr. Samuels. Tom just smiled and thanked everyone for their efforts. He then told the team to be back at 7:00 in the morning to begin looking at the new constraint in the ED. He excused everyone for the day, and everyone except Pete left.

"Tom, I truly do think that the executive team will implement what this ED team has recommended. My question for you is, what do you see us doing in the ED to improve the flow of patients?" he asked. "Tomorrow, as we had originally planned to do, we're going to talk about a new ED scheduling system, Drum Buffer Rope and based upon what we heard today, I have a new idea about how we might go about rolling out," said Tom. "What's your new idea?" Pete asked. "You'll hear all about it tomorrow, so be here bright and early tomorrow morning," said Tom. "Tomorrow could be a very interesting day," he added.

19

Drum Buffer Rope at Maximo

As usual, Tom arrived at the hospital early to begin preparing for the improvement team's new focus: wait times. As he was waiting for the team, he heard the conference room door open as several members of the team had arrived early. Tom walked over, shook everyone's hand, and welcomed them. By 7:00, the team was assembled and ready to begin. Just before Tom was ready to begin, there was a knock on the door and Dr. Samuels walked in. From the back of the room, "Tom, do you mind if I say a few words before you begin?" Dr. Samuels asked.

"No, by all means, take as much time as you need," Tom replied. "Good morning everyone. I wanted to let you know that yesterday the executive team had a meeting to discuss your proposed recommendations. I'm pleased to inform you that the executive team has decided to implement both of your recommendations. They have decided to rework and update the discharge policy and will contact the previous housekeeping employees to see if they are interested in returning. If they aren't available, or they decline, HR will post the jobs and find new candidates," Dr. Samuels said. There were some claps and cheers in the room.

Dr. Samuels continued, "When the executive team met, we talked about why the current discharge policy was written the way it was, and no one could make a strong case for keeping it the way it is. We also considered what Sally had recommended about doubling up on cleaning rooms and it made good sense. I just want to say thank you, to all of you, for all your hard work and the executive team is looking forward to hearing, and reviewing, any new recommendations you might come up with." Everyone was smiling and patting each other on the back. "One other thing, since these were this team's ideas, we would like you to review what we think we need to do before we actually implement any new policies or procedures," said Dr. Samuels. "Are there any questions?" Dr. Samuels asked. No hands went up, so he thanked Tom for the time and left the room.

Sally was the first to comment and said, "I don't know about anyone else, but for me, having the executive team not only accept our recommendations, but also asking us to bless what they put together means that they are listening and accepting what we have to say as important. The fact that they even considered our ideas is a marked change from the past," Sally added. The other team members were nodding their heads in agreement. No one else spoke, so Tom began.

"Today, I want to introduce you to a scheduling concept known as Drum Buffer Rope, or DBR for short," Tom said. "Although DBR was first introduced for application in manufacturing plants, in recent years, other industries have begun incorporating it as well. The basic premise behind DBR is really quite simple, but mostly just logical. And although thinking logically is nothing new, it is simply not the way most people think. The fundamental concept of DBR is to focus on the system as a whole, rather than only a single segment of the system, at least until you have clearly identified the constraint," Tom explained. "And, from what you believe so far, you think the new constraint is the ED physicians?" he stated, scanning the team for concurrence.

Tom continued, "When viewing a system through the eyes of DBR, it becomes quickly apparent that improving every process in the system is not required, nor will the sum total of all of those discrete process improvements equal an improved overall system. When conducting a systems analysis, with the intent of implementing DBR, an important consideration is to know and understand the location of the system constraint, or the slowest operation. In Goldratt's Five Focusing Steps, this is Step 1— Find the constraint! Once you know where the constraint resides, you now have the information necessary to know where to focus your improvement attention," he explained. "In essence, when you look at a system, the entire system can only produce at a rate that is equal to, or less than, the output of the constraint," he added. "What if we're not right about the physicians being the constraint?" asked Jeff.

"I promise you Jeff, if you haven't identified the correct constraint, it will rear its ugly head and let you know where it really is," Tom explained. "So, with the constraint process properly identified, you have effectively isolated the 'drumbeat' of the system and knowing the location of that drumbeat is the first step for implementing DBR. Knowing this location is mandatory!" Tom added, emphasizing this point. "The second consideration is that you must make sure the constraint is busy all the time, not just part of the time," Tom explained. "Why is it so important to have the constraint busy all of the time?" asked Sally.

"Sally, why don't you try to answer that question before I give you my answer," Tom said. Sally thought for a moment and then said, "On the basis of what you've taught us about Theory of Constraints, I would say that any time lost at the constraint is time lost forever; you can't make up that time. If the constraint stops or slows down, then the entire system will stop or slow down," Sally answered. "That is exactly right Sally!" said Tom emphatically. "It's the single point in the system where efficiency really matters." Sally raised her hand again. "So, I guess that the best way to accomplish this is to make sure work is always waiting in front of the constraint?" Sally asked. "Yes!" Tom answered. "In other words, we should create something like a buffer of patients in front of our constraint?" she said in a question-like response.

Tom smiled and said, "Sally, you are correct about the buffer of patients in front of the constraint, but only if you have the right constraint." He loaded a new slide on his screen (Figure 19.1) to be used for his talking points. "I say this because the total system output is not the sum output from each process, but rather only the output from the constraint. In fact, the system constraint not only determines the amount of throughput you can achieve, but it also determines the correct number of patients that can be in the system at any single point in time. The correct number of patients will be reached when patient output is equal to patient input and system subordination is actively pursued and implemented," Tom explained.

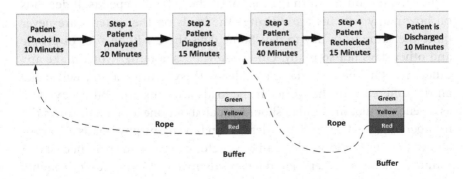

FIGURE 19.1
Traditional Drum Buffer Rope.

"Tom, you have explained the drum and the buffer, but what the heck is this rope that you mentioned earlier?" asked Jeff. "The rope is actually a communication mechanism that controls two different functions," Tom replied. "Can anyone tell me what those two functions might be?" he asked. Jeff raised his hand and said, "First, I would think one of the functions is that the rope determines how many and when to release patients into the system?" Jeff responded in the form of a question.

Tom explained. "In the ED, the most common practice is to tie an artificial 'rope' from the ED physician back to the entry point for patients. When the constraint completes treatment of a patient, the patient is passed on to the next operation, which is either the patient is released to go home, or the patient is admitted to the hospital, or perhaps admitted to another hospital. When one of those three things happens, the signal from the rope is to release another patient into the constraint buffer," Tom explained. "What we're trying to achieve is synchronized patient flow and a smooth transition of patients through the system," Tom explained. "What's the second function of the rope?" asked Jeff.

"The second function of the rope is to make sure that subordination happens at all of the other steps in the process," said Tom. "With active subordination, the non-constraints can only work on what has been released into the system," Tom added. "So, even though the non-constraints can do more work, they are restricted from doing more by the act of subordination and only allowed to work on the patients required to keep the constraint busy?" Jeff asked. "Yes, no more and no less," said Tom. "Tom, I have a question," Sally said. "How do we know how large the patient buffers should be?"

"Great question, Sally. In the case of the hospital, it depends. It depends on how many patients are waiting. The loads on the systems are never quite the same from day to day. Some days there will be a lot of people and other days not so many. On the slow days, a buffer won't make any difference. On the busy days, a buffer with synchronization, will make all the difference in the world. If the loads are constant and heavy, then as a general rule, the buffers should equal about one and a half times the number of patients. It will also depend on how many physicians are available in the ED. For example, if an ED doctor can treat one patient every 15 minutes, then the buffer should be approximately 45 minutes, or roughly three patients. You may decide in time, that the buffer is too large or too small, so you can adjust it either up or down depending on what you've learned from the system and your need," Tom explained.

"Tom, I have another question about our situation here in the ED," said Sally. "Since we have more than one doctor in the ER, does that mean we have more than one constraint?" she asked. "I mean if the ED physicians are the next constraint, does that mean we will have more than one drum?" Sally added as a question.

"Yes, you do Sally and another great observation! You have a situation of multiple drums!" Tom exclaimed. "What Sally has just described is something that I have been thinking about for quite a while. This concept is relatively new, and I refer to it as Multiple Drum–Buffer–Rope, or M-DBR," he explained. "This is a point of separation between traditional DBR and M-DBR. Traditional DBR is based on the fact that the output from a constraint is very predictable. As an example, in a typical manufacturing environment, the constraint usually has a cadence or rhythm that is very predictable and steady, for instance, a constraint machine that is able to produce a part every 7 minutes, or whatever the time may be. Knowing the constraint time allows you to be relatively accurate in establishing a buffer. In other words, there is a constant, but predictable normal variation at the constraint. However, in your situation at the hospital, the constraint time can vary significantly. Each time a patient enters your constraint, there can be a lot of uncertainty for when the patient will finish, depending on what needs to be done. You don't know what patient is coming in with what problem and the ED physician's time can vary greatly form one patient to the next," Tom explained. "Under those kinds of circumstances, it's very difficult, if not impossible, to establish any kind of an accurate buffer."

"Back to Sally's question about having more than one drum," Tom continued. "If the ED physicians are truly the constraint, then how do we manage to keep them fully occupied to reduce wait times?" Tom asked rhetorically.

"It seems to me that we would need to know the real-time status of each constraint," Sally responded. "What I mean by that is, if we knew how much longer each physician believed they had with their current patient, then we could check and see which patient is next and get them ready."

"That's a good possible answer," Tom said. "And, if we already have a buffer in place, then we should know which patient is next. But let's go back and think for a moment about how you establish the buffer," Tom said as he loaded a new overhead on his screen (Figure 19.2). Remember, M-DBR will be different from traditional DBR, mostly because of the uncertainty involved," Tom explained. "Typically, when a patient comes into the ED, you perform a triage to determine severity, or urgency of the situation, is that correct?" Tom asked. "As best we can, that is what we do," Sally said. "What happens during the triage activity?" Tom asked.

"Well, we evaluate the patient and determine a level of urgency. Something like a broken leg would take precedence over a stomach-ache," Sally said. "And that by itself can cause some problems for people already in the waiting room. For example, a less severe patient, who has already been through triage, might end up waiting even longer if two or three more patients show up with a higher priority. For those people, the wait time can be very frustrating! Some people don't seem to mind if it happens once, but when it gets up to two or three times, it starts to wear on their nerves a bit," Sally explained. "It can happen that a patient, who has

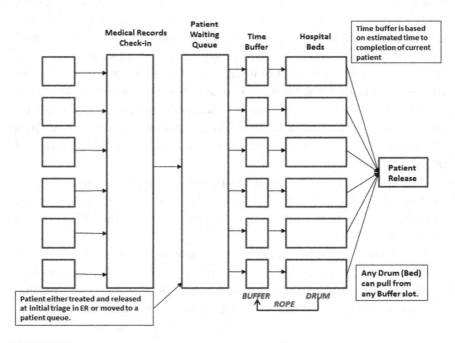

FIGURE 19.2
Graphic of M-DBR.

already been waiting for a long time, might keep getting pushed back because a more urgent case comes in," she explained.

Tom thought for a moment and asked Sally and the team, "What if we had a system that would allow the lower-priority patients to get through faster?" "I'm not sure how you might do that because everyone is waiting to see a doctor and they have to wait their turn," Sally said. "Remember," Tom said addressing the group, "if you reduce wait time, you can also increase the hospital revenue." Sally looked confused and said, "Honestly, I could care less about hospital revenue. I care much more about good patient care." "I couldn't agree more," Tom said. "But what if there was a way to do both?" he asked. "I still can't see how you're going to do that," Sally said. "Everyone still has to see a doctor," she added. "Exactly, and everyone will see a doctor," Tom said with a smile looking directly at Sally.

"Well, I guess you're right; everyone will see a doctor if they wait long enough," Sally said. "But, waiting a long time to see the doctor is the opposite effect that we want," said Sally. "How do you plan on making it faster?" she asked. "Again, you are correct, at least if you keep doing the same things you are doing now," Tom said. "What do you mean?" Sally asked. "Right now, you have everyone on the same priority list, based on a triage ranking, and essentially everyone is in the same buffer location, the waiting room," Tom said. "Yes, that's how we do it, but I still don't understand," Sally said.

"Let me narrate a story to you," Tom said. "Suppose you are in a supermarket and you go in for only a few items. Let's say five different items. You find your five items and move to the front of the store for checkout. You notice there are only four lines open and each line has three or four people already in it. You scan the lines and determine that each person has a fairly full shopping cart with many more items than you have. Through a random selection process, you pick a line and get in it. Now you are forced to wait for those in front of you to finish, and they could take a long time. They do have a sizeable number of items in their cart. Here's what happens; the effects of the system's codependency, has now been passed on to you! What do you do?" Tom asked. Sally put her head in her hands to cover her face. There was a huge smile on her face with an almost audible laugh. She answered, "I'd go get in the express line!"

Tom smiled and said, "I would too! And, any others who were in the other checkout lines, and met the criteria for the express line, could also move that direction. It's possible they could be finished and gone before it would even have been their turn in the other line," Tom added. Jeff was the first to break the silence that followed and said, "But we don't have an express line in the ER!" Tom spun around and faces Jeff and said, "Why not?" "Well, I'm not sure, but it sounds like maybe we should," Jeff said. "Now, it makes sense to me what you said earlier about everyone sees a doctor, wait times can be reduced, and the hospital can bring in more revenue," Jeff added.

"It makes perfect sense to me," said Sally. "We could change how we use our ED capacity to meet the needs of the patient loads. Sometimes, there can be a huge variation between those who can get in and out fast and those who might need a longer time with the doctor. We could decide how many express lines to have, depending on the patient loads and triage classifications," Sally added.

"You know," said Jeff, "I can now see how we might have been unknowingly punishing some of our patients by forcing them to use the system we have in place. In a lot of ways, the system worked for us, but it didn't work for them, at least not to a high level of satisfaction. We made our patients victims of a poorly organized process and system," Jeff said with a much lower voice, almost as if he was talking to himself and he didn't want anyone else to hear.

Tom spoke up. "Remember, this is only one possible idea for the front end of the process. We still need to consider the back end of this process for getting new patients admitted, other patients discharged, and rooms cleaned and ready to a usable condition. Why don't we take a break," Tom said looking at his watch. "Be back in 10 minutes," he added. Most of the team didn't leave the room, but rather assembled into smaller groups with lots of discussion going on.

When everyone sat down again, Tom spoke. "If we change the current system, there are some things that will happen," Tom started. "Basically, we will shift the system from an 'I' configuration to a 'V' configuration." "Change it from what to a what?" Sally asked. "It's not something we have talked about before, at least with this group," Tom said. "But it will be important to understand. With an 'I' configuration, you basically start with one product, or service, and end with the same product or service," he explained. "That's kind of what we do now isn't it?" Sally asked.

"Yes, it is," Tom said. "All of your patients are in the same 'I' line, but if we added an express line, then it will shift to a mini 'V' line. What I mean is, after the triage is complete, a decision will be made if the patient continues in the system down the express side, or do they continue down the regular side. I use the term regular side because I don't currently have a more precise term," he added. Everyone nodded. "Even with the patients who continue down the regular side, there is another decision gate when you decide if they are admitted or released. If you turn the 'V' on its side and consider the bottom to be the start point for the flow of patients through the 'V,' you can now visualize three different paths and each will have its own drumbeat, if you will. Each path will, in essence, move forward based on a different drum or cadence," Tom added. "When you consider a 'V,' there are characteristics and consequences to be aware of. If not managed correctly, this type of improvement can cause a multitude of additional issues."

"The characteristics of a 'V' are," Tom walked to the whiteboard to write, "Number one, the number of end items can be many. In your case, the end items are three. Number two, all items are produced or treated essentially the same way. In your case it's the flow through the ED system. And, number three, equipment to produce the end items or treat patients can be capital intensive. In your case, the X-ray machine, magnetic resonance imaging (MRI) machines, laboratory work and personnel to do the testing, and so on," Tom said.

"It's also important to understand the consequences of the 'V' configuration. They are as follows," he continued to write on the board, "Number one, misallocation of materials or medications. In other words, you commit material or medications too soon. Number two, poor customer service. In other words, it can be easy to get 'stuck' in a 'V' configuration. Number three, priorities seem to change constantly. In other words, you and your system get hung up in the cyclical nature of multitasking. You start jumping from one patient to another trying to get something done. It's not the situation you want to be in," Tom added. "And, number four is the constant complaint that you are being unresponsive to the patient's needs. In the current situation, the patient is continually asking themselves, 'What about me?'" Tom explained.

"If we take a moment and look at the system now, you can see the real goal is not necessarily to create or maintain an appropriate buffer, but rather to have the buffer, or triage priority list, be as close to zero as possible. Does that make sense to you?" Tom asked. He scanned the group and heads were slowly starting to nod in agreement. "This is how an M-DBR system would work. There are different paths, and each path has a different drum. The beat of the drum determines how fast the next patient can be moved forward. If the system loads are present, in your case people waiting in the waiting room, then they need to be assigned a path to get to the finish line," Tom stressed, looking for understanding on the faces of the group. So far, he thought he was seeing it. "So overall, the goal in M-DBR is not to create, or maintain a buffer, but rather to assign the buffer down the different paths and reduce it as quickly as you can. In this case, a zero buffer is the best," he explained and loaded a graphic of M-DBR (Figure 19.3) onto the screen.

"Now, let's work our way down the regular path to the next decision gate. At some point in the system, it will be decided if the patient can be released, or in fact, needs to be admitted, or transferred. This decision is very likely supported by various test results and information gathered from x-ray, or MRI, or whatever. If it is determined that the patient can be released, then they proceed to the finish line and exit the system. However, if it is decided that the patient should be admitted, then a new

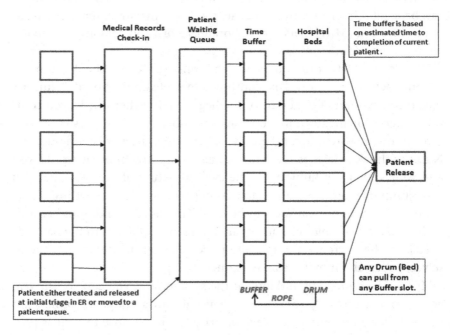

FIGURE 19.3
M-DBR.

set of problems arise, specifically bed availability. You need somewhere to put the patient, in order to admit the patient," Tom explained.

"When my wife Beverly and I came to the ED, getting in and seeing the doctor was not the real problem. We did have some wait time that seemed extreme to me, but I also understand now that I was in a panic mode. I wanted answers!" he said, with a semi-smile. "When we arrived at the ED, it was early afternoon, and according to your then current policy, no more patients were being discharged. What we were waiting for was a room to be cleaned and finished, so my wife could be admitted and put in the room," Tom said. "The entire time we waited for the hospital room, Beverly was in an ED exam room, which meant that because we couldn't move forward, the next patient behind us couldn't move forward either. The system flow had stopped because Beverly had nowhere to go," Tom explained. "We ended up having to wait until 6:00 pm before we finally got her into a room. Once she was in her room, she was considered to be admitted. Before the room becoming available, we were just Work-in-Process inventory that was polluting the ED system. We couldn't get out and no one else could get in. In fact, I can remember seeing some gurneys with patients on them, just sitting in the hallway waiting to be moved somewhere," Tom reminisced.

"So, in order to complete the flow through the system, it is imperative that we spend some time looking at the discharge policy and housekeeping staffing," Tom said. "According to Dr. Samuels, the executive team already approved those recommendations," said Jeff. "They did approve the recommendations, and the recommendations were to change the discharge policy and approval to rehire, or hire, more housekeeping staff," Tom said. "And they did say they want you to look at the new discharge policy before they implement it. My question for this team is, what are you going to change the policy to, and how much more housekeeping staff will be needed?" Tom asked.

"I see your point Tom," Sally said. "We have permission to change it, but we don't know for sure what we should change it to!" Tom smiled. "So, we need to discuss what a good policy looks like, and how better to improve housekeeping," Sally said. "That sounds like an excellent place to start. Does anyone have a comment for that?" Tom asked. "I do," Jeff said. "I'm not a medical professional, but I think it should be based on when the patient is ready, and not what time of day it is," he added.

"I agree," said Sally. "Part of the housekeeping problem right now is many patients are released between 11:30 am and noon. That keeps the release within the policy, but it also creates a situation where many rooms become available for cleaning all at once before a new patient can be admitted. Housekeeping goes from waiting for rooms to clean, to having too many rooms to clean all within the span of approximately 30 minutes. Sometimes, housekeeping can just get overwhelmed," said Sally.

"It's probably true that more rooms would become available in the morning hours, but if you miss the noon deadline, because of some unforeseen issue, then you have to wait until the next day. So, we have a room being occupied by someone who might not have to be there, and there is someone else waiting for a room they can't get into yet. It's just crazy when you stop and think about it," Sally said. "So, what I'm hearing is, remove the deadline and release patients based on good medical protocol, and the patient's comfort and needs, no matter what time it is. Is that correct?" asked Tom. "I think that pretty much sums it up," Sally said. "There will be some details to work out, but overall I think it's a good approach," she added. "So, if we remove the deadline from the policy, does that mean that patient releases will be more evenly distributed?" Jeff asked.

"It's possible," said Sally. "But I still think the morning will be the favored time for release, and that means that a lot of rooms will need to be cleaned at the same time," she added. "What stops them from cleaning the rooms faster right now?" Tom asked. "Honestly, I think they do try and clean the rooms as fast as they can right now," Sally said. "There are several things that must be taken care of before a room is ready for a new patient and it does take some time to do that. And, we did have the layoff. I don't know for sure how many that might have been, but it did have an impact," Sally added. "How long do you think it takes to clean a room right now?" Tom asked.

"I guess that depends, but to do a really good job might take 45 minutes to 1 hour," Sally said. "There is a lot to do. New sheets, new towels, cleaning the bathroom including toilet and shower, or tub, and wiping everything down and sanitizing the room, including the floors," she explained. "Let me relate a story to you," Tom said. "Suppose it's Saturday morning and you want to have four new tires put on your car. You also want to fill the car with gas, and you might even want a Slurpee. How long does it take to get all of that done?" Tom asked the group. Everyone was contemplating the question and formulating an answer. Finally, Sally raised her hand and said, "I'd guess approximately 2 or 3 hours." "Anyone else have a guess?" Tom asked.

"Well, I know a guy at the tire shop, so I think I could get it done in less than 2 hours," said Sally. "Hey, it pays to know people in the right places," she added. Everyone laughed. "I think 2 hours might be about right and I don't even know anyone at the tire shop," Jeff said. "I agree with Sally, I'm thinking more like 3 hours," said Bill Thomas, who had been quiet for most of the discussion. "So, the best time so far is 2 hours," said Tom scanning the group. "Any other guesses?" No one said anything. "What if I told you I know where you can get all of them done in 16 seconds," Tom said. "No way," someone said.

"Yes way," Tom replied. "Think about a pit crew at a race-track. They can change all four tires, fill the tank with gas, and give the driver a drink, all within 16 seconds," Tom said. The faces around the room showed a look of surprise and many broke out with a smile. "He's right!" someone in the room said. "The previous best guess had been 2 hours, but now you know a better way. So, in terms of housekeeping, and the assumption that it takes a long time, ask yourself, 'How can we convert housekeeping into a well-organized pit crew? What is the pit crew doing that housekeeping isn't?'" Tom asked. He could see, if not hear, the wheels turning, and he just smiled.

"I think having more housekeeping people will help a lot," said Sally. "How many more do you need?" Tom asked. "I don't know for sure, but if we want to do it that fast, then we might need three times as many people," Sally said. "Wow!" Tom said. "I don't think the executive team will go for that amount of an increase." "Why not, they promised to follow our recommendations," Sally said. "Yes, they did, but within reason," Tom pointed out. "Let's step back and look at the problem again," he said. "Sometimes, organizations think that the only way they can do more work is hire more people. In some situations, that might be true, but most of the time, it's not. The real trick is to understand how to better use what you have, and not necessarily piling more people into an already bad system," Tom explained.

"Yes, but a pit crew has a lot more people than we do," Sally said. "We only send one housekeeper to do a room, not six or seven." Tom just smiled and asked, "What would happen to the effectiveness of the pit crew if it was only one person doing all of those tasks?" "Well, it would take a lot longer and you would probably lose the race," Sally said. "No doubt,"

Tom said. "What if you considered that when a room was ready for cleaning it was equal to a car being in the pit?" Tom asked.

"We'd still need more people. The current housekeeping staff is scattered all over the hospital on different floors. They assign housekeeping based on areas. Each housekeeper gets assigned so many rooms and hallways and public bathrooms and common areas that they need to maintain," Sally explained. "When we had the layoff, the work increased even more. So, when a room needs cleaning, and it's in your area, you are the one that does it," she added. "Does that mean that at any point in time, some housekeepers could be very busy and some not so much?" Tom asked.

"Wait a minute," Jeff said, "I think I see where you are going with this. If I understand correctly, we probably have the right amount of staff; we just have them in the wrong locations! That could be especially true in the mornings when there could be a surge of rooms that need cleaning," Jeff said. "When we first made our recommendation to increase the house-keeping staff, and we talked about having two people on a cleaning team, I was actually seeing the need to double the staff," Jeff said with a certain amount of doubt in his voice. "I think you might need more housekeeping, but certainly not three times more," Tom said.

Sally looked at Jeff and said, "If a room that needs cleaning is like a race car in the pit, then that makes sense. We can't use the room in its current condition, and somebody might be waiting for it. The sooner it's cleaned, the sooner we can get somebody admitted, which is just like getting the car back in the race!" Sally exclaimed. Then Sally said, "What we need are room pit crews, but maybe just during peak loads, like in the morning. We could pull other staff from other locations until the rooms are cleaned and ready. Then, the other staff could go back to their assigned locations!" Sally explained. "That makes a lot of sense to me," Jeff said. "Housekeeping can still have assigned locations, but if the need is there, we can then move housekeeping where they are most needed. I like it!" Jeff said. "How many people should be on a room pit crew?" Sally asked as a question to the team. "As many as we need," said Jeff. "I agree," said Sally. "But how many is that?" she asked.

"Again, think about the pit crew," Tom said. "Each person on the crew is assigned a specific part of the race car. There is someone on the left front tire, on the left rear tire, and the same for the right side. There is also some-one putting gas in, and someone assigned to jack the car up and down. Now, think about the housekeeping crew. What are the critical areas that need someone assigned?" Tom asked. "Maybe we should talk with the housekeeping supervisor and get the information we need," Jeff said. "I agree," said Sally looking at Jeff. "Let's you and I go do that right now." Both Sally and Jeff left the room. Tom instructed everyone else to go on a break until they got back.

They both returned approximately 15 minutes later and sat in their chairs. "Well, I think we've got what we need," Sally said. "We talked with Nancy, the housekeeping supervisor, and told her what we were thinking about. She seemed a bit surprised that anyone would take any interest in housekeeping. We told her how important this was, and that we needed the information," Sally said. "When she talked about the critical areas, she mentioned all of the linens, including bed sheet and towels, cleaning the bathroom including sinks, toilets, and shower stalls, and making sure the garbage cans are emptied and cleaned with new plastic liners inserted. Also, a top priority is making sure everything is wiped down on all of the flat surfaces. The last critical step is cleaning the floor as you leave the room," Sally said.

"From what I'm hearing, I think we might need three people on a team. We want them to be able to do their work without constantly running into each other," Jeff said. "I think we need to get with Nancy and describe in more detail what we're thinking about. We need to put a practice team together and watch them go through the steps. We can apply Lean and Six Sigma and better define how the process would work and the correct order for doing the steps. We can document our findings and create a preliminary process and work from there," Jeff added. "That's a good idea," Sally said. "Tom, would you mind if we all went back to housekeeping to talk with Nancy?" Sally asked.

"Not at all," Tom said. "It's the next step for what we need to do. Besides, it's almost lunchtime, so we'll meet back here at 2:30 to review your findings. Does that give you enough time?" Tom asked. "I think it might," Sally said. "Even if it's not enough time, it will give us a good start," she added. The team gathered up their things and headed out of the room toward housekeeping. Tom stayed in the room. That would give him time to consider his next steps at Simpson Water Heaters.

Around 2:20, the team started to assemble back in the conference room. There seemed to be a lot of chatter and excitement with the group. When everyone was seated, Jeff was the first to speak. "We talked with Nancy. She seemed okay with the idea, but the first thing she said was, 'We'll need more people to do that.' We explained to her about what we had talked about earlier, that we might have enough people, we just had them in the wrong location. Anyway, she started to warm up to our idea," Jeff added.

"Because it was the noon hour, there were a lot of rooms to pick from. We looked at her list of rooms and picked one on the second floor. Nancy looked at the list as well and determined that the fourth floor had only one room to clean. She called the housekeeping lead on four and asked her to send two people to the second floor. According to the list, the second floor had the most rooms to clean," Sally said.

"When everyone was assembled, we explained to the housekeeping personnel what we wanted to do. We went over the list of critical tasks, and they all agreed," Jeff said. "We divided the tasks among the three, with one person assigned to change the bed sheets and gather towels. We then assigned the second person to the bathroom to clean everything, and the third person was assigned to do the wipe down. The third person would also do the floors when everything else was done, while the other two moved on to the next room," Jeff added.

"When they started, I had a stopwatch on my phone, so I timed them," Jeff said. "They completed the room in 13 minutes. That's almost five rooms an hour!" Jeff said. "We also had Nancy inspect the room when they were finished to see if we had forgotten anything," Sally said. "Nancy said they did a good job and the room was ready!" Sally added. "The other two had moved to the next room and the third person was close behind them," Jeff said.

"I went with the first two and started the stopwatch again when they started," Jeff said. "When they finished the second room it took only 12 minutes," Jeff said. "At that rate, it is five rooms per hour! That's a big improvement over one room every 45 minutes to 1 hour when just one person was assigned," Jeff added. "Nancy inspected the second room and said it was also ready," Sally said. "She was totally amazed at how fast they could do it, and how well it was done," she added. "We did a third room and it was also approximately 12 minutes," Jeff said. "I think if we look at this process a bit closer and apply some Lean and Six Sigma, we can reduce the time even more," Jeff said. "Honestly, I was so amazed to see how fast it could be done," Jeff added.

"I think we might be on to something here," Sally said. "I think we need to fine-tune the process for figuring out which rooms need cleaning, where to assemble the room pit crew staff from, and then notify Admitting which rooms are ready to go," she added. "Excellent!" Tom said, as he walked toward the whiteboard. "Now we have our three injections to help reduce the wait time." He wrote the following on the board:

1. Express lane
2. Update and change the discharge policy
3. Implement room pit crews.

"Now, as a team, you just need to fine-tune these ideas and get ready to make them happen," Tom said. "Unless you have more comments or questions, I think you should get back to working these new ideas," Tom added. No one raised their hand. As they started to exit the room, most seemed excited to get back to what they were doing. Pete stayed behind to talk with Tom for a few minutes. Pete had elected to stay all day and watch Tom do his thing.

"Thank you, Tom, this has been an exceptional day, at least for me. I've come to realize over the past couple of weeks the importance of doing a good system's analysis and applying good systems thinking. I would never have considered any of the things we found without the systems thinking to understand how it was all linked together. I understand much more clearly now how important it is to focus on the real problem and not get caught up in trying to fix everything. There is a lot of leverage in making the system better," Pete said. "Thanks Pete, but let me add that everyone in your group have been exceptional students!" Tom said. "I think you are well on your way to making Maximo Emergency Hospital a world class hospital," Tom added with a smile.

The team returned from their floor exercise and sat down. Tom then addressed the group, "When we started this session today, I explained that I wanted to talk about Drum Buffer Rope. We got side-tracked and, although what we accomplished was fantastic. Drum Buffer Rope is a very important element for your hospital scheduling," Tom explained. And with that brief statement, Tom inserted the same slide he had posted before onto the screen (Figure 19.4).

"As we were discussing earlier, we discussed a new format for Drum Buffer Rope in your Emergency Department which I referred to as Multiple Drum Buffer Rope." "Let's walk through how M-DBR might work in your Emergency Department," Tom said.

"Emergency Department patients enter the ED triage area, are diagnosed and, if appropriate, they are treated and released. If they can't be

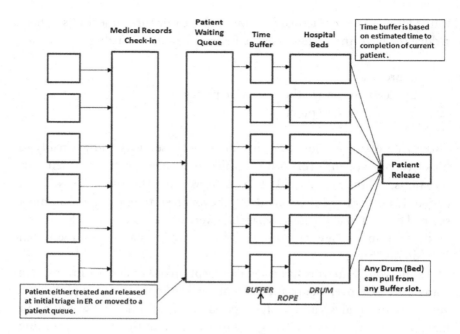

FIGURE 19.4
Multiple Drum Buffer Rope.

treated and released, they are moved to a patient queue area for future testing. When hospital beds become available, they are then transferred to the appropriate section of the hospital for future treatment. The hospital beds, in this case, are considered the drum. The buffer is based upon the estimated time to complete the treatment of the current patient. Because there are multiple drums (hospital beds), any drum can pull from any buffer slot," Tom explained. "The rope is simply the notification that a bed is available for the queue of patients waiting for treatment," Tom added. "Eventually the patients will then be released," Tom said.

Tom continued, "As I explained earlier, the point of separation between traditional Drum Buffer Rope and Multiple Drum Buffer Rope is that traditional DBR is based on the fact that the output from a constraint is very predictable. You'll remember I explained that as an example, in a typical manufacturing environment, the constraint usually has a cadence or rhythm that is very predictable and steady, for instance, a constraint machine that is able to produce a part every 7 minutes, or whatever the time may be. Knowing the constraint time allows you to be relatively accurate in establishing a buffer. In other words, there is a constant, but predictable normal variation at the constraint."

"However, in your situation at the hospital, the constraint time can vary significantly. Each time a patient enters your constraint, there can be a lot of uncertainty for when the patient will finish, depending on what needs to be done. You don't know what patient is coming in with what problem and the ED physician's time can vary greatly depending on the circumstances. It's very difficult, if not impossible, to establish any kind of an accurate buffer, from one patient to the next," Tom explained. Tom repeated what he said to emphasize the point, "Under those kinds of circumstances, it's very difficult, if not impossible, to establish any kind of an accurate buffer."

He continued by asking the same question he had asked earlier in the session, "If the ED physicians are truly the constraint, then how do we manage to keep them fully occupied to reduce wait times?" Tom asked rhetorically. "As I said earlier, it would seem to me that we would need to know the real-time status of each constraint," said Sally. "What I meant by that was, if we knew how much longer each physician believed they had with their current patient, then we could check and see which patient is next and get them ready," she added.

"That's a good possible answer," Tom said. "And, if we already have a buffer in place, then we should know which patient is next. But let's go back and think for a moment about how you establish the buffer. Remember, M-DBR will be different from traditional DBR, mostly because of the uncertainty involved," Tom explained. "As explained earlier, typically, when a patient comes into the ED, you perform a triage to determine severity, or urgency of the situation," Tom said.

"Okay, we are finished for today. What I would like you to do as a team is to assemble the appropriate group of ED doctors, nurses, and other ED personnel and first, explain the M-DBR concept and then work to implement it in your hospital Emergency Department," Tom said. "I will be available by phone for any question that you may have as you're implementing it," Tom added. "In my next session here at Maximo Emergency Hospital, I will present the Theory of Constraints Replenishment Solution," Tom explained. "Do you sometimes run out of supplies and medications here?" he asked. The group, in unison, said, "Yes, that is definitely a problem here." "Then what I will present next time is a way to virtually eliminate stock-outs while at the same time, reduce your inventory by about fifty percent." Tom explained. He thanked the group for all they had accomplished and dismissed them.

When everyone had left, Pete approached Tom and said, "Tom, this may have been the best team session I have ever been involved with and I thank you for everything." "You're very welcome Pete, but I promise you, after the next session you will thank me even more," Tom replied with a smile. "I'll call you later this week so we can schedule my next visit," he added.

As Tom drove home, he had two things on his mind. One thing was that he had to prepare for and schedule his next trip to Simpson Water Heaters. The other thing on his mind was the offer Jonathan Briggs had made to him, whereby he would help the Board decide which new companies they should add to their portfolio. He thought long and hard about the Board's offer on his way home, but he still hadn't decided if he wanted to take this offer. When he arrived home, he decided to put together his presentation on the implementation of Theory of Constraints' Drum Buffer Rope and Replenishment Solution that he would be presenting the next day at Simpson Water Heaters.

20

Simpson Water Heaters' New Initiative

When Tom left Simpson Water Heaters the last time, he explained that when he returned, he would discuss another improvement initiative, the Theory of Constraints Replenishment Solution. Tom arrived at Simpson Water Heaters and walked to the conference room which was already filled with participants. Matt Maloney, the Plant Manager, met him at the door and reintroduced him to his audience. And with that introduction, Tom began today's session. "Good morning everyone," he said. "Today you are going to hear about a parts replenishment initiative that will significantly change the way you order needed materials, supplies, and parts," he explained.

He began, "Most businesses are linked one way or another to some kind of supply chain. They purchase parts, supplies, or raw materials from other companies so they can produce their products, and then pass it on to the next system in line until it finally arrives at the end customer. It clearly depends on what you make and how fast you make it, but keep in mind, the supply chain can be your best, friend or it can be your worst enemy. If it works well, it's clearly your best friend, but if it doesn't work well, then believe me, it can be your worst enemy," Tom explained.

"The problem with most supply-chain systems is that they haven't changed their thinking through time, even though the business reality has changed. There are many new supply-chain software applications, like MRP and ERP, with each one proposing that it will solve the problems associated with the supply chain system. The problem is that while these new software applications have come about mostly because of advances in computer technology, but few have really solved the issues related to the supply chain. It's true that these systems can provide an enormous amount of information very fast, but most times system speed is much less important than having access to the right information. What difference does it make how fast you get the information if it's simply the wrong information?" he asked.

He continued, "The new business reality has created a need for dramatic changes in supply-chain systems, but unfortunately, most systems have not pursued the needed change. In today's worls, businesses are required to build products cheaper, with higher quality, with high on-time delivery rates. These are the new rules of competition, so you either play by the new rules or get out of the way. While the rules in business have changed, many businesses keep on doing business the same 'old' way. If a business owner were to be asked why they haven't changed, the most common answer you would get would be 'Because that's the way we've always done it.' If the supply chain system has not changed to align with the new rules, then the gap between supply-chain output and system needs will grow even larger with very little hope of getting different results."

"Many supply-chain systems were designed to solve a couple of key problems, which were how to avoid stock-outs and how to significantly reduce the size of their inventory of parts or materials. These systems were designed to hold inventory in check, which means don't buy too much, while at the same time avoiding the stock-out situations that always seem to occur. You don't want to run out of parts, and yet, sometimes, you still run out of parts. You don't want excess inventory, and yet sometimes, you have too much inventory. This constant negative gyration between sometimes too much and sometimes too little has persisted through time. Believe it or not, the supply problems encountered many years ago are still the problems being encountered today," Tom explained.

Tom continued, "Many company's system of choice is one referred to as the Minimum/Maximum (MIN/MAX) system. Parts, or inventory, or supplies, are evaluated based on need and usage, and some type of maximum and minimum levels are established for each item. The traditional rules and measures for the Min/Max system are usually quite simple," He said and loaded a Power Point slide onto the screen (Figure 20.1).

- Rule 1: Determine the maximum and minimum levels for each item.

- Rule 2: Don't ever exceed the maximum level.

- Rule 3: Don't reorder until you go below the minimum level.

FIGURE 20.1
Rules for Min/Max system.

"The basic assumptions behind these rules and measures are, as you might have guessed, primarily based in Cost Accounting (CA) and commonly referred to as cost-world thinking. In order to save money and minimize your expenditures for supply parts/inventory, you must reduce, or at least hold in check, the amount of money you spend for these items. In order to reduce the amount of money you spend on these items, you must never buy more than the maximum amount. Also, in order to reduce the money spent on these items, you must not spend money until absolutely necessary, and order parts only when they have reached the minimum level," Tom explained.

"These assumptions might seem valid, and if implemented correctly and monitored, should provide a supply system that both controls dollars spent and maintains inventory within the minimum and maximum levels. However, even in the perfect world, most systems of this type don't seem to generate the desired results that are required. For some reason, there always seems to be situations of excess inventory for some items and of stock-out situations for others. The whole operational concept behind the Minimum/Maximum systems was supposed to prevent these kinds of occurrences from happening, and yet they still do. Let's look at why this happens," Tom said.

"Maybe the best way to make this point is with a couple of examples. The first example deals with a company that measured and rewarded their procurement staff based on the amount of money they saved with procurement purchases. For the procurement staff their primary method to accomplish this objective was to buy everything in bulk. In fact, their suppliers preferred that their customers buy in bulk in order to receive the benefit of 'quantity discounts.' Back then, the more you bought, the less it cost per unit. It seemed like a great idea and certainly a way to meet the objective of saving money. Sometimes, these supply items were procured in amounts well in excess of the maximum, but the company got them at a great price!" Tom explained. "Is that what happens here?" Tom asked. Matt replied, "Yes, pretty much."

Continuing Tom said, "By employing this cost-saving strategy, this company had a warehouse full of low-cost inventory that had used a large portion of their available dollars. The problem was, they didn't have the right mix of inventory to build even a single unit of product. They had too many of some items, even though they were all purchased at the lowest price, and not enough of other items. The bigger problem was they ran out of money to purchase any more parts, especially the parts they desperately needed!"

"The other example is related to a company who was a contractor to the government. Their primary mission was to perform maintenance on helicopters. In their contract with the Government, the Government had offered a very lucrative clause to save money. This company was given a budgeted amount to buy needed parts on a yearly basis. Based on this budgeted amount, the Government offered to split fifty-fifty any amount the company could underrun their parts budget. The company took the total budgeted dollars and divided it by twelve to establish the monthly parts budget. They also held back a percentage of the budgeted amount each month so they could claim cost savings and split the difference. Any parts purchase that would have exceeded the targeted monthly budget was postponed until the next month, even if it was urgently needed. The ability of this company to make money slowed dramatically. They were literally jumping over dollars to pick up pennies. There were many jobs waiting for parts that couldn't be finished until they had the parts to finish, but they had to wait, sometimes for several days or weeks, to get the parts, because of the cost-saving mentality," Tom explained.

Again, Tom continued, "In both of these examples it was an issue of bad cost metrics driving the bad behavior. In both of these cases, cost savings were employed as the primary strategy. In the first example, the company ultimately went bankrupt and went out of business. They couldn't pay back the loans on the money they had borrowed to buy all of the low-cost parts because they couldn't make any products. In the second example the company avoided bankruptcy because they provided a needed service for the Government; they were ultimately spared by seeing the error of their ways, and they decided to spend the budgeted dollars to buy the needed parts."

"Then and now, the functional theory behind the supply-chain Min/Max concept is that supplies, parts, and materials should be distributed and stored at the lowest level of the user supply chain. In effect this is a push system, or one that pushes parts through the system to the lowest possible level. Parts must be available at the lowest level in order to be used. In this type of system, the parts are consumed until the minimum quantity is reached or exceeded, and then an order is placed for more parts. The parts order then goes up the chain from the point-of-use (POU) location back to some kind of central supply center, or orders are placed directly back to the vendor, depending on the situation. When the orders are received at the central supply center, they are pushed back down the chain to the lowest POU locations," he explained as he loaded a new slide (Figure 20.2) which defines a simplified version of this parts Flow activity.

"This flow might not be applicable to all situations, but to most it will make sense. Some companies and smaller businesses will have fewer steps, in that they order directly from a vendor and receive parts back into their business without the need for large, more complex, distribution systems. However, the thinking behind the Min/Max system will still apply, even to those smaller businesses. Larger companies, or those with numerous geographical locations, will most likely have developed some type of a central supply and/or distribution locations that feed the next level of the supply distribution system. The distribution points in turn feed the companies or business segments that use the raw material and parts at the final POU to build products. Some distribution systems may even be more complex than what I have displayed here. But even with increased complexity, the results they are trying to achieve remain the same which is to get the parts to where they are needed and when they need to be there," Tom explained.

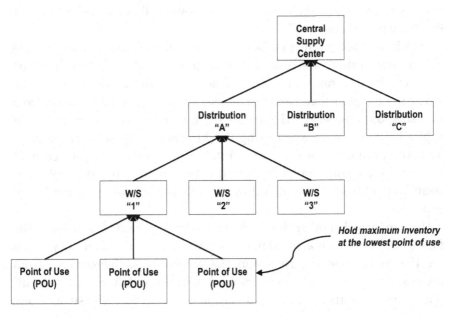

FIGURE 20.2
Simplified parts flow activity.

TABLE 20.1

Top-Level Rules for Minimum/Maximum Supply System

1. The system reorder amount is the maximum amount no matter how many parts are currently in the bin box.
2. Most supply systems only allow for one order at a time to be present
3. Orders for parts are triggered *only* after the minimum amount has been exceeded.
4. Total part inventory is held at the lowest possible level of the distribution chain— the point-of-use (POU) location.
5. Parts are inventoried once or twice a month and orders placed, as required.

"Let's look at some of the Min/Max rules and understand the negative aspects that result from them. Table 20.1 provides a summary of the top-level rules for the Min/Max supply system," he explained.

Tom continued his explanation, "Even though the Min/Max system appears to control your supply needs, and cover the inventory demands, there are some significant negatives effects caused by using this system. First, there is the problem of being reactive to an inventory or parts situation, rather than being proactive. When minimum stock levels are used as the trigger to reorder parts, some supply-chain systems will have a difficult time keeping up with the demands being placed upon them. And there is an increased likelihood that stock-outs will occur and may be for extended periods of time."

"Stock-outs occur when the lead time to replenish the part will exceed the minimum stock available. In other words, the availability of the part between the minimum amount and zero is totally depleted before the part can be replenished from the vendor," Tom explained as he loaded a new slide onto the screen (Figure 20.3). "The figure on the screen is what typically materializes when using the Min/Max replenishment system. The bottom line is that you will wait to reorder parts until you reach, of go below the minimum level. Unfortunately, many times the replenishment time exceeds the replenishment time and stock-outs occur," Tom explained.

He then loaded another slide onto the screen (Figure 20.4) and said, "The figure on the screen is a visual flow of what I just described and as you can see, the distribution of parts is from the top down and the reorder is from the bottom up. The parts come into the central warehouse from the suppliers, and from there, they are distributed to your facility's stock room.

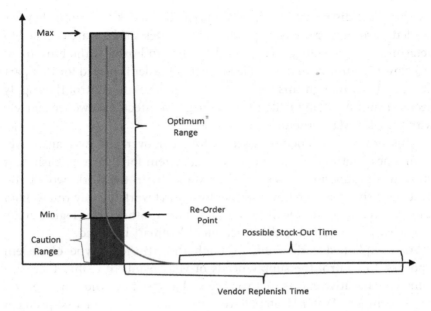

FIGURE 20.3
Stock-out condition with Min/Max system.

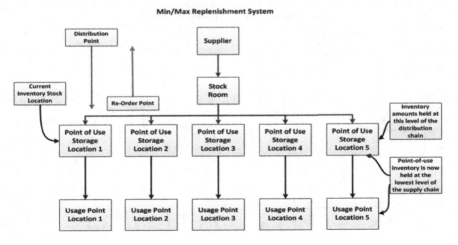

FIGURE 20.4
Parts and inventory flow.

The parts are distributed to the appropriate line stock bins until they are needed in your operations. Typically, once a week the bins are checked to determine the inventory level in each of the bin boxes. If the bins are at or below the minimum defined level, then an order is placed for that part number. Even though this type of system 'appears' to control the supply needs of your plant, in reality there are negative effects that we see and feel with the Min/Max system."

"This problem of stock-outs seems to occur over and over again, yet companies continue to use the Min/Max system for their replenishment of needed production materials. I ask you, why in the world would you continue using a system that continually doesn't work the way you wanted it to?" Tom asked rhetorically as he loaded yet another slide (Figure 20.5). "So, what's the solution to this stock-out dilemma?" he asked.

"As I explained earlier, even though the Min/Max type of system 'appears' to control the supply needs of your plant, in reality there are some very negative effects that you see and feel with it. And I'm sure, you here at Simpson Water Heaters have experienced them. The first problem we experience with this Min/Max System is that you are continuously in a reactive and knee-jerk state, rather than a proactive and practical mode. This is simply because the Min/Max System is almost always assured to

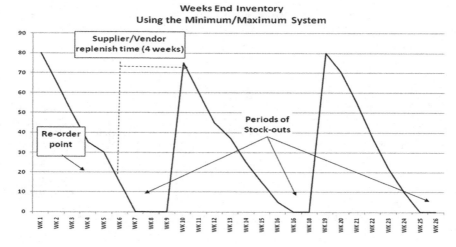

FIGURE 20.5
Repeating periods of stock-outs.

have 'stock-out' conditions regularly and repeatedly. So, the questions we must answer is why do these stock-outs occur and what can we do to prevent them?" Tom asked.

"Very simply put, stock-outs occur principally because it's not unusual for the lead time to replenish the minimum amount of parts left in the bin, quite regularly exceeds the time remaining to build products with what's left in the parts bin. And because of the inherent variation in demand, stock-outs can occur in both shorter or longer times than the Min/Max model might suggest. The problem with this is that when you do have a stock-out, your production stops until new parts arrive, and it usually happens often," he explained.

Tom continued, "As mentioned earlier, the flow in the Min/Max Parts Supply System, where the parts are distributed to the lowest level of the distribution (i.e. to parts bins) and are also reordered from this same low point in the system. So, what must be done differently to avoid these stock-out periods? Wouldn't it be great if we had a system that would operate with much less on-hand inventory without stock-outs?"

"There is such a system, and it comes to us from the Theory of Constraints. The Theory of Constraints Distribution and Replenishment Model states that, unlike the Min/Max system, most of the inventory should be held at the highest level in the distribution chain and not at the lowest level (i.e. the bins). Of course, you must hold some inventory at the point of use (POU) for your assembly work, but this model tells us that the majority of it should be held at the warehouse, from where it's ordered and received from the supplier. The bottom line is this, instead of using some minimum quantity to trigger the reorder of parts, the reorder process should be triggered by daily usage and the time required for the vendor to replenish the parts. That is, it tells us to simply replace what we've used on a very frequent basis, rather than waiting for some minimum quantity to be reached. When this system is used, there will always be enough parts on hand to produce your products and no stock-outs will occur!" Tom explained as he loaded a graphic image (Figure 20.6) of what the Theory of Constraints Replenishment System might look like.

Tom then explained, "Buffers are placed at better leverage points in the supply chain (i.e. Most inventory is held in the factory warehouse). Likewise, each regional warehouse and retail locations have buffers for

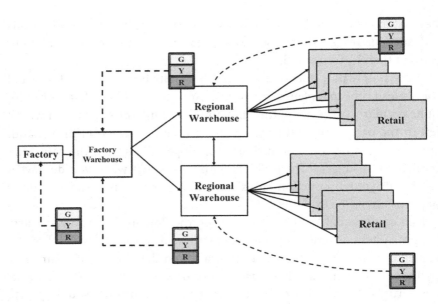

FIGURE 20.6

Theory of Constraints Replenishment System.

each product. These buffers (physical products) are divided into green, yellow and red zones and are located at strategic locations to avoid stock-outs. This replenishment system relies on aggregation to smooth demand and demand at regional warehouses is smoother than demand at retail locations, simply because higher-than-normal demand at some retail locations is offset by lower demand than at other ones. Demand at the factory warehouse is even smoother than demand at the regional warehouses. Goods produced by the factory, are stored in a nearby warehouse until they are needed to replenish goods consumed by sales."

"Because sales occur daily, shipments occur daily, and the quantities shipped are just sufficient to replace goods sold. This might seem to increase shipping costs over what could be achieved by shipping large batches less frequently, but the truth is, the net effect on total shipping costs is that they actually decrease. Stopping the shipment of obsolete goods and reshipment of misallocated goods, more than compensates for increased costs created by smaller shipments of saleable goods," Tom explained.

Tom then said, "The ability to capture sales that would otherwise be lost due to insufficient inventory, makes the Theory of Constraints solution a better alternative. In this system, replenishment is driven by actual consumption and not a sales forecast. As sales are made, the buffer levels at retail locations drop, eventually triggering replenishment from the factory warehouse, which triggers a manufacturing order to resupply the appropriate buffer before it runs out." He continued, "Buffer sizing is based on both variability and the time it takes to resupply the needed parts or materials. So, the more variable the consumption is, the larger the buffer must be to cover this variability. In addition, the longer it takes to re-supply, the bigger the buffer needs to be, so that it is able to cover the demand during the re-supply waiting times," he explained.

"The benefits of Theory of Constraints' replenishment solution can be very striking. For example, a traditional distributor that is 85% reliable, can reasonably expect to increase its reliability to 99%, while reducing its inventory by fifty percent or more. In addition, the average time to resupply retail locations typically drops from weeks or months, to days. A central benefit of Theory of Constraints' Replenishment Solution is to change the distribution from push to pull. That is, nothing gets distributed, unless there is a market for it. Market pull, the external constraint, then optimizes distribution while minimizing inventory," he explained.

Tom continued, "As an added bonus for using this system, the average overall inventory will be significantly lower. This happens because when an order is placed under the Min/Max system, the system automatically reorders, but does so to the maximum quantity. Since the Theory of Constraints Replenishment System simply reorders what's been used, the amount of inventory required to be on hand drops significantly. In fact, you'll see a drop-in inventory levels in the neighborhood of 40–60% while stock-outs drop to nearly zero! Imagine what that means to your cash flow. The figure I just posted (Figure 20.7) is a graphical summary of what you can expect."

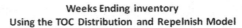

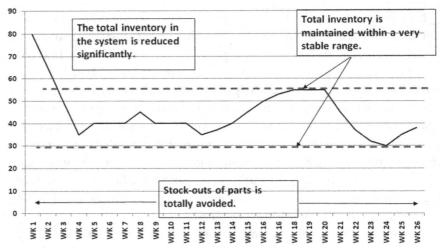

FIGURE 20.7

The benefits of Theory of Constraints' Replenishment System.

Tom then explained, "A simple way to present Theory of Constraints' Replenishment System is by considering a soda vending machine. When the supplier (the soda vendor) opens the door on a vending machine, it is very easy to see what products have been sold. The soda person knows immediately which inventory has to be replaced and to what level to replace it. The soda person is holding the inventory at the next highest level, which is on the soda truck, so it's easy to make the required distribution when needed. The soda person doesn't leave six cases of soda when only twenty cans are needed. If he were to do that, when he got to the next vending machine, he might have run out of the necessary soda, because he made distribution too early at the last stop."

"After completing the daily refill of the vending machines, the soda person then returns to the warehouse or distribution point, to replenish the supply on the soda truck and get ready for the next day's distribution. When the warehouse makes distribution to the soda truck, they move up one level in the chain and replenish what's been used from their supplier. Replenishing in this way, significantly reduces the on-hand inventory, while significantly reducing stock-outs. If a type of soda always runs out, then more should be added to the vending machine (i.e. another row of soda)," Tom explained as he posted another new slide onto the screen (Figure 20.8).

- The Theory of Constraints Replenishment Model holds a small amount of inventory at the Point of Use (POU), while holding the majority of the inventory at the highest level of the organization, typically in a central warehouse. The Min/Max System holds all of the inventory at the POU.

- The Theory of Constraints Replenishment Model re-orders parts based upon real usage on a frequent basis (i.e. typically weekly), and orders parts from the central warehouse. The Min/Max System re-orders to the maximum level, when the number of parts remaining in the parts bin, meets or goes below the calculated minimum quantity, and then orders directly from the POU. Many times, the time required to replenish the part, exceeds what's left in the parts bin and a stock-out occurs.

- Because the Theory of Constraints Replenishment Model re-orders what's been used on a frequent basis, no stock-outs occur and typically the level of inventory is reduced by approximately 50%.

FIGURE 20.8
Summary of differences.

So, to summarize the differences:

"In closing, here is a summary of the benefits from using Theory of Constraints' Replenishment System, rather than the traditional Min/ Max System," Tom said as he posted another new slide onto the screen (Figure 20.9).

1. The reduction of total inventory required to manage and maintain the total supply-chain system is typically on the order of 40-60%, while experiencing the virtual elimination of SKU stock-out situations.

2. Distribution of SKU is made at the right time, to the right location.

3. The frustration caused by stock-out situations virtually disappears. Not only in being able to complete the work, but also the elimination in the time spent looking for and waiting for SKUs to become available.

FIGURE 20.9
Benefits from Theory of Constraints' Replenishment System.

Tom then finished by saying, "Because waiting due to stock-outs virtually disappears, parts flow and synchronization improves dramatically, which improves the throughput of parts through the entire supply chain. And because throughput improves, profitability increases proportionally to the level of sales. Are there any questions about Theory of Constraints' Replenishment System?" Tom asked, and when there weren't any, he continued.

"You will recall during my last visit here to Simpson Water Heaters, we discussed a different scheduling system known as Drum Buffer Rope. We discussed the details of Drum Buffer Rope and the basics of implementing it here at Simpson Water Heaters. One of the most important points you need to understand is that there is an important relationship between Drum Buffer Rope and the Theory of Constraints Replenishment Solution. While Drum Buffer Rope takes care of your scheduling needs, the Replenishment Solution makes certain you won't run out of parts or raw materials," Tom explained.

"I want you to implement both of these improvement initiatives right away here at Simpson Water Heaters and when you do, you will see many benefits happen almost immediately!" Tom exclaimed. "Think, for a minute, what benefits you will see from these two initiatives," he said. "From Drum Buffer Rope, you will see a dramatic reduction in on-time deliveries and a significant reduction in work-in-process inventory. You will also see a significant shift upward in new revenue entering your system, which will translate into a corresponding increase in you company's profit levels," Tom explained.

He continued, "To summarize, the apparent benefits from implementing the Theory of Constraints Replenishment Solution will be about a fifty percent reduction of parts and materials inventory, while at the same time completely eliminating stock-outs. These two benefits will also increase your on-time delivery of orders as well as a significant reduction in the amount of money spent on parts and material's purchases, which also positively impact profitability!" The bottom line is that by implementing both of these methods, your bottom line will improve well beyond what you dreamed was possible.

"As I said, I want you to immediately implement both of these techniques and I will be available for any implementation questions you might have," Tom said. "You've already seen significant improvements in your profits by implementing my Ultimate Improvement Cycle methodology, but when you tie these initiatives together, your company will become one of the best in the portfolio of companies," Tom emphasized. "That is all I have to say today, so go forth and do your thing!" he said.

When everyone was gone, Matt approached Tom and said, "Tom, what you have provided for my team is something that will help us get to the proverbial promised land, and all I can say is thank you!"

"Matt, you have a great team in place, and I am convinced that you guys here at Simpson Water Heaters will become one of the best, if not the best in the Board's entire portfolio!" Tom emphasized. "Think about that Matt, going from 'last place' to 'first place' would be an amazing turn-around!" he exclaimed. "Gotta go now, Matt, but remember, if you need any help, I'll be available by phone or the Internet," he said as he left.

21

The End of the New Beginning

As Tom was driving home from Simpson Water Heaters, a thought entered his mind regarding the offer the Board of Directors had made to him regarding helping the Board select new companies to purchase. He thought to himself, "I'd really like to help them make their purchase decisions, but how should I get paid?" And then he thought back to his favorite TV show, *Shark Tank*. He imagined sitting next to Kevin O'Leary listening to Kevin's royalty offers and that wasn't what he wanted to do this time. "If not a royalty, what if I told the Board that I would take the job, if they would give him an equity percentage instead of a royalty?" he thought. The more he thought about getting paid this way, the more he liked the thought of this approach. He decided to call Jonathan Briggs and discuss this approach with him.

He dialed the number for Jonathan's cell phone and Jonathan answered, "Hello, this is Jonathan Briggs." "Hi Jonathan, this is Tom and I have an answer to your question about helping the Board select future companies to purchase," he explained. "Great Tom, what did you decide?" Jonathan asked. "I decided that I'd like to take you up on your offer," Tom responded. "And how would you like to be paid Tom?" Jonathan asked. "I'd like to get an equity percentage for each company that you end up buying," Tom said. There was dead silence on the other end until Jonathan finally said, "An equity percentage?" "Yes, and I'm thinking something like three percent for each one based upon the new profit levels after one year of turning each one around," Tom explained. "And after the first payout, my equity would drop to one percent and would last forever," he said. Jonathan then said, "I'll have to discuss this proposal with the other Board members." And with that, they both hung up.

Tom had been working for months on the four portfolio companies that the Board of Directors had assigned to him for his improvement efforts. Tom sat down at his desk and pulled up the table of performance metrics

TABLE 21.1

Portfolio Performance Metrics Before and After

Company Name	% On-Time Delivery	% Scrap	% Rework	Stock-Out %	Efficiency %	% Profit Margins
Tamsen Auto Parts Before	68.9	4.8	10.1	11.2	95.4	+5.7
Tamsen Auto Parts After	73.1	3.9	8.8	9.0	81.2	+ 9.2
Simpson Water Heaters Before	68.1	8.8	15.6	19.1	94.7	−1.2
Simpson Water Heaters After	75.2	4.8	10.4	13.7	76.3	+4.1
Watson Rubber Articles Before	70.9	6.8	8.8	9.9	88.7	+7.8
Watson Rubber Articles After	82.2	4.1	6.3	5.2	71.1	+10.1
Jackson Electronics Before	75.4	4.9	14.2	13.4	89.9	9.1
Jackson Electronics After	79.9	3.5	9.1	8.2	70.3	+11.6

that he had started with and had made some improvements in his first few months (Table 21.1). And although he had made some improvements, he was anxious to see what the latest results looked like. He decided to send out a general email to all four portfolio company leaders to get an update. While he had spent the majority of his time at Simpson Water Heaters and Maximo Health Center Complex, he had provided regular webinars for the other portfolio companies as well as the other hospitals within the Maximo Heath Center Complex.

Tom contacted each of the leaders and requested that they update their performance metrics, so he could get a feel for how things were going at each of the portfolio companies. Within twenty-four hours, Tom received feedback from each of the portfolio companies and the results were stunning! He put together an updated table of results (Table 21.2) and he was delighted to see that Simpson Water Heaters, which had been in last place for % Profit Margins at −1.2%, was now leading the group of companies

TABLE 21.2

Portfolio Performance Metrics Update

Company Name	% On-Time Delivery		% Scrap		% Rework		Stock-Out %		Efficiency %		% Profit Margins	
	Bef	Aft	Bef	Aft	Bef	Aft	Bef	Aft	Bef	Aft	Bef	Aft
Tamsen Auto Parts	68.9	94.8	4.8	1.4	10.1	5.1	11.2	1.8	95.4	68.1	+5.7	+29.8
Simpson Water Heaters	75.2	95.8	8.8	1.2	15.6	3.9	19.1	0.7	94.7	61.3	-1.2	+30.3
Watson Rubber Articles	70.9	89.2	6.8	2.1	8.8	4.2	9.9	2.2	88.7	67.1	+7.8	+28.1
Jackson Electronics	75.4	88.9	4.9	1.5	14.2	6.7	13.4	2.2	89.9	64.3	+9.1	+29.6

with profit margins approaching 30% at +29.1%. The remaining three companies in the portfolio now had double-digit % Profit Margins. Tom knew the Board of Directors would be happy with these results, especially because of the short amount of time that had passed since Tom started this assignment.

Tom knew that in three weeks, he had a meeting schedule with the Board of Directors to review the status of the latest performance metrics, so he decided to have a conference call with all four of the portfolio companies. He wanted this call to see what short-term activities each of the portfolio companies had planned, going forward. He arranged the conference call for the day after tomorrow.

Today was the day he had scheduled a conference call with the four portfolio companies, so he logged in to his computer and waited for everyone to join him for their on-line meeting. Matt Maloney from Simpson Water Heaters was the first to log on for the conference call. "Good morning Tom," he said. "Good morning Matt, how are you today?" Tom asked. "I'm actually very good this morning," Matt responded. One-by-one each of the portfolio leaders joined the conference call and the on-line meeting began.

"Good morning everyone," Tom said and everyone in unison replied with a good morning. "In three weeks, I have a meeting with the Board of Directors, so today I want to get an idea of your immediate future plans for improvement. How many of you have fully implemented my Ultimate Improvement Cycle methodology," he asked. Bill Dawson, from Tamsen Auto Parts, was the first to reply and said that his company had fully implemented it and that their scrap and rework levels had improved dramatically, along with their rework levels. "How about everyone else? Have you all seen similar results?" Tom asked. Everyone in the group replied and said they had seen similar results.

Tom then asked, "What about the Theory of Constraints Replenishment Solution?" Tim Selsa, from Jackson Electronics responded and said, "We saw an unbelievable reduction in stock-outs as we reduced it from 13.4% down to 2.2%!" Matt Maloney then said, "You think that was good, ours dropped from 19.1% down to 0.7%!" "Wow!" everyone exclaimed. Then, Tom asked, "How about everyone's Efficiency %?" There was a general laugh that followed with that question as everyone's efficiency had fallen dramatically. Once again Matt Maloney responded and said, "That was the most surprising change for me. I never dreamed that reducing our overall efficiency metric would be a positive result of our improvement efforts!" Everyone in the group had similar feelings on that metric. What they were reporting was the actual average efficiency of their constraint plus their non-constraints.

Tom began again, "I want everyone to know that your % Profit Margins are simply amazing, but not surprising at all. I mean, look at where you are now compared to where you were before you started your improvement initiatives. All of your companies are now approaching a profit margin of thirty percent!" Sarah Johnson from Watson Rubber Articles spoke up and said, "I never imagined profit margins this high Tom and my company is just so thankful to you for teaching us the right way to run our company!" Everyone in attendance agreed with Sarah.

Tom then responded to Sarah's comments and said, "Yes, I did teach you a new way to run your companies, but it was you that spearheaded your improvement efforts and ultimate results. Does anyone have anything new that you want to share with this group?" Tom asked. Matt Maloney then said, "Yes, I have something to share." "And what is that Matt?" Tom asked. "Well, when you taught us about Drum Buffer Rope, I absolutely believed that using traditional DBR was the right way to go and I still do. But after thinking about it more, and relating our multiple production lines, I have a new idea," Matt said. "And what is your new idea Matt?" Tom asked.

"We have five production lines in our plant with each one making a slightly different type of water heater. And in each line, the location of the constraint is different," Matt said as he loaded a figure describing what he had just explained (Figure 21.1).

Matt continued, "In this configuration of multiple drums, there are also multiple ropes, and each has different requirements. There are multiple signal points for the rope as seen in this figure. The signal of each rope would be back to the buffer to release more work for that particular line. The second rope goes back to the raw material release areas to support the needs of the buffer, which in turn releases work at the front of the water heater line."

"It's my belief that the advantage of this concept is to reduce the tendency for economic batch size quantity. Many companies believe when they set up a machine to make parts, they should make as many parts as they can, especially if the machine is expensive, or the setup times seem especially long. The thought that this economic batch size quantity somehow saves money is, at best, absurd, based upon what you taught is about Throughput Accounting. The economic batch size only serves to slow down throughput in the system," Matt explained.

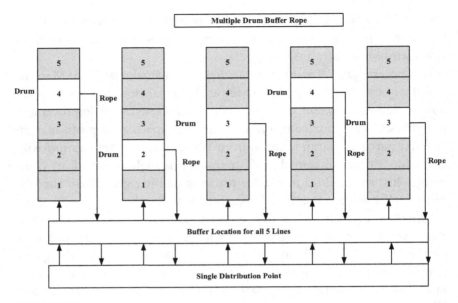

FIGURE 21.1
Multiple Drum Buffer Rope at Simpson Water Heaters.

He continued his explanation and said, "No money has been saved at all! In fact, it will cost additional amounts of money because throughput will have been damaged, revenue is lost, and the dollars will have been spent to buy those raw materials and parts that aren't needed yet. It's my belief instead, that you should manage the constraint, conduct the setups in the sequence and frequency required from the drumbeat in the lines, and solve the problem of shorter setup times as they occur using Single Minute Exchange of Dies (SMED) techniques. The action of the machine should be to support the buffer for the various 'I' line drums, not maintain 'high efficiency' at the expense of making money."

Tom responded and said, "Matt, I believe what you have just presented is a brilliant concept and one that should be shared with all of the Board's portfolio of companies!" There were numerous other positive comments from the other plant leaders. Tim Selsa, from Jackson Electronics, was especially complimentary and indicated that when he returned to his company, he would absolutely want to implement this new concept. He even asked Matt if he would be willing to come to his manufacturing facility and assist them with their implementation of M-DBR, and Matt indicated that he would be happy to help. Tom had one more question for Matt,

"Matt, have you actually implemented this concept?" Matt replied, "Yes, we implemented it four days ago and I can't wait to see what happens to our profit margins." "I have a meeting with the Board in a couple of weeks, so please update your performance metrics before I go," Tom said. When nobody else had any comments, Tom ended the session, and everyone left.

The next item on Tom's agenda was to have a meeting with all of the hospitals within the Maximo Health Center Complex. He wanted to see how each of the hospitals was performing, so he decided he would contact each hospital leader and schedule a joint meeting with all of the leaders of each hospital. He then called Pete Hallwell, the CFO at Maximo Health Center Complex, and his general contact during the improvement efforts. He looked in his desk and found the hospital name and person in charge (Figure 21.2).

The meeting was scheduled for the next day, and he really looked forward to hearing about each of the hospital's improvement efforts. As he talked to each of the hospital leaders, he requested their latest status on the set of performance metrics (Table 21.3) that they had all agreed to keep records of. The next morning Tom arrived around 7:30 am at the corporate office of Maximo Health Center Complex where he was greeted by Pete Hallwell. They took the elevator to the seventh-floor conference room and waited for everyone to arrive. When everyone had arrived, Pete was the first one to speak. "Good morning everyone, I hope you're ready for today's session with Tom Mahanan today. I want each of you to present your results and be ready to answer any questions Tom might have," Pete explained. "Let's start with Tom Jones from Children's Hospital," Pete said.

Tom Jones walked to the front of the room and began, "First, let me say thank you to Tom Mahanan for everything he has taught us over the past

- Maximo Children's Hospital, specializing in children's ailments, Tom Jones

- Maximo Women's Hospital, specializing in pregnancies, Philip Zagst

- Maximo Veteran's Hospital, specializing in military veterans, Marie Thomas

- Maximo Oncology Hospital, specializing in cancer treatments, Terry Sample

- Maximo Surgical Hospital, specializing in surgical operations, Patricia Smith

- Maximo Emergency Hospital, specializing in emergency patients, Ted Simpson

FIGURE 21.2
Maximo Hospitals and leaders.

TABLE 21.3

Maximo Health Center Complex Hospitals

Hospital Name	Avg. ED Hrs of Wait Time for Services		Patient Satisfaction Index		Med Stock-Out %		Bed Occupancy Rate (Days)		% Profit Margins	
	Before	After	Before	After	Before	After	Before	After	Before	After
Children's Hospital	2.5	1.2	82.1	91.7	11.2	0.5	6.7	4.5	+4.2	+9.9
Women's Hospital	2.9	1.5	83.3	90.1	10.8	0.7	5.9	3.4	+2.9	+10.6
Veteran's Hospital	3.4	1.6	78.1	91.1	9.8	0.7	7.8	3.9	+1.8	+14.8
Oncology Hospital	2.8	1.4	82.2	90.8	8.1	0.5	8.2	4.3	+6.2	+17.1
Surgical Hospital	2.7	1.1	80.4	88.8	8.9	1.1	7.3	3.6	+7.4	15.8
Emergency Hospital	1.9	0.7	83.8	93.5	9.9	0.5	3.9	2.4	+3.9	+18.9

several months. As you can see on the screen our before and after results. And while all of these metrics have improved, the one that stands out for me is our Average Emergency Department Wait Time for Services as we have cut this time in half!" "This metric, above all others fully describes our improvement effort results. To think that we have cut the wait time in half means so very much to the parents of the children needing our services. I think it's probably the main reason our Patient Satisfaction metric has improved so much," he explained. He then presented the rest of his metrics and sat down.

Philip Zagst, from Maximo Women's Hospital, was the next to speak, and like Tom Jones, he thanked Tom Mahanan for all of his help in transforming his hospital. Just like Tom Jones, he was especially happy with how much they had reduced their Average Emergency Department Wait Time for Services. He explained that he was also very happy with their new profit margins which were now approaching 11%. Ted Simpson, from Maximo Emergency Hospital, took the floor.

Ted began, "I have been especially blessed to work directly with Tom Mahanan. He has helped us change the course of history at our hospital and I will be forever indebted to him. While all of our performance metrics improved substantially, the one that stands out the most is our new % Profit Margin which is now approaching twenty percent! In all of my years in the medical field, I never expected to see profit margins at a hospital rise to this level," he explained.

Marie Thomas from Maximo Veteran's Hospital then said, "I too want to thank Tom for everything he has taught us, but I'm especially thankful for our new Patient Satisfaction Index which, before we started our improvement journey was at 78.1% and now sits at over 91%. This is a very important metric for us since we specialize in helping our military veterans who don't deserve to wait for our services."

Terry Sample from Maximo Oncology Hospital was next to speak and like the rest of the hospital leaders thanked Tom for his efforts. "Since our objective is to treat various cancer patients, it's extremely important that we always have the necessary meds available when they are needed. Because of Tom's teachings, especially on the Theory of Constraints Replenishment Solution, our stock-out percentage is among the best in our complex of hospitals. Before we started, our Stock-Out % was around eight percent, but now we're down to less than one percent."

And finally, Patricia Smith from Maximo Surgical Hospital stood up and said, "Our Bed Occupancy Rate, before we started our improvement efforts stood at 7.3%, but now, because of our Drum Buffer Rope implementation, it has dropped to 3.6%. This means that we can perform many more surgeries which is reflected in our new % Profit Margin which is now almost 16%!" "So, thank you Tom for everything you have taught us and know that we will be forever grateful to you!" she added.

Pete Hallwell thanked everyone for their presentations and then said, "I'm not sure if everyone knows this, but Tom Mahanan and I first met at, of all places, a golf course. I was part of a foursome and was fortunate enough to have shared a golf cart with Tom. I can't remember exactly how we got onto the subject of system's improvement, but as we continued playing the round of golf, Tom shared the basics of the Theory of Constraints and all that it has to offer. Based upon what I heard that day, I invited Tom to come meet with me and the rest, shall we say, is history. Oh, and by the way, Tom and I won the skins game we played with the other golfers."

Pete continued, "After our meeting the next day, I offered Tom a consulting contract and I must say, I think that was the best decision I have ever made!" "To think how far each of our hospitals in our complex have come, is simply an amazing feat. So, Tom, when we originally signed our consulting agreement, it was to last for a year. But I'd like to extend our contract for at least another year. We would be honored to have you continue to help us get better and better," he said. Tom responded immediately and said that he would be honored to continue working with Maximo. "Great Tom, I have a contract ready for you to sign right now," he said as he reached into his brief case and pulled it out. Without hesitation, Tom signed it and with that, the meeting was adjourned.

As Tom was driving home, he thought about his meeting next week with the Board of Directors and what he had to do to prepare. Upon arriving home, he was met at the door by his wife and kids and received big hugs from everyone. They sat down to dinner and to his surprise, his wife had made his favorite meal, which was chicken divan! The family exchanged pleasantries throughout dinner, and then, Tom let his wife know about the extended consulting agreement with Maximo Health Center Complex. She was very happy to hear about her new agreement, but then, she had a surprise for Tom. "Honey, I have something to tell you," she said. "What's that honey?" Tom asked. "I'm pregnant!" she exclaimed. Tom got the biggest smile on his face, stood up and went over, kissed her, and then said, "I'm so happy to hear that sweetie!!"

Tom had requested updates from the four portfolio companies on their latest performance metrics, and when he checked his emails, he found updates from each of the companies. Tom worked the rest of the week on his presentation to the Board of Directors which was scheduled for Monday morning. He updated his metrics slide and then thought about how he would present it. He also thought about the payment offer he had made to Jonathan Briggs and wondered whether the Board would approve his offer. To think that he could possibly be a part owner of future companies excited him. He worked off and on throughout the weekend, and then, Sunday he flew to Chicago.

As usual, on Monday morning, there was a car ready for him that drove him to his Board meeting. He signed in, and Jonathan met him in the lobby. They exchanged greetings and took the elevator to the conference room which was full of Board Members. Jonathan welcomed everyone and then, once again, introduced Tom to the Board of Directors. Tom thanked everyone for inviting him back to Chicago and began his presentation.

"First of all, when I accepted your offer to improve the results of the original portfolio of companies, I never expected to realize the results that were achieved. After all, my background prior to this had been almost exclusively in the financial world. I learned so much working with the original portfolio of companies which have carried over into the latest four companies," he explained as he posted a table of results onto the screen (Table 21.4). When the results were seen by the Board members, there was a distinct hush that came over the room. They were not surprised with the end results, but they were amazed that the results came as quickly as they did!

When everyone had digested the new data, Jonathan spoke up and said, "Tom, these results are totally amazing!" He continued, "While the actual results aren't surprising to me, the speed at which you have achieved them certainly is!" "I am especially surprised with the results you were able to achieve with Simpson Water Heaters. To think that when you started, they were losing money and now they are the most profitable of all of our portfolio companies is mind boggling!" he exclaimed. "Well, thank you for your glowing remarks Jonathan, but the credit has to go to Matt Maloney," Tom replied. "He actually led his team, so to speak, to victory," Tom added.

They continued discussing the various bits of data Tom had presented until Jonathan spoke up and said, "So, Tom, the Board and I have been discussing your latest consulting payment proposal over the past week. What you requested was that you'd like to get an equity percentage for each company that we end up buying," Jonathan said. "You also suggested

TABLE 21.4

Portfolio Performance Metrics Update

Company Name	% On-Time Delivery		% Scrap		% Rework		Stock-Out %		Efficiency %		% Profit Margins	
	Bef	Aft	Bef	Aft	Bef	Aft	Bef	Aft	Bef	Aft	Bef	Aft
Tamsen Auto Parts	68.9	96.8	4.8	1.1	10.1	3.2	11.2	0.5	95.4	63.1	+5.7	+31.1
Simpson Water Heaters	75.2	98.8	8.8	0.5	15.6	2.2	19.1	0.3	94.7	60.1	−1.2	+34.3
Watson Rubber Articles	70.9	95.3	6.8	1.7	8.8	3.4	9.9	0.6	88.7	63.2	+7.8	+30.2
Jackson Electronics	75.4	94.1	4.9	1.1	14.2	3.5	13.4	0.7	89.9	60.2	+9.1	+30.2

something like three percent for each one based upon the new profit levels after one year of turning each one around," Jonathan continued. "And finally, you suggested that after the first payout, your equity would drop to one percent and would last forever," he explained. Jonathan then said, "I told you that I had to discuss this proposal with the other Board members. Did I get your payment method correct Tom?" Jonathan asked.

Tom responded and said, "Yes Jonathan, you got it absolutely right." "After much discussion, the Board and I have decided to not accept your payment recommendation," he said. He then added, "Our counteroffer goes like this," he said, "Your payment for each company we decide to purchase, will be $200,000 with one caveat, and that is, the profits need to at least double after one year. At the end of the year, assuming the profits have doubled, you will receive the $200,000 plus 1% of the profits forever. And if we were to sell the company, you would receive another payment of $200,000. We think this offer is a fair offer, so what do you think?" he asked.

"I think the offer you have made is a very reasonable offer and I am pleased to tell you that I accept it, but with one additional caveat. On sign-ing this agreement, I want a signing bonus of $500,000 to be payable the day I sign your offer?" he replied. Jonathan looked around the room and saw most heads nodding in the affirmative, so he turned to Tom, and extended his hand, and the two of them shook hands in agreement.

Jonathan offered to take Tom to dinner that night, and he accepted the offer. They decided to meet at a restaurant close to Tom's hotel at 7:00 pm. As Tom walked in the door, he could see Jonathan already seated, along with a couple of the Board Members. They all stood up and shook hands with Jonathan, then ordered a bottle of champagne. When the drinks were in place, Jonathan reached in his brief case and pulled out a piece of paper. It was Tom's new contract and a check for $500,000! Tom immediately signed the contract, and they all ordered and ate their dinner.

As soon as Tom reached his hotel room, he called his wife and said, "Are you sitting down honey?" She said, "Yes I am, what's up?" Tom explained the details of his new contract with her, and she replied, "That's fantastic honey!" Tom replied and said, "I've never been more surprised in my entire life when Jonathan handed me a check for $500,000 tonight!"

"Wow Tom, but I have something to tell you honey that might surprise you even more. I told you I was pregnant, but what I didn't know was that we are having triplets!" "Really? This is the greatest day of my life!" he exclaimed.

22

The Virus

On Tom's flight home, he kept thinking about his future family. "Triplets! I never expected anything like this," he thought. He continued thinking, "Because of our new family size, we'll probably have to buy a new house with more bedrooms. I am so thankful that I received such a huge royalty payment!" As he was sitting there thinking about his new family size, the passenger beside him said, "So what do you think is going to happen as a result of this new virus?" Tom hadn't been watching the news and replied, "What virus is that?" The passenger replied, "It's called the Corona Virus or Covid-19." "Tell me more," Tom said. "Well, apparently there is a virus that supposedly originated somewhere in China and the news reports are saying it's very deadly," said the passenger. "Do you have any idea what the symptoms are for this virus?" Tom asked. The passenger replied, "I'm not sure about all of the symptoms, but I did hear that two of the symptoms are a dry cough and a fever."

Tom decided to log onto his computer and read more about this new virus. He found an article on it with the headline, "Deadly Corona Virus Spreading Quickly Throughout China and is Spreading to Other Countries." Tom immediately thought about his family and how he wanted to get home. He continued searching for more information until his plane finally landed in Pittsburgh. He grabbed his bag and headed for the parking lot to find his car. On his way home, he called his wife. "Hi honey, I'll be so glad to get home," he said. She replied, "And we'll be happy to get you home." They continued talking, and one thing Tom noticed that his wife kept coughing. He then said, "Honey, are you feeling ok?" She responded and said, "I've had this nagging cough for a couple of days and today I have a fever." "Have you called the doctor?" he asked. "Not yet, as I thought maybe my cough was an allergy, but now that I have a fever, I'll call him tomorrow," she replied.

About an hour later, Tom arrived home and hugged his wife and kids. They all sat down and ate dinner together, and then, Tom decided to turn on the news to see if he could hear something about the Corona Virus. What he heard pretty much shocked him as the newscaster focused on the number of infections and the death rate, which were both very high. This menace of a virus apparently hadn't hit the United States yet, but this same newscaster explained that it was just a matter of time before it did. Tom decided to get on the Internet and find out more about this virus. As he was reading, one thing he noticed was the length of time it took to actually get the test results. What he read shocked him, in that after the test was administered, the patient had to wait for two full weeks before finding out if they were infected with the virus. Tom thought to himself, "Well that surely is one of the constraints that must be addressed!"

Tom continued reading and discovered that there was also a shortage of test kits available, and because of this, the medical profession was forced to only test people who had exhibited symptoms of the virus. Tom then thought, "I wonder who the manufacturer of these test kits is? I hope whoever it is, that they've been exposed to the Theory of Constraints so that the throughput of kits can be accelerated." But perhaps the most serious thing Tom read was that there was no vaccination available to prevent this virus from being transmitted and received. Needless to say, the more Tom read, the more worried he became about his wife and her symptoms. "Could she be infected with the Corona Virus?" he thought. He also thought, "If she is infected, what about our two kids? What will be do with them to keep them safe? And what about our unborn triplets?" he thought.

The next morning Tom had his wife call her doctor to make an appointment and scheduled it for later that day. Tom decided to work a bit on some things related to his consulting work, but no matter how hard he tried, he had difficulty concentrating on his work. He kept thinking about the ramifications of his wife possibly being infected with the Corona Virus. He thought to himself, "If she does have the virus, she could be gravely ill, but regardless she will have to be self-quarantined for at least 2 weeks." He kept thinking about all of the problems he read about on the Internet and how he honestly believed that, if given the chance, he might be able to help the medical community speed-up the testing, as well as the company that produces the test kits. He then thought to himself, "I wonder if Jonathan might know anyone in the government that he could call to offer his services for free."

His wife's appointment time arrived, and they traveled to the doctor's office. When they arrived and met with Dr. Thompson, they discovered that her doctor did not have any test kits for this apparently new type virus. Dr. Thompson made several phone calls until he was able to locate a medical facility that did have the test kits available. They immediately scheduled an appointment for Tom's wife, Beverly, to come in for testing. Beverly took the test and was instructed to "self-isolate" for 2 weeks, meaning she should not leave her house and avoid contact with neighbors and other family members. Beverly contacted her mother to let her know her health status, and her mother immediately volunteered to come watch her kids. Beverly instantly explained that in her mother's age group (i.e. over 60), the death rate from this virus is very high and that she needed to stay home and away from her for at least 2 weeks. Her mother reluctantly agreed to do so.

Tom set up the guest room for himself to sleep in, so that his wife could feel more comfortable in their master bedroom during her self-isolation. Because not much was yet known about the impact of this virus, Tom decided to err on the side of safety. He knew that he would have to care for his two children so as to avoid contact with their mother. His two children were ages eight and ten, and although what he had read about the Corona Virus, that they were less vulnerable, again he decided to err on the side of safety. Tom had heard earlier that all schools in Western Pennsylvania were canceled for at least 2 weeks, so he knew he had to stay home during that period of time. Because of the school being canceled, Tom decided to set up some form of home schooling, in the event that schools would remain closed beyond the current 2-week period.

Tom also decided to research as much as he could about this virus so that he would have a much better understanding of the potential impact on hospitals and other medical facilities and the American citizens. "After all," he thought, "if these medical facilities were overwhelmed with patients needing testing and treatment, they should have a clear understanding of how the Theory of Constraints could be used to positively impact patient flow." Tom thought about what constraints might exist and the first one he considered was this 2-week period where the patients had to wait for test results. In order to help shorten this wait time, he needed to understand why the test results were taking so long. The constraint was clearly the existing testing procedure, so someone needed to investigate this and come up with a much faster test method. He then thought about the treatment for this virus, which at this point was a sort of unknown entity and it too should be considered a constraint.

What he read scared him very much, as at this point in time he read that there was no cure for the Corona Virus (aka COVID-19), nor were there any specific medicines to prevent or treat it at this point in time. Tom was very worried about his wife Beverly and what her final outcome might be. He decided to research how things looked in Pennsylvania and found that the Pennsylvania Department of Health reported that there were 3,394 positive cases of the Corona Virus in the state and at least 38 people had died from the virus. Tom and his family lived in Allegheny County, so he looked up the infection rate and found that Allegheny County had reported 265 cases with 2 deaths.

Tom continued thinking about what he might do if he was asked to help solve this mystifying problem. He thought, "This is a very complicated problem that has several constraining factors associated with it. The fact that the test takes so long to get results is a serious issue facing human-ity. We need to very quickly develop a different test that takes hours or minutes to determine if a patient has the Corona Virus." He then thought, "But even if we do come up with a faster test, the most important things we need to discover is first, how do we save the lives of those people already infected? Saving lives must be our first priority! Almost as important is coming up with a way on how to prevent this disease from attacking peo-ple. Prevention truly is almost as important as saving the lives of those already infected."

Tom decided to call the Chairman of the Board, Jonathan Briggs. Jonathan was the man Tom used to report to when he sat on the Board of Directors of Jonathan's portfolio of companies. Tom had worked for one of those companies, Tires for All, and had led major improvements in profit-ability. Because Tom wanted to help fight this deadly virus, he wanted to see if Jonathan might know anyone who might be interested in using his services for free. He dialed Jonathan's number, and after three rings, he answered his phone. "Hi Jonathan, it's Tom Mahanan," Tom said. "Well hi Tom, it's so good to hear from you. What's up?" he asked.

"Jonathan, I've been reading quite a bit about the Corona Virus and how complicated everything is. I'm very interested in helping solve this complicated disease and I was wondering if you knew anyone at the fore-front of this disease that I could call and offer my services for free," Tom explained. "That's very kind of you Tom, so let me check into just who

I might know, and I'll get back to you with the names of several people that might be interested in your free services," Jonathan replied. "Thanks Jonathan and I assume you are feeling ok?" he asked. "Yes, no problems so far," he replied. And with that, the conversation ended.

Several hours later, Tom received a call back from Jonathan with the names of two medical professionals that could possibly be interested in working with Tom. One of the doctors, Dr. Samuel Johnson, was from New York City, and the other doctor, Dr. Timothy Wasso, was from Chicago. Both doctors were in hot bed areas where the virus was flourishing. Jonathan had provided Tom with their phone numbers, so Tom decided to call both of them, just to offer his services for free. During the conversation, Tom let both doctors know that he probably couldn't help them in the medical field, but that he could help them receive medical supplies at a faster rate. Dr. Johnson explained to Tom that he was in great need of ventilators, while Dr. Wasso explained that facial masks were critically needed. Both doctors gave Tom the names and phone numbers of their contacts at two of their suppliers.

Before Tom called these two contacts, he decided to do a little research on respirators and facial masks, just so he could speak intelligently to both of the contacts. Tom first researched ventilators and found that ventilators are the machines that push and pull air through a tube connected to the lungs, allowing people with limited pulmonary capacity to breathe better. He also read that for people with severe infections from this Corona Virus, which attacks respiratory cells, these machines can literally be the difference between life and death.

Tom then researched facial masks and discovered that the Surgeon General's official post stated that "They are NOT effective in preventing general public from catching the Corona Virus, but if healthcare providers can't get them to care for sick patients, it puts them and our communities at risk!" Tom thought after reading this that, "Clearly we need to protect our healthcare workers first, so our country, and the world, needs to make sure that our healthcare workers aren't in jeopardy." So, with his new information on these two products, Tom decided to call both contacts to see if they were interested in his assistance.

He first contacted the ventilator company, Jefferson Ventilators. "Hello, this is Steve Thomas." Tom replied, "Hi Steve, my name is Tom Mahanan. I am an independent consultant and I specialize in helping companies improve the output of their products." Steve immediately replied and said,

"Hi Tom, sorry but we can't afford to hire a consultant at the moment." "Steve, I'm offering my services for free, if your company is interested," Tom said. "For free?" Steve said. "Yes, for free! I want to help with this pandemic in any way I can and since I'm not a doctor, I see the only way I can contribute is to help companies make major improvements in their output rate, without spending major amounts of money," Tom replied.

The two of them continued talking, and Steve thanked Tom for his generous offer. "In all my years in manufacturing, I've never been given an offer quite like the one you just made me. So, Tom, how would we go about doing this?" Steve asked. Tom replied, "I've given this a lot of thought and I think the best way to do this would be for me to have a webinar with your company with your key manufacturing personnel in attendance." Steve then asked, "So, what would be included in your webinar?" Tom responded, "Not sure how familiar you are with the Theory of Constraints, but this will be the focus of the webinar. I'll demonstrate how you can combine the Theory of Constraints with Lean and Six Sigma that will result in significant improvements to your product throughput."

"Tom, it would be great if you could help us increase our output of ventilators!" Steve said. Tom replied, "When would you like to have our webinar?" "The sooner the better Tom!" Steve exclaimed. "Why don't you talk to your key people and get back to me as to when you'd like to have our webinar Steve," Tom said. "Who do you think should be in the audience for this webinar Tom?" Steve asked. Tom replied, "You need to invite your production managers, supervisors, your Industrial Engineers and anyone else that you think might benefit from our webinar." "Okay Tom, I'll have a meeting here and get back to you on when we could have your webinar," Steve said.

Tom then contacted the company that manufactures facial masks, The Mask Makers. "Hello, this is John Watson, how can I help you?" Once again, Tom explained who he was and made the same offer to John, and as with Jefferson Ventilators, The Mask Makers were very interested in Tom's offer for a free webinar on how to maximize their company's output. "How soon could you have this webinar Tom?" John asked. Tom then said, "As we were talking, what if we could hold a joint webinar with your company and Jefferson Ventilators?" "I have no problem at all with that," John replied. "Once I hear back from Jefferson Ventilators on when they want to have the webinar, I'll call you back and see if the day and time works for your company," Tom explained. "Sounds good to me Tom and thank you for your offer," John said.

While Tom eagerly awaited his call back from Jefferson Ventilators, he began planning his webinar. He thought to himself, "Now what should I include in this webinar?" He assumed that both of these companies would have experience with Lean and Six Sigma, so he needed to focus the webinar on the Theory of Constraints. He could then explain just how to go about combining the Theory of Constraints with Lean and/or Six Sigma. He knew he wouldn't have time to explain either Lean or Six Sigma, but he could lay the foundation on how to use these three improvement methodologies in combination. And with these thoughts in mind, he began preparing a series of Power Point slides that he would deliver during his free webinar.

Just then, Tom's cell phone rang, and he answered it, "Hello, this is Tom Mahanan." "Hi Tom, it's Steve from Jefferson Ventilators. Would it be possible to have the webinar tomorrow at 3:00 pm?" Steve asked. "Yes, absolutely. I hope it's alright with you, but I've invited a company that produces facial masks to join in my webinar?" Tom asked. "Yes, that's actually a great idea! Killing two birds with one stone is better," Steve added. "I'll send you the login details later today Steve," Tom said. Just as Tom hung up, his phone rang again, and it was John from The Mask Makers. "Tom Mahanan here," Tom said as he answered his phone. "John from The Mask Makers here," said the voice on the other end. "Any idea on when you plan on having your webinar?" John asked. "Yes, our plan is to have it tomorrow at 3:00 pm," Tom replied. "Sounds great for us Tom," John replied. "Great John, I'll send you the login information a bit later today. Oh, and it's going to be a joint webinar with Jefferson Ventilators," he added.

Tom called both John and Steve back just to get an idea of what improvement methods both companies were using and discovered that Jefferson Ventilators was deep into Lean Manufacturing while The Mask Makers were using a combination of Lean and Six Sigma. He also asked each of them how much time he should plan on for the upcoming webinar. Both of them said that they thought an hour and a half would be the ideal amount of time. Using this information, Tom completed the preparation of his slide deck. Tom was very anxious to help both companies improve their rate of finished product generation and hope that what he presented would result in a meaningful new methodology for both companies. Tom put together the login information and sent it on to John and Steve. He also thought it would be a good idea to send a copy of his Power Point presentation to distribute to all of the webinar participants to make it easier to follow and to use it to train others in both companies.

23

The Webinar

It was now time for Tom's webinar to begin, so he logged in and waited for both companies to also login. When both companies were on-line, Tom welcomed everyone and began presenting his slide deck. "Today, because of time limitations, what I will present will be a 'fast' version of what normally takes several hours to present. What you see on the screen (Figure 23.1) is a simple cross section of a piping system used to

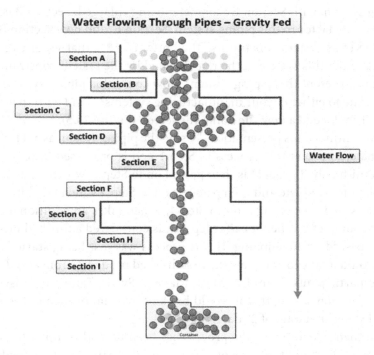

FIGURE 23.1
Piping diagram.

deliver water. It is a gravity fed system with water entering Section A, then flows into Section B, and continues downward until it collects in the receptacle at the base of the system."

Tom then asked the group, "If you wanted a higher rate of flow of water through this piping system, what would you need to do?" One of the participants from Jefferson Ventilators, Tony Jefferson, responded and said, "Based upon what I see in this diagram, it looks like Section E is limiting how much water can flow through this system. So, I would say that you would have to increase the diameter of Section E?" he said in a question-like manner. "Does everyone see what Tony has pointed out?" Tom asked. When everyone in attendance seemed to agree with Tony, Tom asked a different question. "Tony, since your last name is Jefferson, and you work for Jefferson Ventilators, are you part of the Jefferson family?" Tom asked. Tony replied and said, "The man who started this company was my grandfather, so the answer is yes." With that response, Tom loaded a new Power Point slide onto his screen (Figure 23.2).

Tom continued, "Based upon Tony's suggestion, here you see the same piping system, with Section E's diameter being enlarged. Section B is now the limiting factor in this piping system. Section E, and now Section B, are referred to as system constraints. The bottom line is that water can only flow through this system at the rate dictated by the system constraint. So why did I present this piping system? How could this piping system possibly relate to either of your manufacturing systems?" And with that comment, Tom loaded a new slide onto his screen (Figure 23.3).

Tom continued his presentation, "Using the piping system as a reference, raw material enters this process in Step 1 and is processed for two days. The semi-finished product is then passed on to Step 2, which takes seventeen days to complete and then passes it on to Step 3 which takes five days to process before passing it on to Step 4, which takes an additional three days to complete. When it exits Step 4, it is considered a finished product and is passed on to shipping. If this process was just being started, how long would it take to complete the first finished product?" Tom asked. One of the participants from The Mask Makers, Sylvia Tammers, answered Tom's question saying that it would be the sum total of each of the individual steps for a total of 27 days.

Tom then asked, "Once the process has been up and running for some time, what is the output rate of this process?" Again, Sylvia replied and said, "My guess is that it would depend upon what you referred to as

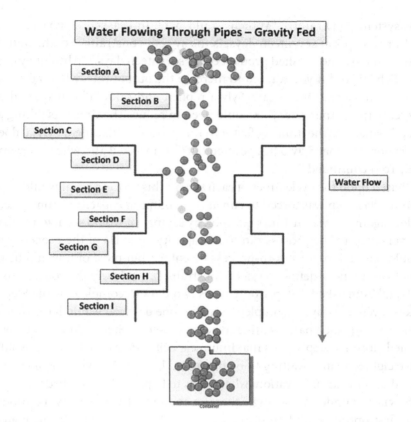

FIGURE 23.2
Piping system with a new constraint.

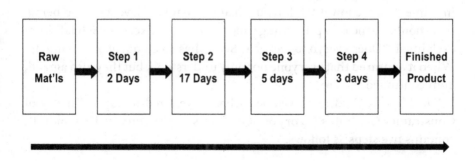

Total Cycle Days = "X" Days

FIGURE 23.3
Simple 4-step process.

the system constraint?" "Which would be?" Tom asked. Sylvia replied, "Clearly, Step 2 at seventeen days, is the system constraint. So, the output rate would be one finished product every seventeen days." "Absolutely correct Sylvia! And if you wanted to increase the output rate, what must you do?" Tom asked. Once again Sylvia replied and said, "If you wanted to increase the output rate, you would need to reduce the time it is taking at Step 2, since it is the limiting factor in this process." "Excellent Sylvia, does everyone see what Sylvia has pointed out?" Tom asked and when everyone did, Tom continued.

"Based upon the cycle times of each step in this process, what would happen if every step was forced to run at its maximum capacity?" Tom asked. Sylvia again, answered Tom's question by saying, "It would seem to me that if every step in the process ran to its capacity, in parts of the process you would have a ton of work-in-process inventory, but most of it would be in front of our now defined system constraint." "And why do you say that Sylvia?" Tom asked. "Step 1 only takes two days to complete, while Step 2 takes seventeen days to complete. So, after one day, you would have almost nine semi-finished parts waiting to be processed by Step 2. And if you continued running Step 1 at its maximum capacity, after two days, you would have eighteen parts waiting to be processed by Step 2," Sylvia replied. "So based upon your observation, what needs to happen?" Tom asked.

Sylvia responded by saying, "It seems to me that you have two options. The first option would be to increase Step 1's processing time to match that of the constraint. But that wouldn't make much sense. The second option, which is a much better option, would be to reduce Step 2's processing time to some lower level. And whatever that new level ends up being, that should be the new processing time for Step 1." "Excellent Sylvia!" Tom exclaimed. "Does everyone see what Sylvia has so eloquently explained?" When it appeared that everyone not only understood, but they also agreed, Tom continued.

"Dr. Eliyahu Goldratt developed what he referred to as the Theory of Constraints. Goldratt's Theory of Constraints, as presented by Dr. Goldratt, contains five steps as follows:

- Step 1: Identify the system constraint.
- Step 2: Decide how to exploit the system constraint.
- Step 3: Subordinate everything else to the system constraint.
- Step 4: If necessary, elevate the system constraint.
- Step 5: Return to Step 1 to identify the new system constraint."

"If you think about our four-step process, there is a huge gap between the cycle time of Step 1 and Step 2. So, my next question for everyone is, how could you reduce the cycle time of Step 2 to make it more in line with the other steps in the process?" Tom asked.

Jeffrey Holstein, an employee at Jefferson Ventilators said, "It seems to me that since there is such a huge difference in cycle times between Steps 1 and 2, that you might have to add another Step 2 to this process. What I mean by that is, if you set up an identical Step 2 beside the current Step 2, you would reduce the total cycle time by half, so instead of it taking seventeen days to complete, Step 2 would now take just eight and a half days to complete. And in so doing, you would have doubled the output of this process?" Jeffrey said in the form of a question. Tom replied, "Jeffrey, that is an excellent idea! Does everyone see what Jeffrey is saying?" Tom asked and everyone did.

"This is Step 4 of Goldratt's Five Focusing Steps, which says if necessary, elevate the system constraint," Tom explained. He continued, "And if you added two additional Step 2's, you would reduce the effective cycle time to four and a quarter, days which would make the new constraint be Step 3 at five days. This is the concept of elevating the system constraint, to create a new system constraint. And to increase the throughput of this process, you would then need to focus on the new constraint, which is what Step 5 tells us to do."

Tom's time for the webinar was almost complete, so he decided to stop and ask for comments and questions. Steve, from Jefferson Ventilators, was the first to comment and said "In all my years in manufacturing, I had never been introduced to the Theory of Constraints. But I must say going forward, it will become an integral part of our improvement efforts. I personally want to thank you Tom for such an enlightening session today." Tom thanked him for his comment and let everyone know that as they work to produce more ventilators and facial masks, if they have questions, everyone must feel free to contact him.

John from The Mask Makers asked another question, "Tom, not sure about Jefferson Ventilators, but at our company we have been using Lean and Six Sigma to improve our process. Is there a way to combine our current improvement efforts with the Theory of Constraints?" "Excellent question John and the answer is a resounding yes!" Tom replied. "Could we take a few more minutes to answer this important question?" Tom asked. Both John and Steve said yes, so Tom continued and flashed a new overhead onto the screen (Figure 23.4).

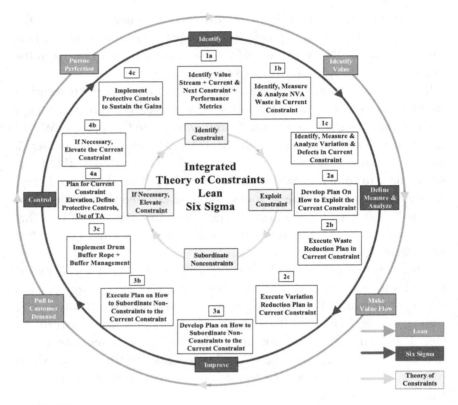

FIGURE 23.4
How to integrate Theory of Constraints, Lean, and Six Sigma.

"What you see on the screen is what I refer to as the Ultimate Improvement Cycle or UIC. In it you will see the steps required to integrate all three of these initiatives into a single improvement initiative." Tom then loaded two slides on the screen, which summarized the tools, actions, and focus of combining these three initiatives (Figure 23.5) and the expected deliverables.

"In this first slide I have outlined the basic ingredients of the UIC, or those tools and actions needed to use the UIC," Tom explained. Tom then explained that the second slide (Figure 23.6) outlines the expected deliverables from this combination of improvement initiatives. "So, if you were to combine these three improvement initiatives, there are a host of expectations you should expect to see when you are successful in doing so," Tom explained. "I have tried to keep this simple for everyone to understand,

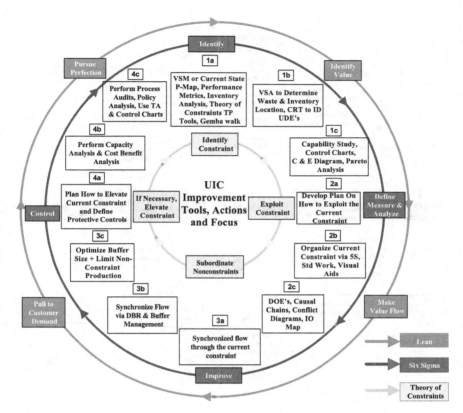

FIGURE 23.5
Tools, actions, and focus of the UIC.

and since we don't have much time left in today's session, I want everyone to study these three slides and consider how your processes might use them to improve the output of your processes and system," Tom explained.

"I know you'll have quite a few questions going forward and I want everyone to know that I will be available to take phone calls or emails any time you need answers. What I've explained to you today, is just part of the Theory of Constraints, so I wish you much luck. We can overcome this terrible virus, so take what I gave you today and apply it to your processes," Tom stated. And with that, the webinar ended. John and Steve stayed on-line to have a few words with Tom.

Steve was the first to speak and said, "Tom, I personally want to thank you for all of the valuable information you gave us today. And to think you did this without any kind of charge is mind boggling!" John then added,

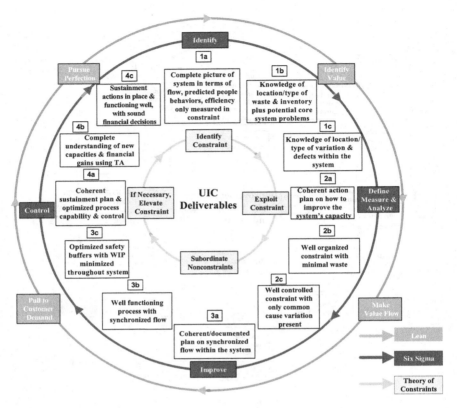

FIGURE 23.6
Expected deliverable from the UIC.

"I totally agree with Steve. In the future I can see our facial mask business being able to supply many more masks to not only the medical community, but to the citizens of America and the world in general." He then added, "I also appreciate you being available for assistance as we implement our new improvement methodology." Steve then chimed in and said, "Tom, would it be possible for us to have a weekly, on-line update?" "Yes, absolutely Steve!" Tom replied. "Just let me know when you both would like to schedule it and I will make myself available." Tom added.

It has now been two weeks since Tom's wife, Beverly, had been tested for the Corona Virus and they were both eagerly awaiting the test results. Later on, in the day, they received a call from her doctor's office with the news that Beverly did not have the virus, and needless to say both were excited to hear this news. Finally, Beverly could get back to her normal life of caring for her children. Tom was thankful because he could get back to focusing on virtually helping companies improve their profitability, especially Jefferson Ventilators and The Mask Makers. Tom hadn't heard anything back from either company on how their improvement efforts were progressing, so he decided to contact both companies to get an update.

As he was sitting on his couch watching television, the broadcaster provided the latest infection and death rates on the Corona Virus and they were staggering. Apparently 200,000 Americans had been infected with nearly 4,400 deaths being recorded. Worldwide, there are nearly 1,000,000 confirmed cases with nearly 46,000 deaths. The announcer also talked about the apparent shortage of both ventilators and facial masks which prompted Tom to make the call to Steve and John, so he called Steve first. Steve answered the phone, and Tom said, "Hi Steve, it's Tom and I was wondering how you're doing on implementing the Theory of Constraints?" Steve replied, "Tom, I don't know how we could have supplied enough ventilators without incorporating the Theory of Constraints. As a result of your webinar, we have actually tripled the rate of ventilator production!" "That's fantastic Steve!" Tom replied. "But Tom, we're just getting started. We think that at the end of the day our throughput rate will have increased by a factor of five!" Steve added. "Let me know if you need anything Steve," Tom replied, and they both hung up.

Tom then called John from The Mask Makers. "Hello, John here," John said as he answered the phone. "Hi John, it's Tom and I was just calling to see how things are going since you learned about the Theory of Constraints?" Tom asked. "Tom, all I can say is that they're going fantastic!" John stated. "Since leaving your webinar, we have been able to triple the rate on the number of facial masks we can produce, and we truly believe that this rate will increase substantially over the next month." "You remember Sylvia from the webinar?" John asked. "I sure do John," Tom replied. "I was so impressed with her answers to the questions you asked in the webinar that I put her in charge of incorporating the Theory of Constraints and that was a great move!" John explained. "After the webinar, on her own, she went out and purchased a couple of books and then stayed up all night reading them," John added. "Which books did she buy?" Tom asked. "She bought *The Goal* by Eli Goldratt and Jeff Cox and *Epiphanized* by Bruce Nelson and Bob Sproull. I was so impressed with her work that I bought all of my supervisors a copy of both books," John explained. "Thanks for the update John and if you need anything, call me," Tom said.

After he hung up, Tom became curious about what a ventilator is and why they are so important in some coronavirus cases? He logged on to the internet to see what he could find. According to a man named David Hill, a Pulmonologist who sits on the board of the American Lung Association, "A ventilator is a fairly fancy piece of technological equipment which is designed to breathe for somebody who is unable to breathe effectively on their own." Apparently, a ventilator essentially helps a patient's lungs accomplish this task. He continued reading and read that modern ventilators consist of a pump machine and a tube that healthcare professionals slide into a victim's windpipe to control airflow. Tom also read that it's important to understand that ventilators do not cure the Corona Virus, but they help support lung function while a patient's body is fighting the infection. "Wow, no wonder ventilator companies are trying to produce more," Tom thought.

The next day, as Tom was working on a new slide deck, his cell phone rang. He answered it and said, "Hello, this is Tom Mahanan." "Hi Tom, it's Steve. I have a question for you about the Theory of Constraints," he said. "Sure Steve, what's up?" Tom asked. "I was wondering whether or not the Theory of Constraints has anything that addresses parts shortages?" Steve asked. "It most certainly does Steve, why did you ask that?" Tom asked. "Well, with our new improvement methodology, we have been running into problems with parts not being available for our ventilators. We could actually be producing more, but we don't have all of the parts we need," Steve explained. "Why don't I set up another webinar to explain the Theory of Constraints Replenishment Solution," Tom responded. "Sounds great Tom," Steve said. "Why don't I call John and see if he wants to be a part of it?" Steve added. "That would be a good idea, so let me know what he says," Tom said. "I will Tom and thanks," Steve replied.

Fifteen minutes later Tom received a call back from Steve who explained that John was having the same problem with parts availability, so he wanted to be a part of this webinar. They discussed when they should have this webinar, and both agreed that tomorrow at 2:00 pm would work. Tom told Steve that he would send him the login details for the webinar, and as soon as they hung up, he began preparing a slide deck for tomorrow's webinar. Once again, Tom decided that he would not go into great detail, but rather he would provide the basics of what needed to happen to implement this important effort.

The next day, at 2:00 pm, Tom logged into the site and waited for both companies to join him on-line. When everyone was on-line, Tom began. "Most, if not all, businesses are linked one way or another to some kind of supply chain system. Companies need parts or raw materials from somebody else, in order to do what they do and pass it on to the next system in line until it finally arrives at the end consumer. Depending on what you make and how fast you make it, the supply chain can be your best friend or worst enemy. If it works well, it's your best friend. If it doesn't work well, it's your worst enemy."

Tom continued, "The fundamental problem with most supply-chain systems is that they have remained stagnant in their thinking through time, while business reality has flexed in a cycle of constant change, sometimes at an exponential rate. There are many new supply-chain software applications, each proposing that it will solve the problems associated with the supply chain. These new software applications have come about mostly because of advances in computer technology, but few have solved the real issues of the supply chain. While it is true that these systems can provide an enormous amount of information in very fast fashion, sometimes system speed is not as important as having access to the correct information. What difference does it make how fast you get the information if it's the wrong information?"

Tom asked if everyone was understanding what he had explained so far and when they indicated that they did, he continued. "Many supply-chain systems were designed to solve a problem, and the problem they were trying to solve was the needed availability of parts, raw materials, or inventory. Companies need the right parts or material, in the right location, at the right time. The bottom line is that you don't want to run out of parts or materials, and yet, many times you do. You don't want excessive inventory, and yet sometimes you have way too much inventory. This constant negative cycle of sometimes too much or too little has continued through time."

"For many companies the supply chain/inventory system of choice is one referred to as the minimum/maximum (MIN/MAX) system. Parts or inventory levels are evaluated based on need and usage, and some type of maximum and minimum levels are established for each item. The traditional rules and measures for these systems are usually quite simple," and with that Tom loaded a new overhead on the screen (Figure 23.7).

- Rule 1: Determine the maximum and minimum levels for each item.

- Rule 2: Don't exceed the maximum level.

- Rule 3: Don't reorder until you go below the minimum level.

FIGURE 23.7
The rules of the Min/Max system.

"Is this what rules you're using at your companies?" Tom asked. Both Steve and John responded and said, "Yes, pretty much so." Tom continued, "The thinking behind these measures are primarily based in Cost Accounting and commonly referred to as cost-world thinking. In order to save money and minimize your costs, you must reduce the amount of money you spend for these items. In other words, you must never buy more than the maximum amount. In addition, you must not spend money until absolutely necessary, which means you only order parts only when they reach or go below the minimum level," Tom explained to a very captive audience.

Tom continued, "These assumptions seem valid, and if implemented correctly and monitored closely, they should deliver a supply system that controls dollars and maintains inventory within the minimum and maximum levels. The problem is that most systems of this type, don't seem to generate the desired results that are required," and again, Tom checked to see if most in attendance agreed with his comment and they did. "For some reason, there always seem to be situations of excess inventory for some items and of stock-out situations for others. "Is that what your companies are experiencing?" Tom asked. Steve and John replied that it was. The whole operational concept behind the Minimum/Maximum systems was supposed to prevent these kinds of occurrences from happening, and yet they still do," Tom explained.

Tom continued, "If the system, as a whole, isn't producing the desired results, then what segment of the system needs to be changed to produce the desired results? Perhaps the minimum and maximum levels are the wrong rules to engage, and saving money is the wrong financial measure to consider. In order to solve today's problems, we must think at an order of magnitude higher than we were thinking when we developed yesterday's solutions. In other words, yesterday's solutions are causing most of today's problems."

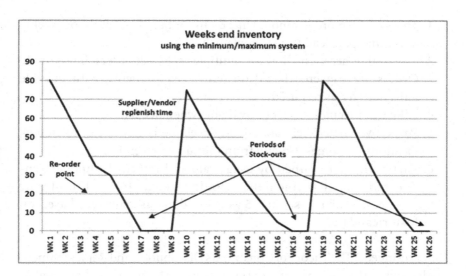

FIGURE 23.8
Min/Max system results.

"Stock-outs occur most often when the lead time to replenish the part exceeds the minimum stock available. In other words, availability of the part between the minimum amount and zero is totally depleted before the part can be replenished from the vendor," Tom explained and flashed a new figure on the screen (Figure 23.8). "So, you end up with periods of stock-outs that occur when you least need them. So, what's the answer to this dilemma?" he asked.

Tom continued, "One of the primary operating functions of the supply-chain system is to build and hold inventory at the lowest possible distribution level. This assumption is both correct and incorrect. The correct inventory should be held at the point-of-use location, but not based on minimum or maximum amounts. Instead, the necessary inventory should be based on the vendor lead times to replenish and maintain sufficient inventory to buffer the variations that exist in lead time. The Theory of Constraints Distribution and Replenishment Model is a robust parts replenishment system that allows the user to be proactive in managing the supply-chain system. It's also a system based on usage, either daily or weekly, but not the minimum amount. Some parts/inventory will require much more vigilance in day-to-day management." Tom said and posted the rules for Theory of Constraints' Replenishment System on his screen.

1. The system reorder amount needs to be based on daily or weekly usage and part lead time to replenish.
2. The system needs to allow for multiple replenish orders, if required.
3. Orders are triggered based on buffer requirements, with possible daily actions, as required.
4. All parts/inventory must be available when needed.
5. Parts inventory is held at a higher level, preferably at central supply locations, or comes directly from the supplier/vendor.
6. Part buffer determined by usage rate and replenish supplier/vendor lead time. Baseline buffer should be equal to 1.5. If lead time is 1 week, buffer is set at 1.5 weeks. Adjust as required, based on historical data.

Tom continued, "The Theory of Constraints Distribution and Replenishment Model argues that the majority of the inventory should be held at a higher level in the distribution system and not at the lowest level. It is still important to keep what is needed at the lowest levels, but don't try to hold the total inventory at that location." Again, Tom checked for understanding and when he was comfortable that everyone was following what he had just said, he continued.

Tom continued his presentation, "The Theory of Constraints Distribution and Replenishment Model also argues that the use of minimum and maximum amounts should be abolished. Instead the inventory should be monitored based on daily or weekly usage, with replenishment occurring, at a minimum weekly, and possibly daily for highly used items. The end result of these actions will be sufficient inventory in the right location at the right time, with zero or minimal stock-outs to support the activities that take place within your hospitals. Instead of using the minimum amount to trigger the reorder process, it should be triggered by daily usage and vendor lead time to replenish," Tom explained and posted a new slide on his screen (Figure 23.9).

Tom continued, "The figure on the screen demonstrates the effects of using the Theory of Constraints Distribution and Replenishment Model. One of the most notable things you see in this graph is that total inventory required through time has decreased from ninety items to approximately forty-two items or roughly a forty-seven percent reduction. In essence, the required inventory has been cut in half. The other notable feature is that even though the inventory level has been cut in half, the number of

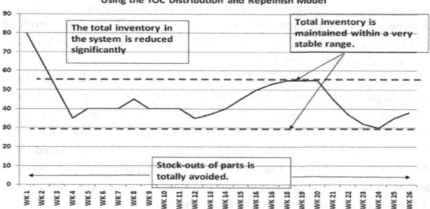

FIGURE 23.9
Theory of Constraints Replenishment Results.

stock-out situations has been reduced to zero!" Tom said with vigor. The group was somewhat flabbergasted in that by reducing the inventory by half, there were no stock-outs!

Tom continued, "When the Theory of Constraints Distribution and Replenishment Model is used to manage the supply chain, there is always sufficient parts inventory to continue your work in your companies. The total inventory is also much more stable through time, without the large gaps and gyrations from zero inventories available to maximum inventory as noted on the minimum/maximum system. So, there you have it. A system that will typically reduce inventory by 50% while virtually eliminating stock-outs."

With a smile on his face, Tom remembered an analogy he had presented to another company and said, "Perhaps the best way to explain the Theory of Constraints Distribution and Replenishment Model is with a very simple and common example you're all familiar with. Consider what happens with a soda vending machine. When the soda vendor opens the door on a vending machine, it is very easy to see what's been sold since the soda vendor last replenished the vending machine. The soda person knows immediately which inventory has to be replaced and to what level to replace it. The soda person is holding the inventory at the next highest level, which is on his soda truck, so it's easy to make the required distribution when needed. He doesn't leave four cases of soda when only twenty cans are needed. If he were to do that, think about what would happen. When he got to the next vending machine he might have run out of the necessary soda because he made distribution too early at the last stop." Tom noticed that the faces in his audience were smiling, meaning that they immediately related to this simple example.

"After completing the required daily distribution to the vending machines, the soda person returns to the warehouse or distribution point in order to replenish the supply on the soda truck and get ready for the next day's distribution. When the warehouse makes distribution to the soda truck, they move up one level in the chain and replenish what's been used from their supplier. This type of system does require discipline to gain the most benefits, but it assumes that regular and needed checks are taking place at the inventory locations to determine the replenishment needs. If these points are not checked on a regular basis, it is possible for the system to experience stock-out situations." Tom explained.

"So, let's summarize our conclusions from what you've heard today," Tom continued. "The distinct contrast in results between simulated data runs using the Minimum/Maximum supply system and the Theory of Constraints Distribution and Replenishment Model are undeniable. The true benefits of a Theory of Constraints-based parts replenishment system are many, but the most significant impact is realized in these two areas. The first benefit is the reduction of total inventory required to manage and maintain the total supply-chain system by nearly fifty percent. This inventory reduction could lead to a significant dollar savings in total inventory required, perhaps thousands of dollars. And think about what would happen to your profit levels, but more importantly, what would happen to your ability to supply more ventilators and facial masks?" Tom said.

"The second benefit is the elimination of stock-out situations. Without a doubt, not having parts available is an expensive situation because it slows throughput through the systems you have at each company. Process steps sit idle, waiting for parts to become available. Stock-out situations increase frustration, not only in not being able to complete the work, but also in the time spent waiting for parts to become available. So, think about what might happen to your capacity and on-time delivery," Tom suggested.

Tom completed his presentation by stating, "Looking for parts and experiencing shortages are a continuing problem in most supply-chain systems. These problems are not caused by the operators, but by the negative effects of the supply-chain system and the way it is used. If your current Min/Max supply system is maintained, then the results from that system cannot be expected to change. However, if new levels of output are required from the system, which they clearly are, then new thinking must be applied to solve the parts supply-system issues. The concepts and methodologies of the Theory of Constraints Distribution and Replenishment Model can positively impact the ability to produce ventilators and facial masks in larger quantities. Are there any questions or comments?" Tom asked as he completed his presentation. It was clear that everyone had understood the basics of Theory of Constraints Distribution and Replenishment Solution as there were no questions and with that the webinar ended.

As with his previous webinar, Steve and John stayed on-line to chat with Tom about what he had presented. John was the first to speak and said, "Tom, I have a general knowledge question for you." "Sure John, go ahead and ask away," Tom replied. "Why is it that the Theory of Constraints is not presented in colleges as part of a degree program?" John asked. "That's a very good question, John, and I wish I had a good answer for you. I will tell you that there are quite a few graduate programs that offer it as part of their curriculum," Tom explained. "One other question for you," John said. "Are there other tools and methods that are part of the Theory of Constraints body of knowledge?" he asked. "Yes, there are many other facets within the Theory of Constraints body of knowledge," Tom replied. "For example, the Theory of Constraints has its own version of accounting known as Throughput Accounting. While traditional Cost Accounting focuses on saving money to enhance profitability, Throughput Accounting focuses on how much money a company can make, and trust me, these two approaches are entirely different," he explained.

Steve then asked, "What other things does the Theory of Constraints offer?" Tom replied, "If your company uses project management, Theory of Constraints has its own version known as Critical Chain Project Management or CCPM. There is also another side of Theory of Constraints known as the Thinking Processes which are a series of logic tools which can be used to analyze a business to identify areas in need of improvement. I could go on and on, but my time is limited today. My advice to you is to get a copy of the book *Epiphanized* and focus on the appendix as it summarizes many of the tools and techniques associated with the Theory of Constraints. Before we hang up, let me know if you need any help implementing what I presented today." And with that, their conversation was over.

It had been two weeks since Tom's webinar, and needless to say, Tom was very curious about how things were going at Jefferson Ventilators and The Mask Makers. Tom decided that instead of wondering how things were going, he would call Steve and John to get an update. He called Steve first and Steve answered the phone. "Hello, Steve here," he said. "Hi Steve, it's Tom. I was wondering how things were going at your company?" he asked. "Things are progressing nicely, thanks to the Theory of Constraints and you too Tom," Steve said. "In what way Steve?" Tom asked. "Well, we're just starting to see the results from our new replenishment system and based upon what we've seen so far, our number of stock-outs are rapidly approaching zero. Plus, our inventory levels have decreased by thirty percent so far. But the thing that is most important is that our new capacity is six times what it was before we started this effort! And that's the key to success for us!" Steve exclaimed. "Thanks Steve, for the update and if you need anything, just call me." Tom replied. "Will do, Tom, and thanks for everything," Steve replied.

Tom next called John and asked him the same question. And like Steve's response, John indicated that their output of facial masks had accelerated upward at a very fast pace. But then, John completely surprised Tom by saying, "One thing else, Tom. You remember Sylvia, well she has taken the Theory of Constraints to a new level. She has been working with our accounting people and we now have implemented Throughput Accounting to make our financial decisions. And she did this all by reading the book, *Epiphanized*. She was able to glean enough from the book to be able to convince our financial people that we needed to try it. We can already see an improvement in our profitability." "That's amazing John!" Tom exclaimed. "Let me know if you need anything from me John," Tom added. "I will do that Tom," he replied and they hung up.

When his calls were complete, Tom turned on his television to get an update on the Corona Virus. The pandemic was clearly out of control now as 4,000,000 people were now infected worldwide, with nearly half of the infected residing in the United States. The death rate was clearly out of control with the number of reported deaths worldwide now over 700,000. And nearly one third of the reported deaths were from the United States. But even though these rates were shocking, there was some relatively good news. According to the announcer, the pandemic had finally reached its apex, and the infection and death rates were on their way down. This was very refreshing for Tom to hear.

Another bit of good news was that the number of ventilators was now sufficient to treat the people that were severely infected with the Corona Virus, as well as the facial masks being in sufficient volume to aid in the prevention of this deadly disease. While this was all great news, there were two other pieces of news that truly struck a positive cord with Tom. The first bit of news was that doctors in the United States had developed a vaccine which could be easily administered to the general public that would prevent this pandemic from returning in the future. But the best news of all however was that his wife was now experiencing labor pains and that he would soon be the father of three new children.

The End

Index

Note: **Bold** page numbers refer to tables and *italic* page numbers refer to figures.

Printed in the United States
by Baker & Taylor Publisher Services